ADVANCE PRAISE FOR

The Visionary's Handbook

"Tired of abstract theory about chaos and acceleration and predictions of future? Fasten your seatbelt for this personal, rock & roll journey into your own future. As usual, Jim and Watts don't disappoint."

—Candice Carpenter,
Chief Executive Officer, iVillage

◆

"I've seen the future, and it's in the pages of this eye-opening book. The most powerful asset in business is a strong point of view about the future. *The Visionary's Handbook* will help you figure out your future."

—William Taylor,
Founding Editor, Fast Company

◆

"Should find an important place on any thoughtful manager's desk."

—James Abernathy,
Managing Partner, The Abernathy MacGregor Group

◆

"*The 500-Year Delta* was an interesting book. *The Visionary's Handbook* is an important book. Not just a quick read, this book requires an intellectual engagement from the reader, a full involvement working through the exercises and aggressively absorbing and processing its contents. The personal return on such an intellectual investment will be endless, continuing as far in the reader's future as can be imagined. I can see no way that your life and business future could fail to be enriched if you take the time to really think through the principles and issues presented in this book. What a lucky circumstance! About how many books can we say that?"

—Frank Lane,
President, Pyramid Consulting

◆

"The world changed. Click companies want to build brand as though they were mortar companies. Brick and mortar companies are striving to be on-line click companies. The world of click and mortar companies is emerging. All the rules changed. *The Visionary's Handbook* is a mandatory source of guidance necessary to visualize and manifest success."

—Lee H. Stein,
Chairman, Virtual Capital, LLC

◆

"As a University professor and one of the originator of the Third International Mathematics and Science study, I have a strong appreciation for both breadth of view and focus (that is vision) in creating something new. This book is one of the most creative and thoughtful discussions of what it means to be a visionary in today's world. I encourage every person who is placed in a leadership role, whether in business or some other field, to especially read the first chapter of this book."

—William Schmidt,
Professor, NRC U.S. TIMSS, Michigan State University

◆

"You will never be the same after reading this exceptional book. Thought provoking and inspiring and great value. New insight of our realities and futures come to light each time the book is read one to keep by the bedside."

—Keith Todd,
Chief Executive, ICL PLC

◆

"*The Visionary's Handbook* removes much of the mystery and uncertainty about the future. It's as exciting and as fun as learning a magician's secrets."

—Jim McCann,
CEO, 1-800-FLOWERS.COM

◆

"The form of the book perfectly mirrors its message that inherent truth has yielded to individual 'neotribe' realities and that it is only in embracing your own present reality that you can forecast any viable future. I must say that you've given me a lot to think about both professionally and personally, and I look forward to hearing the presentations that will evolve out of this book."

—Don Epstein,
President, Greater Talent Network

THE VISIONARY'S HANDBOOK

THE VISIONARY'S HANDBOOK

Nine Paradoxes That Will Shape the Future of Your Business

JIM TAYLOR and WATTS WACKER

with HOWARD MEANS

HarperBusiness
An Imprint of HarperCollinsPublishers

HarperCollins books may be purchased for educational, business, or sales promotional use. For information please write: Special Markets Department, HarperCollins Publishers Inc., 10 East 53rd Street, New York, New York 10022.

First HarperBusiness paperback edition published 2001.

Designed by Stanley S. Drate/Folio Graphics Co. Inc.

The Library of Congress has catalogued the hardcover edition as follows:
Wacker, Watts.
     The visionary's handbook : nine paradoxes that will shape the future of your business /
   Watts Wacker and Jim Taylor with Howard Means.—1st ed.
       p.   cm.
     ISBN 0-06-661987-4
     1. Business forecasting.   2. Management,   3. Organizational change.
   I. Taylor, Jim, 1947 Apr. 25   II. Means, Howard B.   III. Title.
   HD30.27.W33 2000
   658.4′06—dc21   99-049663

ISBN 0-06-661988-2 (pbk.)
01 02 03 04 05 RRD 10 9 8 7 6 5 4 3 2 1

To Cal and Lee Wacker,
the source of my inspiration.

To my wife, Judy, my parents,
and every other teacher
who took so much pleasure
in helping me to know
how wrong I can be.

And to the memory
of Katharine Bursk Means.

What lies behind us and what lies
before us are tiny matters
compared to what lies within us.

RALPH WALDO EMERSON

"But what am I to do?" said Alice.
"Anything you like," said the Footman,
and began whistling.

LEWIS CARROLL, *Alice's Adventures in Wonderland*

Contents

◆ ◆ ◆ ◆ ◆ ◆ ◆ ◆ ◆ ◆ ◆ ◆ ◆ ◆ ◆ ◆ ◆ ◆ ◆

ACKNOWLEDGMENTS   *xi*

PREFACE TO THE PAPERBACK EDITION   *xiii*

I

THE PARADOX OF THE VISIONARY   *1*

II

PARADOXES OF THE EVERYDAY   37

1 ◆ The Paradox of Value   39
    BOX 1: The Brand Promise   57

2 ◆ The Paradox of Size   61
    BOX 2: What Color Is Your Disaster?   71

3 ◆ The Paradox of Time   77

4 ◆ The Paradox of Competition   97
    BOX 3: Global Metaphors and Global Brands   113

5 ◆ The Paradox of Action   115

6 ◆ The Paradox of Leadership   135
    BOX 4: Governance, Patriotism, and Loyalty   151

7 ◆ The Paradox of Leisure 155

III

THE SERIAL FUTURE 173

IV

THE PARADOX OF REALITY 227

INDEX 245

Acknowledgments

◆ ◆ ◆ ◆ ◆ ◆ ◆ ◆ ◆ ◆ ◆ ◆ ◆ ◆ ◆

The trouble with thank-you lists is that they can never be long enough.

We are indebted to literally thousands of people for this book: to everyone who helped us see beyond the cage of our experience, everyone who enriched our understanding by sharing their own, everyone who let us inside their stories long enough for us to try to find our own.

Some people, though, do need mentioning by name. Raphael Sagalyn of the Sagalyn Literary Agency brought us up short whenever we failed to live up to the potential of our ideas. His assistant, Ethan Kline, gave us the title for this book, and the title helped dictate structure. Adrian Zackheim, publishing director of HarperBusiness, wouldn't let us take the easy route, either. Many thanks to them for their wisdom and friendship. Many thanks also to Mary De Vito for coordinating three far-flung authors, and to Bernadette Sherry for her help in the same often thankless task. Many people have helped us think about what it means to be a visionary. We would especially like to thank Ted Briscoe, Candace Carpenter, David Ford, Mike Grobstein, Frank Hall, Tom Heintz, John Heubusch, Michael Hudes, Mary Ellen Keating, Sandy Kemper, Frank Lane, Ryan Mathews, Jonathan Nelson, Harriet Rubin, Geoff Shaw, Jim Sierk, Lee Stein, Keith Todd, Ted Waitt, Chip, Charley, and Chuck. Their inspiration is a well we are privileged to drink from every day. Rolf Jensen, head of the Copenhagen Institute for Future Studies in Denmark, deserves a special mention, too, for helping us to see that the Information Age was ending, not beginning. Thanks to him, to Candy Means, and to all our families, for their patience first and foremost. Authors are not always fun to live with.

We also need to thank each other, for never agreeing so much that the spark of inquiry went out and for never disagreeing so much that civility suffered. As balancing acts go, that's a tough one to pull off.

WW
JT
HM
Summer 1999

Preface to the Paperback Edition

In the year that passed between the hardcover edition of this book and its release in this paperback version, polls found that three in five of us believe simultaneously in both creationism and evolution. The world's greatest amateur athletes gathered in Sydney, Australia, for the Summer Olympics—an event celebrated for its purity, reviled for its drugs, and condemned for the corruption of its governing body. In November, Americans handed Al Gore a convincing win in the popular vote only to see George W. Bush inaugurated, thanks in large part to the tireless machinations of an obscure Florida Secretary of State and one-time chicken dancer. The dead Old Economy suddenly came back to life, while in the New One, some of the most successful companies were vultures buying at deep discounts the inventories of their failed dot.com competitors.

What we said in our first edition is even more true now. We live inside a continuous collision of opposites that change us and the terms of our business and personal lives every moment we are alive. This is a book not about avoiding those collisions, but about recognizing and living with them. It's a book about managing the paradoxes that manage you.

In Part I, we introduce you to the paradoxical world of the visionary, and we invite you to join us in what we call the "Fool Box" so that you can determine your own tomorrow instead of letting tomorrow determine a place for you. A word of warning: It's not easy work.

Part II takes up the contradictions that are almost impossible to see because they surround us every moment of every day. Stated along with their controlling paradoxes, they are:

- The paradox of value: Intrinsic worth isn't.

- The paradox of size: The bigger you are, the smaller you need to be.
- The paradox of time: At the speed of light, nothing happens.
- The paradox of competition: Your biggest competitor is your own view of your future.
- The paradox of action: You've got to go for what you can't expect to get.
- The paradox of leadership: To lead from the front, you have to stay inside the story.
- The paradox of leisure: Play is hard work.

Part III introduces the concept of serial futuring. So far as we know, the concept is unique to us. Simply stated, it is that when change is constant, our approach to the future and our understanding of what it holds must be constantly changing. The model we use is built on our own reality. We hope, though, that by the time you are through with this section, you will understand your own reality well enough to build a model that fits it.

"The Paradox of Reality" is the title of Part IV. By Part IV, we think you will have no trouble understanding what that means.

This is also an interactive book. Through nearly forty "Future Exercises" and "Exams" (self-graded), we try to provide you with the tools and understanding to become the architect of your own future. Go on this trip with us, use our tools, make them your own, work the exercises, take the exams, and we think you'll be a better person for the experience.

We don't know if we are right about the future—how can we until it happens?—but we do know that none of us is allowed to drift through life without paying a price. Take control of what lies ahead and it belongs to you; let what lies ahead take control of you and you will always be fate's pawn. That's our argument and our justification. Enjoy.

WATTS WACKER
Westport, Connecticut

JIM TAYLOR
Santa Fe, New Mexico

HOWARD MEANS
Bethesda, Maryland

I

THE PARADOX OF
THE VISIONARY

*The more you are right,
the more wrong you will be.*

Welcome to the Age of Possibility.

Welcome to the first time in the history of the planet when you truly can choose what you want to be, what you want to do, what you want to know, and where you want to go.

Welcome to a world in which reality is whatever we make it, a world in which you both can and must immerse yourself in your own possibilities, a world in which you—you the person, you the business, you the organization, you the government, and you the society—can write your own story and walk into it and become whatever it is you imagine yourself becoming. Life has never been easier, and because it has never been easier, life has never been more hard.

Emancipated from group-think and collective fate, people have the capacity today as never before to claim their own futures and to shape those futures to suit completely idiosyncratic wants and needs. You really are free, and as all truly free people are, you really are responsible. Fail to build your own future, and someone is going to build one for you, whether you want it or not. Fail to bind all the disparately emerging futures within your organization—be it company, school, government, or family—to a shared set of goals, and its future will be forfeit, too.

Our job as consultants is to help top executives look into the future and prepare themselves for the paradoxical nature of the world they must learn to operate in—the world that lies just around the corner and the world that is waiting decades down the road. Far more than that, though, our job is to introduce CEOs and their companies to the tools we use as visionaries so that they can become the custodians of their own destiny. No one can predict the future, but no one afford to be unprepared to meet whatever does arrive.

We can do the same thing for you and for your business. We can give you the same tools and show you the same frames of mind you'll need to master, and instead of charging you the tens of thousands of dollars consultants charge the corporate top brass, you will have had to pony up only the price of this book. But to become your own visionary, you will need to help yourself along the way. You can begin that process right now by taking the pretest below, and you can enhance the value immensely by being utterly honest with yourself, on this test and on all the tests and "Future Exercises" that follow. It's your destiny, not ours, that you are pursuing, and the only person you finally have to please is yourself.

♦ Pretest

TOTAL TEST TIME: 4 MINUTES

This test consists of four sections. In the chapters ahead, you'll have time to ponder all four sections in far greater depth. For now, go with your gut and take no more than sixty seconds to complete each one.

- ♦ On a clean sheet of paper, freeze your reality at this precise moment in time and list all the things you are—not yesterday or tomorrow, but right now. This is your benchmark against which to measure future change.

- ♦ On a second sheet of paper, declare a major in your future by listing all the things you will be. This is the reality you hope to invent.

- For Section 3, start another list, your postulates about the future: "Things that have to be true in order for me to be what I will be." Fill the list out.

- Finally, write at the top of a fresh sheet of paper "The following things mark me as a radical among my peers." Take no more than sixty seconds to list them all.

When you're through with the pretest, store your answers somewhere handy. We're going to ask you to complete a similar exercise at the end of this book, and comparing those answers to these should give you a good road map of the trip you've taken through these pages. For now, though, give yourself a good pat on the back because you've just attacked the four critical issues in becoming your own futurist:

- You have to know who you are.
- You have to know where you want to go.
- You need to recognize your own seminal moments.
- And you must have an attitude of insurgency.

For a visionary, these four principles are the beginning of knowledge. You might not get where you want to go by following them, but you can't control your destiny without them.

A New Grammar

In this book, we also explore what it means to live not in the past or the present or even in the future, but to live in a new grammar: the future expressed in the present tense, because this is where and how we must live today, with a foot in both tenses.

Just as important, we invite you to be our colleagues on this exploration, to find yourself and the story of your business in the stories we have to tell, and to write your own story as we tell ours. There are times we ask you to do that literally, as we have just done: times when we encourage you to take out a pencil and pad and work an exercise. We hope you also jot notes in the margins as you read along and that you constantly inject yourself and your company into the anecdotes we tell and the situations we describe. The more you choose to participate as you read along, the more you are likely to have produced an accidental diary of your own future by the time you come to our final page.

Because we humans are the categorizing animal, we divide our species up in every conceivable way: by race, by sex, by ethnicity, by size, by wealth, by geopolitics, by left-handedness and the length of the forehead and the thickness of the cranium. Finally, though, there are only two kinds of people in the world—optimists and pessimists—and there is one difference between the two: An optimist thinks he is having a great future, while a pessimist thinks he is having a lousy one. It's how you organize your view of the future that determines what sort of future you have.

To an optimist, marriage presents the opportunity for a happy life; to a pessimist, it poses a threat to the same thing. And whatever the course of either marriage, that view of its future is likely to be fulfilled. Is the growing role of the United Nations in the management of conflict a sign that peace is upon us or that Big Brother is here? Does Chile's decision to make the dollar its currency standard provide more proof of U.S. economic imperialism, or does it give Chile the chance to participate fully in the global economy without sacrificing nationalism? Is there always going to be an England, or is England just an offshore state of the European Union?

There are no answers to such questions, only ways of approaching them, and there are no universal approaches either. No one is one type of person or another, an optimist or a pessimist, 100 percent of the time. Life doesn't break down that neatly. In fact, here's a paradox of life to ponder on that very score, from Yankelovich Partners: 82 percent of Americans say things are getting better, and 82 percent say things are getting worse. Thus, we live in contradiction with even our own understandings.

Events don't write our future. Whether you subscribe to an optimistic or a pessimistic view of the world, the same events are happening to you over the same time span. Events are the given even though we have no way of knowing what the events will be. What isn't given is how we react to unknowable and unpredictable events as they arrive. It's the response, not the events, that determine both our future and our satisfaction in the present with the future we expect.

If the stock market were to crash tomorrow, would you be depressed because your vision of a stable retirement had been shot to hell? Or would you change your perception of how you are going to be effective in the future? We can't tell you which to do or which to be. But we can point you to the former Iron Curtain countries. The reason a free-market economy failed in Russia was that the critical mass of Russian people were unprepared to redefine themselves: Their future is hostage to their history. The reason a free-market economy has prospered in the Czech Republic is that nearly everyone there was prepared to embrace a new definition of themselves.

The future is never what we think it will be; jobs, relationships, cancer, an inheritance, war, El Niño, IPOs launched or unlaunched, stock options vested or unvested, new discoveries, antitrust suits—something always intervenes. The more we measure our progress through life as a series of approaches to a constant future, the more dissatisfied we are when the real future intrudes into the present. Instead of looking to the same fixed point on the horizon, we need to rewrite the future serially as events change the likelihood of any particular future arriving. Doing so can be brutally difficult—sometimes there's nothing harder—but by the end of this book we hope that you will know how to do that if it is your choice to do so.

Collisions with Chaos

We all walk through collisions with chaos every day, and we walk through them equally. That's what it means to be alive at the beginning of this new millennium: Chaos is what we breathe.

Maybe it's observing a street mugging in New York and trying to factor that into our reality. Did we really see it? What did we do, or fail to do? Maybe it's a stop sign we didn't stop at, or one that someone failed to honor at the only moment in all of time when our reality and that person's reality could have possibly coincided. We collide with chaos when the airplane we are strapped into flies into a dead-air pocket and suddenly plunges one hundred feet, or when we walk into the Alfred P. Murrah Federal Building in Oklahoma City at the infinitesimally brief moment in history when where we are is exactly the wrong place to be. Or we collide with chaos when a random $5 investment in a Powerball game turns into $14 million in the blink of an eye.

For some people, each of those collisions is proof of an uncaring god or a cruel fate, or that the great moments in life arrive only serendipitously. For others, every collision with chaos is potentially a systematic collision with opportunity, a chance to change, a new start on a life that is always serially starting anew until it ends. How you choose to write the story that you are living in—*your* story, personal and business—makes all the difference.

For some people, too, every collision with chaos is a seminal one. For others, no collision is. The truth is, neither is right. Only for the very frantic or the very crazy is every elevated moment of life an epiphany, but learning to pick out the elevated moments that do matter—the seminal ones—from the ones that don't is a vital life skill. Being hauled into federal court by the Justice Department was not a seminal moment for Microsoft, but faking a courtroom videotape involving the company's Internet Explorer browser was. And the difference between the two is huge. Being hauled into federal court happens when you're the most powerful company in the world. Faking it, though, changes the equation because faking it creates the real possibility that the company will lose the case or have to settle on very unfavorable terms (quite possibly by the time this book appears in print). Unless Microsoft is prepared to serially adjust its future in a way that allows it to contemplate losing the case de facto or de jure—unless, that is, it has a vision of the future that allows for a different outcome than it contemplates in the present—it and its stock- and stakeholders are in for a very long ride.

Some moments ring big but change very little. Other moments change everything because from the instant they happen all bets on prior considerations of your future are off. Still other moments change everything because they are exactly the right or exactly the wrong point in time: Ask too early, and you get the wrong answer. Ask too late, and it doesn't matter anyway.

Every life, individual and corporate, is also a constant collision between present and future, and how you choose to live in the space between the two tenses makes all the difference, too.

A company called Organic is the largest online business development company in the world today, but the skills that helped Organic become so successful at incubating new Web companies also have made it one of the best Web technology businesses going. In order to build and maintain Websites for clients such as Daimler-Chrysler and Home Depot, Organic has had to skew resources toward the booming Web technology side of the business, and with handsome rewards. The company has grown into a billion-dollar enterprise in just a few years. Yet the more resources it throws into supporting its present success, the more Organic disinherits its incubation side and risks disappearing as a player in the Web company invention world. And the closer it gets to that possibility, the more convinced Organic is that its real future lies where the company began: as an Internet incubator. Thus, its present success poisons the future; thus, the future poisons present success. Thus, too, Organic's culture is endangered by the fictions it must tell about the future in order to build the teamwork necessary to succeed at present tasks. And thus, companies as well as people are required to live in the future in the present tense, in the new grammar of our chaos world.

Visions False and True

This is a book about vision, as well: true vision. The "true" is important because most of what passes for vision in the world today is anything but.

Corporate "vision statements" are all the rage these days, and yet virtually every such vision statement we have ever seen is not a statement about the future but a projection forward beyond the present of an idealized past, an idealized workforce, an idealized marketplace functioning perfectly in an idealized and unchanging economy. "We here at General Widget aspire to utilize empowered workers and cutting-edge technology to continue our domination of the global widget market. . . ." Really? And what if widgets fall out of fashion, or are replaced by wadgets, or the Asian market for widgets goes up in flames as North Korea rains missiles and biowarfare agents down on South Korea and Japan in a desperate effort to break out of its peninsular fortress and find some food for its people?

What if the Reverend Jerry Falwell discovers evidence of Satanic influences embedded in your widgets—666 separate welds!—and all the fundamentalist Christians at your Clarksburg, Tennessee, assembly plant suddenly walk off the job? Or what if the Reverend Jesse Jackson discovers evidence of racism in your packaging—the black's always on the bottom!—and all the African American employees at your Gary, Indiana, distribution facility suddenly walk off the job in protest? Improbable? No more so than that one of the reverends or their many acolytes won't find something similar in a world so deeply tribalized. Yet where is the space in the average corporate vision statement for such events? Their denial of chaos and its possibilities is not merely profound; it approaches pathological.

What if, for that matter, widgets aren't the business General Widget will be in ten years down the highway, or at least the business that will be driving its bottom line? Side businesses migrate to the center if we let them. Owens-Corning migrated from pots and pans to glass cookware to fiber optics; Westinghouse, from air brakes to radio to an independent subscriber broadcast network, and from there through appliances to a TV network (CBS) with attendant cable and Internet operations. The name "Motorola" comes from motoring victrolas, but Motorola hasn't made a record player in decades, to the great joy of its stockholders. The fastest-growing division at Hallmark is a side business—corporate communications programs—that is migrating into a main business. Examples are legend, and in many cases legendarily profitable, but the more we lock in a "vision" that is really just a new iteration of ancient history, the less room we leave for movement of any sort.

The key to a false vision is that, in the face of knowing for sure that the world is going to change, a company or an organization or an individual aspires to stay the same. The key to a true vision is that, in the face of knowing for sure that the world is going to change, an organization or a company or an individual aspires to change with it and stay the same simultaneously. And the reality of a true vision is that, unlike a false one, pursuing it is such difficult work.

Whatever the vision statement of Boeing might say, the vision of Boeing has to be that it aspires to dominate the motion of human beings across the planet in ten years, and in every possible way: by plane and aeronautic design, but also by train and surface transportation design, and by telepresence and thus by satellite and Internet design, too. Anything less is compromise. Yet to say so is to acknowledge the need to dominate the Chinese market—the numbers leave you no other choice. That, in turn, means committing resources that may jeopardize financial performance in the present. Do that, and you risk compromising share value and thus your capacity to attract money at favorable terms. Compromise that and you may lack the resources to dominate the Chinese market in the first place.

How do you bet on your vision of the future and allow yourself to survive in the present? That is a large part of what this book is about.

Most "visionary" books are failures of imagination, too, and the more they ring of "truth," the greater the failure they are. Why? Because that is the first paradox of the visionary: The closer your vision gets to a provable "truth," the more you are simply describing the present in the future tense. Global connectivity, real-time information, and the other usual suspects of visionary business books won't change the business world. They already are changing it, they have changed it in the past, and they've been on their way to changing it for more than three decades, ever since the Pentagon's Advanced Research Projects Agency first successfully tested its ARPANET, the forerunner of today's Internet.

Even the provable "truths" about the future rarely turn out quite as expected. A quarter century ago, we attended a conference sponsored by IBM to introduce the integrated electronic architecture that was going to create the paperless office. Was IBM "right" about the future? Completely. The models on display that day reflect the modern office environment with an uncanny degree of accuracy. And how about the "paperless" office? Well, in 1975, the year of that presentation, U.S. businesses purchased about 5.3 million tons of what's known in the industry as "office paper." By century's end, the U.S. population had grown by about 26 percent, and the amount of office paper sold to U.S. businesses had grown almost threefold, to about fifteen million tons.

Almost twenty years ago, we were also present when John Diebold proclaimed the invention of the automatic teller machine, and the subsequent death of the paper check. Diebold was right: ATMs are everywhere today, and his name is on many of them. But he was also wrong: In 1981, about forty-four billion paper checks were presented to U.S. banks for payment. By 1998, that figure had grown to almost sixty-four billion checks, or almost six times the 11.2 billion ATM transactions that year.

◆ Future Exercise

We'll get to the mythologies of businesses later. For now, let's kick off the series of "future exercises" that run throughout this book by having you calculate your own myth.

On a legal pad, list all the things that are said about you, all the qualities ascribed to you, and all the stories you have reason to believe are told about you by your colleagues. Throw in everything you can think of—the good, the bad, the ugly: is brilliant, drinks too much, was an all-American in college, loves her husband, has a mistress, studied under Marshall McLuhan, can calculate complex percentages in his head, fluent in German, spent the late 1970s stoned in an ashram, a boss who really respects women/men/gays/blacks, a suck-up, a great mentor, whatever.

Now, go down the list and cross out all those items you know to be factually true. Myths are public dreams. Like actual dreams (which are in fact private myths) they are about the truth, not about a truth. What's left is the legend that has been created about and around you thus far in life. Finally, go through what remains and put brackets around all the items that reflect your own deeply held belief system. The ratio of bracketed items to those that are neither bracketed nor crossed out (that is, items that are neither factual truths nor true to your own beliefs) will tell you how much you have allowed your myth to be created by others and how much the myth is a reflection of the core person within, and that, in turn, will tell you how valid your own mythology is.

We have no magic numbers in mind, no figure you need to fall above or below, but if half of all the "mythic" truths about you are being written by others, you're not in control of your own story. And if you're not in control of your own story, you can't possibly be in control of your own place in the future.

Destabilizing the Present

The second paradox of the visionary follows from the first: The more successful you are at predicting the future, the more you destabilize your present, in every way. Suppose you are Kodak, and you truly believe, as we do, that by the year 2010 thirty-five-millimeter film will be a luxury available only to the few as a sign of their artistry, that photographs generally will be a thing of the past, and that virtually all image capturing, reproduction, and storage will be done digitally. Do you shift all resources from film to digital imaging right now? No, the world is not adopting digital-image technology fast enough in the present to absorb the cost of managing for the future. If you believe that you are right, though, then you also believe that your film people will be less prominent in the future, and you need to begin to make them less prominent today by systematically downgrading their role in decisions about the future. Thus, the realities of the present day collide with expectations about the future and the allocation of resources among and between the two to produce a massive future-based political problem with huge consequences for the present. Fun, eh?

Or take a more ready example: the book in your hand. The book-publishing industry is predicated on paper—paper for the pages, paper for the cover, paper for the dust jacket. The economics of the industry revolve around predictions about the type and amounts of paper that will be consumed. Yet if two things seem predictable about a future that resists prediction, they are that, despite the examples we cited above, (a) environmental pressures will render paper a diminishing resource and (b) cyber-publishers will rush to fill the gap as paper publishers increasingly scramble for the paper to print on. One technology, still in experimentation, would allow students to download a textbook onto a disk while simultaneously encoding a date for the expiration of the material. Students, in effect, would rent the book for two weeks, two months, or whatever, at the end of which time the text would disappear without destroying the disk.

Is that necessarily where the future is headed for the book industry? We don't know, although we will point out that Jimmy Buffet now operates a Website (www.parrot.com) where you can buy direct from him and download any song that he has recorded and owns the rights to. And from there it is not a very large leap to the cyber-publishing enterprise we were just describing. Whether or not our vision of the future of publishing is "true" in any final sense, though, the elements of possibility in it are such that to truly contemplate them is to question the survival of virtually every element of the business.

Books and music and movies that are available in cyberspace for downloading are available there for pirates, too, which means that artists negotiating over the future use of their material may well have to sacrifice money in the present to get their record companies and book publishers and movie distributors to agree to a more limited exposure that might well hurt sales but will not run the risk of cyber-piracy. In effect, artists will have the choice of surrendering present control to protect future value, or of creating present value by surrendering future control.

Then again, if we can publish our book in cyberspace, why do we need a publisher at all? At best, a publisher will give us a 15 percent royalty on each book sold, but we can set the cyber-subscription price for our book at whatever we choose to set it at, and our production costs, once we've written the book, approach zero. And if we don't need a publisher, we don't need the editors who work for publishers, or the agents who represent us to publishers. And then what happens to the cut of the distributors and all the other middlemen whom Jimmy Buffet's record Website so deftly sidesteps?

Follow our vision to the nth degree, and we disintermediate the publishing industry just as surely as Henry the Navigator and the other Age of Exploration sailors disintermediated the sultans and pashas who grew fat as middlemen on the old land-trading routes between Europe and the Far East. We know one company that took a hard look at its $3 billion in sales in 1998 and discovered that over $1 billion of that had gone to intermediaries: more than a third—*poof!*—gone. Today, that company's primary strategy for increasing profit margin isn't to sell more goods; it's to squeeze out the fat.

Bye-bye, middlemen, in short. And then what? And then the middlemen can either keep heading into the future they had once envisioned for themselves or they can rewrite their futures, too, and reintermediate themselves as on-line advertisers for our on-line books or as information editors or in any one of hundreds of other ways that will keep our prediction of their imminent demise from coming true because that is the corollary of this second Paradox of the Visionary: The more accurate a vision is and the more it destabilizes the present, the less likely it is to come true.

Altering the Future

Imagine a truly visionary work—in fiction or nonfiction form, as a movie, book, or play, it doesn't matter—that in 1950 predicted accurately and in minute detail what the United States of America would be like in the year 2000: California well on the way to being a majority nonwhite state and the nation following not all that far behind; astronomical divorce rates; women flooding into the workforce despite an absence of war and great general prosperity; roving bands of latchkey children; cocaine, marijuana, and other narcotics widely prevalent throughout society; the coarsest sort of pornography ready to leap off your computer monitor any time of the day or night; many of the largest urban governments turned over to African American mayors and bureaucrats and most large urban school districts in severe disarray.

If Americans had been allowed to "see" in a convincing and unavoidable way where each incremental step of the last half century has brought them, would they have ever arrived where they have arrived? Or would the compelling specter of such a future have led the white male European descendants who then dominated the body social and the body politic in entirely an opposite direction—toward an almost Islamic conservatism? Did the Big

Brother world limned by George Orwell in *1984* fail to materialize in Western democracies because it was a failed vision or because it was a great one? If we had to vote, we'd vote the latter. Orwell, after all, got the technology almost exactly right.

In effect, Orwell's vision was a worst-case scenario that the Warren Court, foremost among many forces, assured would never materialize through its spirited defense of civil rights and free speech—the same spirited defense that also laid the legal framework for the rampant pornography and broad drug use of today.

You can read the future preventively or prescriptively, and you can adjust serially for every new wrinkle the future-present throws at us, but you can never allow yourself to look in just one direction. Read the future solely to prevent the worst possible things from overwhelming your career or your company or your nation, and you will be blind to opportunity and to all the ironies your vigilance spawns. Read the future solely in light of the best possible course of action, and you will be blind to the potential for disaster. Pursue either route to the exclusion of the other, and you will never understand one more thing: that opportunity and disaster are both headed your way, and that they may be the same thing.

Today, we need to live with a foot in both the preventive and the prescriptive camps, just as we need to live in the present and future simultaneously, and we need to be constantly in touch with three other Paradoxes of the Visionary as well:

- The more we are certain of the details of the future, the more we are likely to be wrong.
- Whatever we expect to be in the future, we must anticipate we won't be.
- And a final one that should serve as a warning before you read further: The more we come to understand our future, the more we alienate ourselves from the present and those who live in it.

Will a religious demagogue take over American politics when the next wave of bad times rolls over the land? Is the Internet an interim technology? Will gays and women in the military eventually dilute the ancient warrior spirit of fighting men? We have inclinations in all three cases, but our future isn't yours. If you see yourself in any of these futures and begin to express yourself in the present on the basis of that future, and thus begin to live in the future you foresee, you will by your very nature become alienating. And the closer you get to the present that your future would destabilize—to the religious right, to Internet investors, to ACT-UP or NOW—the more you will be met by denial, anger, and opprobrium.

Remember: Your reality is yours alone.

Self-contradiction

Obviously, too, this is also a book about paradox, a book about the self-contradictory state we all exist in today.

At one level, nothing is new about that. Contradiction is as old as the human experience, which is why synthesis is as old as humanity, too. Business, corporate, personal, even national life has always been proceeded by the steady blending of seemingly opposite experiences. One condition arose, one set of data, only to be confronted by its own negation, and the challenge was to resolve the difference, to find middle ground, all in the service of determining what was most valid and most useful to pursue. If achieving synthesis meant abandoning old ideas and practices, so be it. If it meant embracing new practices, so be it, too. Progress is a tossing out and an adding to. The point is: There was time, there was space for resolution.

The difference today is that the acceleration in the rate of change coupled with the acceleration and massification of input has created a state of seemingly permanent paradox. A condition and its negation, a set of data and its apparent contradiction, a course of action and its own anticourse, no longer arrive incrementally or sequentially; they arrive instantaneously and simultaneously, and because they do, there is no time to resolve the difference between them by traditional methods. The space between seeming opposites—physical space, psychological space, space in time and emotion and logic—has shrunk so dramatically in the last decade that every condition, every course of action, every possibility has come to be permanently juxtaposed between its own polarities.

As we mentioned earlier, the world has never been more connected. People have never had more choices. Never before in human history has there been so much information on which to base choices. The great library of Alexandria, in Egypt, that was burned by Julius Caesar's forces in 47 B.C. is said to have contained six hundred thousand papyrus scrolls—virtually all the recorded knowledge in the world. Fifteen hundred years later, the entire library collection at Queen's College, Cambridge, amounted to 199 volumes. Thomas Jefferson's collection of six thousand books, one of the great personal libraries of his age, became the basis of the Library of Congress. Today, the Library of Congress contains 113 million items, and 20,000 more arrive every day. Fifty thousand books are published annually in the United States; something like four hundred thousand journals are in publication globally. And all that is just the print information. The number of satellites in space is expected to grow tenfold over the next decade. The bandwidth of the average channel will multiply by a hundredfold over that time, and the compression of the average message will grow by another thousandfold. By the start of the second decade of the twenty-first century, the information available to the average individual at any given point in time will be a hundred thousand times what it is today.

And what do we do with all that information, all those choices, all that connectivity? We choose our own reality and we simplify. From among the tens of thousands of possible soft drinks we could choose, we choose the one that requires the least thinking: Coke. From among the thousands of fast-food franchises we could stop at, we stop at the one that delivers the most predictable promise: McDonald's. It's not connectivity that creates global branding. It's the fact that brands penetrate information spaces and edit for us. They allow us to disconnect from connectivity, and that's what makes them transcendent across reality barriers.

◆ Future Exercise

This is the first of three exercises meant to measure the breadth of your interaction with the world around you: On your pad, write down all the professional journals and trade publications you read on at least a semi-regular basis. (Once a month will do so long as you do more than glance at the cover.) Next, take a look at the list that follows. Collectively, these fifteen "industry" groups account for half of the world's gross domestic product, which means that chances are very high you are employed in one of them.

- Agriculture
- Banking/Finance
- Construction
- Education
- Government
- Hospitality
- Information Technology
- Utilities/Power/Fuel
- Media/Entertainment
- Medicine/Health Care
- Military
- Retail Sales
- Telecommunications
- Trade
- Transportation

Now go back to your list of trade and professional journals, and count up how many of these fifteen groups are represented among your reading. Whatever the answer—one of fifteen, a fifth, a third, two-thirds—that is your professional bandwidth, the range of work experience you are exposing yourself to through your media choices.

Is there a bandwidth that we consider satisfactory? Failing? Good? Outstanding? No, as we said earlier, these are ungraded exercises. Everyone gets to make a private accommodation with the world around him. But the more truncated your range, the less ready you are for change, and the less ready you are for change, the greater the chance that, instead of determining your own place in the future, the future will determine a place for you.

When we do this exercise with executives in any particular industry group, by the way, we always recommend that they call friends in other industries, ask them what journals they read in their own fields, and then start looking at them on a regular basis. Almost inevitably, we find, they discover issue after issue that relates to their own business and provokes their thinking because it comes from a different direction.

Migrating to the Extremes

The global dispersion of information has also made global ideas possible. Never before in history have so many people aspired to one political and social concept as now aspire to principles of self-determination. From Islamic women to the sweatshop workers of Southeast Asia, the drive to emancipation is universal. And yet we live, too, in a world of ever-increasing extremes: extremes of wealth (the richest three people on earth have assets in excess of the combined gross domestic products of the forty-eight poorest nations), extremes of resources (the corn-and-beef-fed 340-pound linemen of the National Football League versus the haunting wraiths of famine-stricken Somalia), ethnic tribal extremes that have made genocide (Rwanda, Serbia, take your pick) almost commonplace, and moral tribal extremes (the Christian Coalition versus People for the American Way versus Larry Flynt) that are turning national politics into a charred landscape from which almost no reputation escapes unscathed.

A hundred wars of nationalism are being fought at the same time the World Trade Organization, the World Bank, the International Monetary Fund, and the United Nations near their peaks of influence and power. Atlanta Falcons safety Eugene Robinson is arrested for propositioning an undercover police officer for sex on the eve of the Super Bowl, and on the very day he is awarded the Bart Starr award for outstanding moral character. Yasser Arafat is filmed sitting not in a desert war camp but at an Israeli peace table. Lucent has a higher market capitalization than its parent company, AT&T. Cisco has a market cap five times that of General Motors. The Greeks help their ancient enemies the Turks to apprehend a Kurdish leader in Kenya, and riots erupt in Europe. Every condition, every news story, every new human event comes slamming into town or onto the television screen or into the newspaper with its opposite firmly in tow, and the only choices we have are to go mad, die laughing, or try to live inside the contradictions.

Every fall, Beloit College in Wisconsin puts together a list for its faculty of all the things the incoming freshman class does not know about or has never experienced. Among the more than forty items on the list for the freshman class of 1998–99 were these entries: Tiananmen Square, the Reagan era, and the Persian Gulf War mean almost nothing to them, nor do they have any idea that Americans were ever held hostage in Iran. McDonald's never came in Styrofoam containers. They have always known MTV and compact disks and VCRs and cable, although they have never owned a record player, and ever since they were in middle school, there has been but one president.

Fair enough. What the list doesn't include, though, are all the things that the freshman class of 1998–99 knows that the faculty doesn't know because that is another extreme: the knowledge extreme, not between the knows and know-nots, although that's worth worrying about, but between the generations. Such is the pace of change, so transient is technology, that adults have stored in their head a near past that is already ancient history: wars, machines, "defining" events (Woodstock, Watergate), inventions, presidents, disasters, all of them meaningless or nearly so to their offspring. Meanwhile, for the first time in history, children have something that their parents desperately want: not youth, not vitality (you can buy both of those at the nearest General Nutrition Center), but *knowledge:* an understanding of the way things work, the ability to write software codes, to install memory in the CPU, to set the VCR so it will record the basketball game at the same time that the TV is showing *ER.* Kids also know one other thing that their parents had no idea of at their age: that sex can not only get you in trouble; it can kill you.

How do you move inside such a world? How do you market to kids and adults simultaneously when their neurons are so differently occupied? How do you operate a global business in a deeply interconnected world that is so divided and tribalized? How do you create heroes when role models that apply to specific demographic or economic sectors refuse to translate to other sectors?

◆ Future Exercise

Here's another exercise you can use to test your level of truncation. Turn your computer on, double click on the hard drive, and then start opening up the folders that appear—system folder, application folder, whatever they are called and however they're configured. As you do so, keep a running score of how many items on your hard drive are immediately intelligible to you and how many are not. (Being able to decipher the name isn't enough; you have to have some grasp of what the function of the item is likely to be.) Then calculate what percentage of all the items on your hard drive made sense to you.

Now, find a reasonably computer-literate fifteen-year-old—a son or daughter, or just the bright kid down the street—pay him a little money for his time, and have him perform the same exercise. Finally, put your score on top of the fifteen-year-old's score to create a fraction. This is, in effect, your generational-technological bandwidth, and once again, the more narrow it is, the greater the chance your future will be created for you.

How can you improve the bandwidth? Instead of hiring a college senior to intern for you this summer, hire the fifteen-year-old who helped you do the test. And listen to what he has to say. (We'll get to listening in our next future exercise.)

Managing Paradox

Whether it's in our personal or our corporate or our national lives, each of us is confronted today with the management of paradox as a fundamental and critical part of our daily life. We prepare for careers that we know will be obsolete. We have to leave our organizations in order to find the opportunities that will lead to promotion and advancement. We take drugs to stay healthy, knowing full well that drugs jeopardize our health. We buy guns to protect our houses, knowing full well that guns make our houses dangerous. As companies, we grow our net worth by dematerializing our assets, or we compete successfully by ignoring our competitors. As nations, we foster the right to self-determination by brutally imposing the collective will of the powerful—U.S.-led economic boycotts, NATO military actions—upon the individual will of the weak.

On occasion, we do create movies like *Saving Private Ryan* or *Titanic* that seem to transcend demographic and economic sectors, but almost invariably, the heroes that inspire us in such movies are characters from the digital era who have been projected into the past to help us understand the conflict in the present. Kate Winslet making an obscene gesture to her rich-but-brutish fiancé in *Titanic* isn't about the doomed luxury liner or even about 1912, when the movie is set. It's about the values and attitudes of the mid-1990s reinterpreting the past in a way that makes it politically and intellectually acceptable to us.

At the turn of the twentieth century, all that was good in Western thought could reasonably be contained in what was advertised as a "five-foot shelf of books"—the *Harvard Classics*, edited by none other than the president of Harvard himself, Charles W. Eliot. A generation later, in the 1920s, you could have access to virtually everything there was to know, again by Western lights, by owning two sets of volumes: the *Encyclopedia Britannica* and the *Oxford English Dictionary*. Even a generation and a half ago, most people watched the same things, read the same things, knew the same things, and were at least predisposed to agree on the same things: patriotism, job, career, the inevitable value of a Harvard education, the inevitable fact that human beings reigned at the top of the animal kingdom. The certainty of the future could always be predicated upon the certainties of the present because the certainties of the present were shared and known. Today, not even a husband and wife have a shared media life, and almost no one has a shared reality.

What is the meaning of government when the agenda of the middle is being defined by the extremists of the left and right? What is the meaning of corporate structure when the desires of management will go unrealized unless they can be married to the desires of the disparate tribes that make up the workforce? What is the meaning of reality when no two people occupy the same knowledge space or have the same understanding of the same object or fact?

The world is so awash in paradox and contradiction that each of us is forced to choose on a daily basis whether we are going to deal with the simultaneous validity of both sides of the same continuum or whether we are going to deny one side or the other. We have to learn to live in a world in which multiple realities are both true and reliable. And yet as sentient creatures, we also need to have a single sense of reality to operate from, to call home base. If we give ourselves over to the pure randomness of experience, if we allow ourselves to Ping-Pong continuously between the extremes of choice, there's no chance of a decent future: We ourselves will become the pure randomness that we've embraced. If we fail to give ourselves over to the randomness, though, we'll find ourselves living in a present that is an absolute denial of reality.

How do you manage that? How do you choose in such a world? How do you structure a life—of action, of the intellect—that allows you to function among all these collisions of chaos, in this swamp of possibility? We'll get to specific strategies in Part II of this book: "Paradoxes of the Everyday." For now, let us paint the broad picture, which is itself full of examples because one of the nice things about the fungibility of reality is that you can make it serve any purpose you choose.

◆ Future Exercise

Here's a last exercise to prepare you for what lies ahead. Ask your secretary or assistant to tape a one-on-one meeting in your office of at least fifteen minutes' duration. The choice of the meeting is up to your assistant—you shouldn't know when it will be. Then immediately afterwards, do two things:

First, write down everything you remember about the meeting, in bullet fashion. Then listen to the tape and write down everything you had already forgotten. The ratio of the two—remembered/forgotten—is a measure of your attention bandwidth.

Number two and more important, as you listen to the tape, measure the amount of time you spend talking and the amount you spend listening. That ratio is your learning bandwidth, for a very simple reason: When you talk, you tell people what you know; when you listen, you open yourself to the possibility of learning.

The Immunization Fallacy

One way to manage paradox is to immunize yourself against it. We call this denial, but we recognize the necessary role of denial in helping us abridge the choices we have to make.

Maybe you have immunized yourself against paradox by simply denying its existence. If you believe in the inevitable triumph of Islam, for example, you have denied that the United States controls the world's largest arsenal of nuclear weapons and would in the right circumstances be willing to use them. You are wrong, of course, but at least you have escaped the contradiction. If you believe in the inevitable triumph of the sporting man, you have denied that all the money has gone to the geeks. But you're wrong about that, too. And if you have invested all your money in the belief that food is the most important human commodity, you are wrong again. You can't eat software, but over the last decade of the twentieth century you could have gotten filthy rich by betting on it in the stock market.

Live in a world that denies the other half of every equation, surround yourself physically and psychologically with the neo-tribe of people who believe as you do, and you can almost escape paradox entirely. The reawakening of religious fundamentalism across much of the world is, at heart, an attempt to cleanse the world of its ambient contradictions. The belief in an idealized family unit that drives much of American political conservatism serves the same purpose. Both create benchmarks against which all reality is measured. Believe rigidly enough, accept deeply enough, apply the benchmark at every turn, and you'll never have to confront the choices that living fully in paradox requires of you.

Maybe you have immunized yourself by raising paradox to a spiritual level. Much of New Age religion, at least as defined by Deepak Chopra and others, makes paradox a kind of food of the gods—a mystical yin and yang that together form the portals to the mysteries of life, death, and the universal whole. Do we buy into it? Buying into it isn't the point. Make New Age religion your reality, and you will have co-opted paradox according to what will be for you a worldview every bit as consistent and omni-explanatory as that of William Bennett or Al Sharpton or Patricia Ireland. And every bit as limiting, too.

Maybe you have immunized yourself by defining yourself in a career. I am Doctor. Therefore the systems of the human body are all that I will attend to, and everything else can float around me. I am Lawyer, and therefore the systems of law and jurisprudence are all that I will concern myself with. I am CEO, economist, teacher, artist—whatever will allow you to limit your scope to a very narrow range of knowledge deeply mastered while the rest of the world bounces around you. Do we lack Renaissance men and women today because the world requires such specialization of us? Or do we lack them because so many people retreat into the sanctuary of specialization to avoid fully living in the world and its contradictory pulls and tugs?

Or maybe you have immunized yourself against paradox with the simplest expedient: money, lots of it. Get rich enough and you can buy a separate peace. Buy a separate peace—a $60 million fortress, your own private amusement park—and chaos can slam around all it wants outside your walls, or at least until the Justice Department decides it wants to break apart your empire or the father of one of the boys you import inside the walls of your amusement park for your own amusement decides that it's time to make you pay. And in one form or another, the Justice Department always does arrive at your door; someone always does file a suit. The career that we have immunized ourselves in—or the corporation or the marriage—fails, and all that our denial has done is leave us unprepared for the debacle.

Living with the Opposition

Not long ago we were riding in a cab outside Moscow when the driver stopped and bought a bottle of vodka. Ah, well, we thought, it's Russia. But instead of drinking it, the driver poured the vodka into the windshield wiper reservoir so he could see where he was going! And thus he returned vodka to its etymological roots, if not its routine purpose: The word traces back to the Sanskrit *udan,* for water. Was our experience just an amusing anecdote of a strangely resourceful person living within an economy that was in free fall? Did it portend the revival of a communist orthodoxy? Should we read into it the beginnings of a drift through a barter economy back to the rule of the czars? Or will the Russia that emerges from the post-Yeltsin era be a free-market KGB state? Or a brutally repressive realization of Adam Smith's fondest dreams? We don't begin to know the answer, but we do know that if you hope to do business in Russia or even understand it, you better not deny any of the possibilities. Bet on the communists, and it's critical that you ask yourself both what you should do in the present to prepare for that future and what the effect of what you do will be if the future belongs instead to the czarists, or to KGB-trained capitalists, or to the gangster-CEOs of present-day Moscow.

Across the Great Wall, post-Mao China has been clinging all along to an absolutely heterodox view of communism while encouraging capitalism at every level of society. What is the principal reform of the future that the Chinese government is promoting? Ownership, private control of the means of production. And what is the one inviolable bugaboo of communist economic doctrine, the one thing that cannot be countenanced? Ownership, private control of the means of production. Is China on its way to becoming the world's largest officially communistic economic democracy or the world's largest democratic communist state? Both are possible, and unless you entertain the possibility of both, you will be prepared for neither.

How about if you hope to do business in the Middle East? Well, you can assume the status quo will last out your lifetime, or even that peace ultimately will triumph. You can bet that an isolated Jewish state eventually must be swallowed up once again by its Islamic neighbors. Or you can entertain the possibility that, in its struggle to survive, Israel will adopt the politics of national socialism and eventually come to resemble the German Motherland from which so much of its horrible history derives. Whatever future you are landing in—Israeli citizen, Likud terrorist, Arab imam, petroleum executive, desert cartographer, Raytheon missile salesperson—will be profoundly affected by the future that Israel and the Middle East land in. And unless you are prepared for all of them, you are prepared for none.

The Triumph of Paradox

We cannot control outcomes anymore, no more than we can wish paradox away or defeat its contradiction. All we can do is attempt to influence our own future or the future of our own business, absorb the paradoxes that our personal or professional life presents us with, and be prepared for whatever tomorrow does arrive. To do that, businesses and individuals have to answer two fundamental questions about themselves: What am I? And what will I be?

Doing so is the first act of the visionary, but it is only Act 1. Getting from now to then also requires you to recognize your postulates about the future: the things that have to be true for you to become what you think you will be. And it requires you to change your understanding of your future whenever one of your postulates becomes less likely of achieving truth.

For a pessimist, this constant revision will be a source of depression: He had hoped that he could control the universe, and in the space between "I am a" and "I will be a" he is finding out that he cannot. Our counsel: Don't be disappointed that the future is going to be different, because it always will be. Instead, revel in the certainty of change and in the realization that with each change you are opening up to the full range of your own possibilities.

Individuals will have to perform the following steps on their own. As for organizations, everyone, no matter what work or service it is in, needs to assemble a Future Council and to trust to its care the following functions and conditions:

♦ You need to define your values because when everything else changes, your values cannot. More about this in Part II, but if you don't know what you believe in, as an individual or a company, stop right now, figure it out, and make sure those values are embedded in moral certainty and disproportionately rewarded. We here at Citibank believe in innovation, and so certain are we of the value of innovation that we will pay greater attention, time, *and* money to the clever among us than we do to the loyal, the fair, and the trustworthy. We here at Motorola will understand the electron. That is our value above all values, and because it is, we will reward physicists over nonphysicists. And thus your value, whatever it is, becomes readily and consistently identifiable within the organization. Thus, too, as you change and change and change, you always know who you are.

♦ To review your future effectively, you need to repackage the concept of time within your own life and within your organization. Do something every month, quarterly, or even annually, and you are tying it to rituals of the past. Review your future every nineteen weeks or every five months or at some other asynchronous interval, and you've placed your review at odds with the normal rhythms of both business and your life, and made it disjunctive instead of conjunctive. That's part of what it means to have the attitude of an insurgent.

◆ When you review your future, look at the seminal moments that have occurred since your last review. Ask yourself how those moments need to change your perception of what the future is going to be and what has to now be true for you to become what you now think you will be. Then ask yourself how your renewed view of the future should change the decisions you are making in the present, and what will happen if you are right or (and this is critical) if you are wrong. What if you invest in a future that turns out to be false, or underinvest in one that turns out to be true? What are the probable consequences of either course of action because either course of action is likely to be the right one? You can't look in just one direction: You have to live in both tenses, and to do that you have to make the future live in the present, and the present live in the future.

◆ You need to manage relations, internally and externally, so that you allow yourself the latitude to change when you need to change. Internally, that means building both a culture that can respond to constantly altering horizons and a communications matrix that doesn't measure the worth of a vision by the length of its shelf life. Everybody inside the company has to understand that the future is going to be reassigned as often as the horizon changes. Be true to your values, honor them in everything you do, and what seems like constant change will simply be constant consistency. Externally, you need to be yourself and not yourself. Every action you take, every decision you make has to be informed by the opposite point of view and has to recognize the potential for an opposite outcome. Companies today have to be global. You can't just sell in the Pacific Rim and India and Poland; you have to be in Warsaw and Delhi and Hong Kong and Malaysia, which means that you can't stop your global expansion. But globalism is also spawning an outbreak of virulent nationalism, and unless you are equally ready for that, you are ready for neither condition. Instead of economic imperialism, practice economic diplomacy. Marry the countries you move into. In Spain, be Spanish; in China, be Chinese; in Brazil, Brazilian; and in all those countries, be global, too. Find the people in each venue in which you operate who share not just your goals but your beliefs, and make your belief system their belief system, and their belief system yours. And then be utterly prepared for the possibility that no matter how right every step you take is, the outcome might be utterly wrong.

- You should take a few very visible actions that make it clear where your future bets are placed, but never find yourself so deeply in the future that you can't change your vision of it without looking like a hypocrite. Whether it's the allocation of human or financial resources, you've got to finally put your money where your mouth is. Just don't put too much there, or leave it there for too long.

- When you assemble your Future Council, be certain that its membership reaches down deeply into the organization, that it includes potential future stars as well as present ones, that it crosses organizational barriers to the future, and that it includes a fair representation of what we call "Socratic gadflies"—people who have been traditionally excluded from important councils because their point of view is likely to create friction. Leave the future up to your executive team, and you will find them agreeing about things that have already been decided on. You need outsiders looking in and insiders looking out. You need to reward them for their time and effort, and reward them significantly to show the significance of their work. And you need to shuffle the group constantly because membership on the Future Council can be no more predictable than the future itself.

- Finally, make certain that it's not just answers but questions that are driving your decision making. Answers describe only today. Questions describe tomorrow, and the future by its very definition is in opposition to the present.

Problems and Solutions

If you follow the seven steps we've outlined above, your Future Council should produce on a continuing—and continually changing—basis a set of problems and solutions that reflect your company's current vision of the future. Sometimes, you will have discovered problems that you have no solution for; sometimes, there will be solutions in search of problems. Issues will have emerged that you understand the meaning of, and issues will have surfaced that you can identify only as issues because their meaning leaves you completely in the dark. The question, at this point, isn't what you know and what you don't know: Life isn't a quiz show. The real question is, how do you apply company (and personal) resources to both nurturing and understanding your current vision of the future? And for that we suggest using the two-by-two matrix below as your guideline. Take a moment now to look at it before we go on. We'll be returning to this schematic numerous times throughout this book.

PROBLEM	**don't know the problem**	listen	question
	know the problem	attack	leverage
		know the solution	**don't know the solution**
		SOLUTION	

Take a look at the lower left-hand box of the matrix. The Future Council has identified a problem raised by its current vision of the future, and it has identified a solution to that problem as well. Great. Attack. Assemble an action team from the inside or put together the best invited team from outside you can find, and get to it. This is life in the present tense: problems in real time, solutions in real time.

The lower right-hand corner represents life in the present-future tense: real-time problems awaiting future solutions. The Future Council has raised an important issue—our logo no longer reflects the future as we now understand it—but you lack the specific resources to solve the problem internally because graphic design is not one of the things you do well. Here's where you outsource. But don't just find one body shop and send the problem its way. Outsource it to multiple body shops and have them produce simultaneous alternatives. That way you're applying leverage at the same time you're outsourcing. Once you have chosen the best of the simultaneous alternatives, you've converted a situation where you know the problem but not the solution to one where you know both problem and solution. Now you're back into the lower-left box of the matrix, and you can attack this one, too.

Take a look next at the upper left-hand corner. The Future Council has identified a solution to a problem it can't define. Maybe the solution is a paradigm: quality circles, reengineering, internal customers, whatever the flavor of the day happens to be. Maybe it's something else. But in either event, it's time to bring a guru in—from inside or outside the organization—and to sit at his or her feet and listen while he tells you what problems the solution will fix. This, as we wrote earlier, is life in the future-present tense: answers for the present day wrapped in the language of the future, which means that by the time you implement whatever paradigm you buy, you will be living in the present-past tense: employing yesterday's answers to address today's problems.

Don't get us wrong: If listening to a guru feels good—and it often does—then by all means do so. Just don't confuse the verb tenses, and don't forget that most great "answers" about the future are serendipitous in any event. Chester Barnard, who headed up New Jersey Bell for twenty-five years until 1952 and also served as president of the Rockefeller Fund, is one of the great futurists of the twentieth century. He is the one responsible for double-twisted phone lines being installed in every house from the very beginning of telephone service, long before there was any need for them, and even today that twisted-pair line dominates the architecture of information delivery. But Barnard didn't insist on the twisted line because he foresaw computers and faxes and modems at the century's end. His reason was far simpler: He believed that eventually most houses would subdivide into duplexes, and he wanted to have a second line ready when that happened. Right answer, in short; wrong reason, and a huge leap forward because of a misguess about the future.

Now take a look at the upper right-hand corner: Neither the solution nor the problem is known, and so there can be no answers, only questions. Among ourselves, we call this the Fool Box because it was the job of the fool in medieval royal society to always be at the king's elbow, tempering his vanity and reminding him (at risk to the fool's own life) of his royal mortality. "I am Ozymandias, King of Kings: / Look on my works, ye Mighty, and despair!" the ruler (actually the thirteenth-century B.C. Egyptian pharaoh Ramses II) roars in Percy Bysshe Shelley's famous poem of the same name. "Not so fast, buster," the fool says in response. "You think that ticker of yours is going to last forever? Or this empire? Look at the dinosaurs! Not to mention sandstorms. . . ."

For a king in a monarchical world, a fool was indispensable. We tend to think the fool is indispensable for CEOs in a corporate-driven world, but if the concept of the fool bothers you, just think of it as the Opposition Box, because this is where you build questioning into your organization. This is how you live in the present and future, how you are yourself and not yourself, how you move inside and absorb paradox institutionally. You embed contradiction in your organization by being certain that someone inside it is living outside it, beyond here and now, carrying your story line out five, ten, twenty years—even, we would argue, a hundred and five hundred years ahead of you.

Maybe you hire from the outside to fill the Fool Box; maybe you do so from inside. But if you do fill from inside, it's critical that you relax constraints so thoroughly on those who occupy the box that they can speak truths and think thoughts and contemplate without fear of retribution heresies that are forbidden to the normal run of mortals within your organization. The fool also has to be able to say the sky is falling and be wrong and look ridiculous and not be punished for doing so. It's not the answers that count in the Fool Box so much as it's reinventing the future on a continuing and serial basis. Do that well, and the fool will destabilize on a regular basis everything your organization thinks about itself.

Welcome to the Fool Box

If you think you know your problem and the answer you seek, this book is probably not for you. Nor is it necessarily for you if you don't know your problem but want to be told an answer—the bookshelves are full of works by learned gurus who will try to do just that—or if you want to outsource a problem you are incapable of solving to someone whom you think can. There's plenty of help for that available also.

We admit it up front: We don't know your problems. We don't know the solutions, either. We can't, in either case. Your reality and our reality have many points in common because we share the same fundamental base of experience and sensory stimulation and because we live in the same moment in space and time, but our reality and yours are not now and never will be parallel. All we know are the questions you need to be asking, and all we can sense is that if you have picked up this book and read this far in it, you must be feeling something like the same uneasiness that sent us on our journey. Maybe your business feels out of control, or your career. Maybe it's your life generally that's on the edge. You don't know your problem, nor do we. We don't know your solution, nor do you. Climb into the Fool Box with us and let's see what we can find together, but as you do so, keep in mind the following axioms:

- The closer a vision gets to a provable "truth," the more it is simply describing the present in the future tense.
- The more successful you are at predicting the future, the more you destabilize your present, in every way.
- The more accurate a vision is and the more it destabilizes the present, the less likely it is to come true.
- The more we are certain of the details of the future, the more we are likely to be wrong.
- Whatever we expect to be in the future, we must anticipate we won't be.

♦ The more we come to understand our future, the more we alienate ourselves from the present and those who live in it.

In Part II, we take up the paradoxes you encounter in your daily life: those of value, size, time, competition, action, leadership, and leisure. We'll meet you there. Meanwhile, we encourage you to spend a few minutes on the concluding exam for Part I.

♦ First-Quarter Exam

Turn your pad sideways and divide the page into four columns. Label the left-hand column "Issue." The next two columns, heading left to right, should be labeled "Know Problem" and "Know Solution." Finally, label the right-hand column "Action Taken."

Under "Issue" list the six to ten most vexing matters in your business and/or personal life—"payroll is unresponsive," "boss doesn't realize what I do," "marriage is no longer exciting," whatever fits your reality right now.

Next, go to the "Problem" and "Solution" column for each issue and place an X if you know either or both. Under "Action Taken," use a shorthand to indicate what steps you have instituted to bring the issue to closure.

When you're done with that, turn back to the matrix on Page 31 and compare your actions to the ones we suggest. If you think you know the problem and the solution—sales are slow in the Midwest and your Midwest sales manager is incompetent—are you attacking it? If you know the problem but not the solution—your son won't talk to you but you don't know why—have you gone outside for help, and are you leveraging the people you are consulting? Have you found a guru on the bookshelves or in the wilds of cable TV who can help you find the problem you think you have the solution for?

Finally, take a hard look at any issues for which there are no Xs marked under "Problem" and "Solution." Who's asking the questions that need to be asked? And is that person (or persons) sufficiently removed from the issue—sufficiently outside the box of the matter troubling you—to think independently? If not, who is going to occupy the Fool Box? Don't leave this exam until you've written down at least two names for each such item on your "Issue" list.

II
PARADOXES OF
THE EVERYDAY

*The more change becomes
constant, the less daily it seems.*

1

◆ ◆ ◆ ◆ ◆ ◆ ◆ ◆ ◆ ◆ ◆ ◆ ◆ ◆ ◆ ◆ ◆ ◆

THE PARADOX OF VALUE

Intrinsic worth isn't.

What is the value of an Oscar Mayer hot dog? Intrinsically, a figure is easy to arrive at. The hot dog is worth the cost of the sum total of its parts and assemblage: a tenth of a penny in nitrates and other preservatives, let's say; another two-tenths of a penny for the casing; a full penny's worth of pork by-products; another half a cent for other filling; plus a penny for the tiny fraction of a work minute necessary to manufacture the hot dog and for depreciation of the machinery involved. Maybe a little less than three cents in all.

But does the intrinsic worth of the hot dog tell us anything about its value? Not really. More and more, intrinsic worth isn't.

Just as corporate valuation has come uncoupled from intrinsic value—the liquidation value of amazon.com, to cite one famous example, is virtually nothing—so the value of the products businesses make bears less and less relationship to the physical assets contained in the offering.

Everything is duplicatable. The world is awash in products. Almost everything can be bought round the clock—by phone, by Net, in person. The expectation is that almost everything will be cheaper tomorrow, and even if it's not, somewhere a discounter or a gray marketer is waiting to sell you what you want or its generic equivalent at half what you'd pay down the street. Buyers control the sales equation, and they control it with an iron fist. And thus the value of any product—from a hot dog to a luxury car—becomes inseparable from the buyer's perception of worth. Instead of intrinsic value, we have relative value.

In theory, every product has a spot price—a price a customer is willing to pay to achieve ownership—but the spot price changes in relation to the customer's experience and history and the circumstances at the moment the transaction is to take place. What's more, the changes cannot be measured across market segments because concepts of value have become idiosyncratically embedded in individual value codes that are themselves the reflection of highly distinct orientations toward an unshared reality.

How many realities does the manufacturer of a product destined for broad American consumption have to keep in mind when he values it for the marketplace today? As of late April 1999, 272,381,040 of them. Is it possible to keep all those realities in mind as you set a strike price? Absolutely not. Is it possible to ignore the fact that 272,381,040 different realities are waiting to judge your price in the marketplace? Absolutely not that, either. Welcome to the fun house.

Back to the hot dog.

At Sam's Club, an individual Oscar Mayer hot dog—shrink-wrapped and packed a dozen to the container—would have a value of twelve cents if that's the unit price a shopper is willing to pay. But what if the shopper is a vegetarian or eats only kosher or is a mother who has read one of those articles about how hot dogs are perfect plugs for little throats or sees hot dogs as phallic symbols representative of millennia of male domination? Then the hot dog has negative value. You would have to pay any one of those shoppers to carry it out of the store, and the more loathsome she found it, the more you would have to shell out.

Now take that exact same hot dog to a major American airport, smother it with a few pennies' worth of catsup, onions, mustard, and relish, tuck it between a few pennies' more of bun. What is its value now? Up to $5, depending on toppings, the last we looked, and they were flying off the stand.

How is it that a product that he can be had in the supermarket for twelve pennies—and has an intrinsic value perhaps a quarter of that—comes to be valued at a multiple maybe forty times that at Hartsfield International Airport? Because circumstances change the spot value of any product and they change it continuously. At the marketing window called Sam's Club, the hot dog has a value set by the needs of a grocery shopper. At the marketing window known as Hartsfield International Airport, the time value of money suddenly gets thrown into the equation. You could perhaps get a better lunch snack at Hartsfield—but nowhere so quick. And it's not just the time value of money that has to be factored in. There's also the money value of escaping the cage: If you don't eat this hot dog now, you will be forced to eat whatever you are served on your airline flight, and the chance of that food being anywhere near as satisfying as a hot dog smothered in onions, catsup, relish, and mustard is slim to none.

Is $5 all you would pay for an Oscar Mayer hot dog smothered with the works at Hartsfield or O'Hare or LAX or whatever transportation hub happens to have you trapped at the moment? Maybe yes, if you were about to get on a Delta flight, or another airline where the food occasionally can be tolerable. But maybe not, especially if you were about to board a plane run by an airline notorious for its bad or almost nonexistent in-flight food— Southwest, AirTran, the list goes on. Then $10 might seem perfectly reasonable. The value of the product changes not just according to its marketing window but according to the consumer's own immediate future.

And why is it that of every food vendor vying for business at America's airports, Oscar Mayer is outselling nearly all of them with a product priced at such a high multiple of its supermarket value? Because amidst all the uncertainty of air travel—the rush between flights, delays at the gate, canceled flights, bumpy rides, inedible in-flight lasagna, flammable insulation, global terrorism—the absolute predictability of the Oscar Mayer experience is an island of calm. You know what the hot dog will taste like the minute you see the sign, and because you do, and because your speed needs are being met and your fear of cage-eating is being assuaged, you'll tolerate a price that is, on its face, ridiculous.

That's a second paradox of value: The more stable its brand, the more unstable the value of a product is, and the greater the potential to maximize price margins.

Coca-Cola, perhaps the world's strongest brand, is said to be considering experimenting with spot pricing on its vending machines. Sensors on outdoor machines would read temperature and humidity and set the price accordingly. On a dry, one-hundred-degree day, a twelve-ounce Coke might cost you $1.25. The price might be 65 cents on an average day—about what a vending-machine Coke now costs—and maybe 25 cents on an optimally poor day to sell soft drinks. Will the company actually go ahead with the plan? We have no idea. Could it succeed with spot pricing if it did? We have no doubt. Whether a Coke costs a quarter—roughly 25 times its intrinsic worth—or $1.25, the brand Coca-Cola delivers a promise of refreshment so consistent that it could sustain prices changing by a multiple of 5 times at the same machine, perhaps even on the same day.

Why not, for that matter, set the value of a vending-machine Coca-Cola by region and hour of day? In the Deep South, Coke is a common substitute for morning coffee. Price the product according to customer demand in, say, a Birmingham office building, and you could easily get a dime more a drink, with an offsetting reduction later in the day when demand is slack. Strategically located weight sensors would allow the vending machines to ratchet up the price of a Diet Coke when an obese customer shows up, or of a regular Coke when a skinny one does. Again, the needs and conditions of the immediate marketplace would be determining value, and thus price, and microprocessors, would be doing the grunt work.

Or spot pricing could be used for machine-by-machine inventory control. If a vending machine senses that it has only three regular Cokes left but fifteen Nestea Iced Teas, and if it knows there will be no new deliveries for another half a day, it could set the price of a Coke at $1.50 and the price of a canned iced tea at, say, a quarter, and it could readjust the equation hourly, or by the minute, to assure that the last drink in the machine of whatever sort is being sold just as the delivery truck pulls up.

We would even argue that there are times Coca-Cola should consider pricing its product at its intrinsic worth of almost nothing because among the circumstances that determine value in a relative world are history and memory. Share a Coke from a chilled bottle with the first date you've kissed at your first teenage dance, and the drink forever after will remind you, at some deep interior place, of the moment. Give the drink away at that moment, and it will be your brand that fills that place in personal history. Provide each bottle with a straw, and provide each straw with a double sipping head, and you'll also assure that two sets of lips get close enough to graze one another. Of such moments are memories made.

Pepsi-Cola, by the way, could do the same thing with its vending machines, but only after Coke had led the way. As a brand, Pepsi isn't strong enough to support spot pricing on its own. When value becomes externalized, it's the internal strength of the product that determines how widely the value to the customer will fluctuate.

What's the premium a customer will pay for a fully assembled bike versus one that comes with those ominous words: "Some assembly required"? Nothing, if the customer is handy with tools. Nothing, if he has time to figure out the curious language that always seems to accompany "some assembly required." Almost anything, though, if it's Christmas Eve, you've just gotten the children to bed, and you want to have something waiting by the tree the next morning that looks as if a human could actually ride it.

What's the value, for that matter, of a prostitute? Once again, it all depends. If a ship has just come in from six months at sea, a prostitute can pretty much set her price. If the ship has been in dock for a week, a different pricing structure obtains. If the ship is leaving the next morning for another six months at sea, the price changes again. It changes for bachelor parties, too, and in repetition, and depending on the location and the medium of the meeting: the Plaza Bar at 10:00 P.M. versus the corner of 13th and L at 3:00 in the morning.

What's more, the price changes, and everyone knows why. There are still virgins in this world, but there are no virgin consumers any longer. Charge an extra 50 cents a gallon for your gas in the Mojave Desert, and no one is going to think he's being ripped off because he forgot to fill up the car in L.A. before leaving for Vegas. Value today exists in a triangulation between brand, consumer, and circumstance, and because it does, every product has both a Price Discrepancy Threshold and a Contextual Price Discrepancy Threshold.

Go back to soft drinks. At your neighborhood Wal-Mart a six-pack of Classic Coca-Cola might sell for $2.39, while in the rack right beside it, a six-pack of Sam's Cola (actually, repackaged RC Cola) sells for $1.79. If the customer chooses the Classic Coke over the Sam's brand, you have begun to establish a residual brand value. The Price Discrepancy Threshold is the point at which the customer will make the opposite choice—that is, she will choose Sam's Cola over the "real" Coke based solely on price. Maybe it's a price differential of a dollar a six-pack; maybe it's $1.50. But at some point the scales will tip, and you'll know what your brand is worth. But only in that context.

Change the circumstance, and the discrepancy slides up or down depending on the relative value of the product as a result of its probable absence in a particular environment. In a store, you have to imagine the future excess satisfaction a Classic Coke might give you over a generic one, and thus you're willing to tolerate less of a price difference between the two. But in an airport faced with a sea of uncertainty or at a football game where you have gone just to have fun, both the brand promise and the implicit brand fulfillment are directly in front of you. Then the differential between what you'll pay might rise to 200 percent or more—who wants to take a chance in such circumstances?—and that's your Contextual Price Discrepancy Threshold.

There's one more wrinkle we have to mention as well. To the extent that you can fuse product and service, what you are putting on the market is an offering. And to the extent you can create offerings and use your advertising to show the offering at the moment of brand truth, the price discrepancy grows still greater. Taken solely as a physical entity, a Michelin tire is just a tire, nothing more: a combination of synthetic and real rubbers, belting, threading, and valve stem that you could buy at a cheaper price from many other manufacturers. Michelin tires, though, are not perceived as just products. Embedded in them is also a service—safety—that is constantly reinforced by an ad campaign that shows that service at the moment when you most want to imagine the promise of the brand will come true: when your baby's life is in danger. Thus, Michelin tires are also an offering, almost a religious one to those for whom the life of their baby is a sacred holding. Thus, too, the premium the brand Michelin allows the manufacturer Michelin to charge for its wares.

When intrinsic worth disappears as a measuring stick, the value of anything migrates to need, at the moment of need. In 1998, CBS, Fox, and ABC paid a collective $12.8 billion for the rights to broadcast National Football League games through the year 2005. At the time, the most recent sale of an NFL team—the Minnesota Vikings—had fetched $250 million. In short, for what the networks collectively paid, they could in theory have bought all thirty NFL teams then extant, voted themselves the broadcast rights for free into perpetuity, and had billions of dollars left over. Nuts? Looked at one way, it's nuttier than a fruitcake, but the need of the networks at the time of the transaction wasn't to own football teams; it was to fill airtime and be perceived as a player in the world of professional sports broadcasting. And it was that need that drove the value.

An older example: Way back at the beginning of the 1950s, CBS found itself in a deadlock with Philip Morris over the *I Love Lucy* show. CBS wanted to follow the then-standard procedure of broadcasting live on the West Coast but filming the show from a TV screen for distribution elsewhere in the country. Philip Morris, the show's sponsor, knew that such a procedure produced grainy images for East Coast consumption and didn't want its name associated with second-rate quality in the market where it was doing most of its business. To solve the dilemma, Desi Arnaz came up with the idea of filming the series in the studio so that viewers everywhere could enjoy the same pristine quality. When CBS balked at the cost, Arnaz sweetened his offer: Desilu, the production company he and Lucille Ball had formed, would pay for the filming itself in return for retaining the rights to the series. Was CBS wrong in its calculations? Horribly so, in retrospect. The network has lost millions upon millions of dollars in the years since *I Love Lucy* went into syndication. Do those millions and millions of dollars represent the show's extrinsic worth? Hardly, either. But ratings create need, and need establishes value.

In effect, everything has a floating worth whose margins are determined by which of the many variables is weighing on a buying decision at any given moment you are able to maximize. Or almost everything.

What's the worth of a year of undergraduate education at Harvard? At the bottom of the price range, the value is zero—that's what a full-scholarship student pays to attend the university for a year. And at the top? Well, as of the 1999–2000 school year, the figure was $32,164—that's for tuition plus room and board. Who pays that figure? Anyone who fails to qualify for a merit scholarship or has annual family income in excess of the threshold for need-based scholarships. Roughly four million students were expected to receive Pell Grants, the most widely used federal college-assistance program, in 1999–2000. Of those, 90 percent were expected to have annual family incomes below $30,000, which is why a lot of families earning in the range of $55,000 to over $100,000 annually go seriously into debt to fund their children's college education at Harvard or elsewhere.

But what if Harvard were to use tier pricing instead of flat pricing? What if the value of a year's education in those hallowed halls were allowed to float to the level of consumer need and circumstance as does the value of other products. What then?

For simplicity's sake, let's say that Harvard takes in a thousand freshmen a year, and that, when scholarship aid is figured in, the average payment for tuition, fees, room, and board is $15,000 annually. That leaves a total tab for the freshman class of $15 million. Now, let's price things differently. Instead of a one-tuition-size-fits-all approach, we're going to offer admission at various pricing levels. As a brand, Harvard is nearly as golden as Coca-Cola—it will withstand wide pricing margins. So we'll earmark ten spots in the freshman class for qualified students whose parents are willing to pay $100,000 a year for them to attend the university. As a tuition payment, that's nothing to a Michael Eisner if his son or daughter wants to attend. Children seeking those $100,000 slots will apply for them and them alone. Probably the competition will be laxer than it is at lower tuition levels. Certainly the gene pool will be far smaller, which should make it easier to gain admission. But here's the key thing: We're making the value of a Harvard education extrinsic to the customer.

Next, let's fill in the other tuition slots: twenty-five places at $75,000 a year, fifty places at $50,000, a hundred at $40,000, two hundred at $30,000. We've taken up fewer than four hundred slots in a class of a thousand; yet we've already produced $15.375 million in tuition, fees, and accessories—an excess of $375,000 over our current theoretical total. And guess what? Because we've let value float to need and circumstance, the rest of the class, all 615 of them, can attend for free. Instead of saddling the cost of scholarship programs on the backs of everyone who fails, however marginally, to quality for aid, the cost is borne by those most able to do so.

Now, let's take our tier-pricing program and convert it, in effect, to spot pricing. In short, let's have value *really* float to the purchasers' circumstances and the perceived need for a Harvard degree. Instead of being admitted to the college at the $100,000 level, students will be admitted at the Tier A level, and instead of admitting just ten students at that level, we're going to admit twenty—Harvard material, everyone of them. Here's the catch, though: Those twenty students (and their parents) will be bidding against each other for only ten slots, with the bidding to open at $100,000 per annum for four years. We'll do the same thing at the Tier B level, with bidding to begin at $75,000, and so on.

How quickly will the aggregate tab for tuition, fees, room, and board get to the $15 million level? How many of those thousand students being allowed into the freshman class will be able to attend for free now? And what about the would-be Tier A students whose parents had to drop out of the bidding at, say, $150,000 a year? Well, how about if we let them buy an admission slot from one of the students who had been admitted at a free tier level? The Tier A parents had been willing to pay a bare minimum of $400,000 for their children to attend Harvard for four years, and before the bidding began, the children had been found to have adequate intellectual capacity. If they now want to buy an admission slot for that same $400,000 and if they can find someone willing to sell it, why not?

And why shouldn't the student who sells the slot be allowed to convert his or her intellectual capital to real capital at the front end of an academic career instead of at the back end? For $100,000 of the $400,000 their admission slots would fetch, students who sold their places in the Class of 2004 could put themselves through seven years of undergraduate and graduate work at an excellent state university. Maybe another $100,000 would go to taxes. The other $200,000 they could put into a tax-deferred bundle of mutual funds that, even at a modest 7 percent return per annum, would be worth more than $3 million by the time they began to pull within sight of retirement age. Is the differential value between a Harvard degree and one from the University of North Carolina at Chapel Hill or the University of California at Berkeley possibly greater than that? And even if it is, shouldn't the student have the right to make the choice?

There's a third paradox of value: The more brutally it is determined by marketplace factors, the more democratizing it can be. When value becomes unhinged from intrinsic worth, dismeritocratic means produce meritocratic ends.

Is the Harvard Board of Governors likely to adopt a pricing policy such as we have just described anytime soon? No, not at all. The thought of having their educational service product treated like pork-belly futures would send Harvard faculty members and alumni to the swooning couches by the tens of thousands, we suspect. But if the school's alumni were to consult their own daily experience, they would find abundant examples of exactly the same pricing principles.

The price of an airline ticket can change more than half a

dozen times in a single day. Gasoline prices rise and fall according to a logic seemingly all their own. Thanks to the Internet and twenty-four-hour shopping, sales prices on anything from cars to TVs to mail-order sport coats strike at any moment around the clock, anywhere around the world, and disappear just as fast. And, of course, the most closely watched indicators of value in America today—the prices of stocks and mutual funds—can change not just by the minute or second but by the nanosecond.

In such a spot-price world what most determines the value of any product or any service is not the product or service itself, not its intrinsic worth, not even external circumstances under which buyer and seller meet, but the information attendant upon the transaction at the moment the transaction takes place.

What do we mean? Let's start with the buyer. Jayne and John both want new windows for their houses. They live in average neighborhoods, in average houses, in average climates, and both would like their new windows to provide the maximum insulation necessary for the climate they live in—enough insulation, that is, but not too much, at too great a price. At the beginning of their purchase journey, both also know as close to nothing as it is humanly possible to know about exterior windows. Insulating capacity is expressed by an "R" rating—the higher, the better—and where "R" ratings are concerned, John and Jayne are both babes in the woods.

But not for long. Thanks to the World Wide Web, global connectivity, and the proliferation of special-interest publications, it is now possible for anyone of average intelligence to become an expert in almost any field he or she chooses to pursue, without ever leaving home. And so Jayne does. She pays *Consumer Reports* a modest on-line fee to download its most recent ranking of exterior windows, complete with an exhaustive description of "R" ratings. But Jayne doesn't stop there. She joins a chat room that consists largely of housing contractors who have been unlucky in love, and there, under the guise of flirtation, she further enriches her knowledge of the subject. Calls to the toll-free consumer information numbers of several manufacturers of exterior windows deepen her awareness still further. Finally, Jayne feels fully confident: She knows not just the "R" rating necessary for her climate zone but the best window casing for the money to give her the needed "R" rating and the best grade of glass to accomplish her goal.

John, meanwhile, can't be bothered. Time, not money, is for him the one irreplaceable commodity. Or maybe he's just lazy. How do you find *Consumer Reports* on the Internet? If not the Net, where would it be in the public library? And where exactly might the nearest library be?

Who's going to make the better buy? Who's going to get the most value for his or her money? Jayne, obviously. She's bringing a very specific set of needs to the marketplace and letting the marketplace bid to fulfill her wants. Andersen windows? Pellas? Who needs the top-of-the-line models so long as the "R" rating is right? It's the casing and glass that determine insulation capacity, not the brand on the window. In effect, Jayne has informationalized the transaction, and it's the information she holds that is determining value and price.

John, by contrast, has elected to let the marketplace hold the information. In his ignorance, he is likely to migrate to brand— Pella, let's say—and because he is coming to the brand instead of forcing the brand to come to him, Pella will be able to value its windows at the absolute top of the margin. Ignorance may be bliss, but it is expensive bliss.

Or maybe not. Maybe the money value of the time John saved *not* learning about "R" value was worth every extra cent he paid for his Pella windows over a cheaper generic that would have accomplished exactly the same purpose. That's why we say that the value of every transaction is extrinsic to the customer's needs at the moment the transaction takes place.

And as with windows, so with everything from TV sets to deck shoes, macrobiotics, and even medical treatment for life-threatening conditions. Medline—the extensive database of medical information maintained by the National Library of Medicine at the National Institutes of Health—can take you on an on-line tour through decades of learned articles on the subject of prostate cancer. Chat lines and support groups will give you the latest on radiation therapy versus cryogenic surgery versus a radical prostatectomy. If you want to watch a radical prostatectomy, the

Discovery Channel probably will be glad to oblige. Consumer watchdog groups will tell you what to expect to pay. Health care watchdog groups will tell you which hospitals are the best at urological surgery, and various surveys in which doctors rate other doctors will tell you which urological surgeons physicians themselves would go to if they were diagnosed with prostate cancer.

The more complete the information the customer holds, the more the customer controls the transaction. And the more the customer controls the transaction, the more the value of the transaction is determined on the buyer's side of the sales equation. But what is true for buyers is equally true for sellers.

How do you manage the value of your product today? In part, certainly, by managing its intrinsic worth. The less you can manufacture a product for or provide a service at, without diminution in value, the better. That's as it has always been. What's different is that managing intrinsic worth is only one piece of the pie, and an increasingly small share.

Managing value requires that you manage the time the product is most demanded, the time it is least demanded, and the time that it's consistently demanded. The more you understand about the buying cycles of consumers, the more you can manage your price margins to the rhythm of their shopping.

You also can manage value by asking the customer to work for the transaction. What is the brilliance of FedEx? Well, part of it is understanding intercity exchange rates, but a larger part is that FedEx has managed to turn its entire customer base into their own shipping clerks. We'll give you the materials; we'll pick up the package; we'll deliver it to and for you. But you do the wrapping and you do the packaging. Customers pay an extreme premium not because FedEx has saved them time but because it has involved them, relatively painlessly, in the process.

Dell does the same thing: You design the machine, and we'll build it for you. And the more intricately you design it—that is to say, the harder you work at doing our work—the more work we will do for you, and the more we will charge you for doing it. Judged by the classic rules of how consumers are to be served by the marketplace, this approaches madness: The customer is always right, and the customer never lifts a finger. In the contemporary marketplace, though, consumers will lift far more than a finger so long as they think their singular needs are being uniquely served.

The same broad principles of customer involvement apply to on-line book sales. Amazon.com owns the market—and more critically the market value—not because it sells a book any faster than the on-line Barnes & Noble (www.bn.com) and not because it has a larger inventory. It owns the market because almost from the beginning it has involved customers in the transaction. You want to be an unpaid book reviewer? Post it on amazon.com. You can do it at bn.com, but because Barnes & Noble was late getting into the cyber-sales game, you are far more likely to do so at Amazon. Amazon will also pay you if you sell its books via links from your own Website, another stroke of brilliance that is turning sites all over the Internet into satellite stores.

Maybe most important, managing value requires understanding the information horizon in which transactions are likely to take place. You may not know that AirTran has terrible in-flight food—it might have been a dozen years since you even considered flying an airline so lowly as AirTran—but the public knows, and the public is merciless in its judgments. Fail to know what the public knows and you will miss an opportunity to value your product according to your customers' circumstances and needs.

In theory, as we wrote earlier, that should mean that you could price your Oscar Mayer hot dog at $10 next to AirTran gates, instead of the customary $5. Add in the fact that AirTran has one of the worst on-time records in the industry, and the window for a $10 hot dog would seem to be expanding indefinitely. But both sets of data have to be weighed against other data: that AirTran customers are generally willing to sacrifice promptness for lower fares and thus, presumably, are generally from a lower economic demographic: students, let's say, many of whom exist on such tight budgets that $10 begins to seem like a serious sacrifice; a percentage of whom, too, are likely to be vegetarians. Is your hot dog still a $10 value? And does it make sense in any event to set up an Oscar Mayer stand next to an AirTran gate? As one of the

Johnny-come-latelies to the industry—AirTran was born from the ashes of ValuJet—it tends to be located at the far ends of terminals, in what amounts to air-transportation Siberia. How many customers are you going to get at whatever value you set on your hot dogs?

Information is power, and power creates value. Sometimes, indeed, there is no value but information. The battle for even marginal value on commercial Websites grows more intense with each passing day, but about www.persiankitty.com there is really no question. Run by a Seattle housewife, persiankitty was grossing roughly $800,000 a month by the summer of 1998. Its product? There is no product, only links. Persiankitty is the biggest clearinghouse in the world for sex Websites, and every one of them pays that Seattle housewife for the right to be linked to her site.

The radio personality Don Imus converts information to value in a different way, by acting as an editor for his listeners in the economic marketplace. By commenting on books, movies, and the products that lend commercial support to his show, and by being consistent in his point of view about such items, Imus has established himself as his listeners' intermediary. He saves them time and money, and spares them the hassle of excessive choice; and they pay him with attention to his program, which converts into rating points, which converts into direct economic value derived from the information that Imus assembles and edits.

Whether a product or service stands behind the information or not, the deeper the data can go, the more it can be layered and cross-referenced and cross-fertilized—the more, that is, it is not just data but *meta*data—the more powerful it is, and the more anticipatory it can be. Manage that, and you are managing not just an information flow. You are managing value, at the heart of where it is created.

Imagine a relationship whereby parents of a newborn would surrender genetic information about their child to a pharmaceutical and toiletries conglomerate in return for the conglomerate's attending to the child's seminal moments. A week before the likely emergence of a first tooth, the company would send its equivalent of Ora-Gel. A week before the genetically encoded onset of puberty, it might send girls a package of sanitary napkins and a videotape about feminine hygiene. Boys would get similar information on acne and pimples, plus samples of the products for treating both. Maybe, too, the coverage would be extended. The pharmaceutical firm might continuously monitor a child's genome into adulthood, looking for signs of incipient disease.

Would the company charge for this service? Maybe, but maybe not. Just as Coca-Cola could tie itself to memory by giving away its products at eighth-grade dances, so the pharmaceutical firm could tie itself deep into a family's history by giving away the Ora-Gel, the first box of Tampons, the first tube of Clearasil—even by providing the first warnings of measles or worse. Like an allegory, the pharmaceutical company would be there physically and symbolically at each of the turning points in forming lives. The net worth of the transaction would be so great that the price of the product could be calculated in negative numbers yet still create value for the company because worth is no longer determined intrinsically. What you are seeking to maximize is the value of the purchase to the organization, not profit-margin maximization.

The more you can use information to tie your story into your customer's story, the greater that value will be. And the more you can follow the information that flows back from customers to your core competencies, the more likely you are to discover hidden strengths and even new centers of value within your business.

What if, say, Johnson & Johnson were to launch a successful partnership with new parents such as we described above? Wouldn't it make sense, then, for the company to move into child care? How could you not trust your children to the people who make Band-Aids? In the same spirit, shouldn't Procter & Gamble be opening a virtual marketing university on the Web? Its customers tell it every day that no company on earth has been more successful at marketing over a longer period—and its stock price confirms its customers' opinion. Maybe Coca-Cola shouldn't just give soft drinks away at middle-school dances; maybe the company should get in the business of actually staging the dances themselves, along with bar mitzvahs and Sweet Sixteen parties. Following your own bliss might land you in Tahiti, like Paul Gauguin. Following your customers' bliss could help you fuse product and service into an offering, and in doing that, you could open up whole new value realms.

Maybe the greatest publicity stunt of the last twenty years was the one designed to promote Captain Morgan's Rum. For virtually nothing, the company bought a tiny, two-bit Caribbean Island, declared it an independent republic, wrote a constitution with one peculiar caveat—"Everyone of this island shall have the right to party, man"—and petitioned the United Nations for admission. Meanwhile, back on Captain Morgan's island, the constitution was being upheld with a vengeance. As the cameras whirred and the waves lapped gently against the white sand shores, the partying was continuous.

A loss leader? Absolutely in the short term, but the stunt tied Captain Morgan's Rum to precisely what rum was created to be tied to: sun, fun, the Caribbean, young women in scant bathing suits, young men with washboard abdomens. It embedded the product, in short, in youth and the instinct of youth to party, and in so doing it created value that has sustained the brand as a market leader ever since. All rums cost essentially the same to make. Blindfold a panel of average tasters, and they couldn't begin to distinguish between the five or ten top-selling labels. It's the information that attends the transaction that creates price differentials—the information that creates and sustains value.

Let the drones who know both the problem and the solution worry about average margins and average costs. Both are important, and they'll keep the drones occupied. But put the people in the Fool Box to work on information because that's where value really lies. It's not just that the value of the information of the transaction is worth more than the value of the goods and services being transacted, although that's important in itself. It's also that the specific point at which the customer interacts with the product and with the product environment produces the greatest understanding of the net margin possibilities of the organization. There's the final paradox of value.

◆ Future Exercise

Spot-price yourself by filling out the following questionnaire.

What promises do you deliver or fail to deliver as a product that cause your value to be:

Maximized? _____
_____
_____

Average? _____
_____
_____

Minimized? _____
_____
_____

Under what conditions of need is your value most likely to be:

Maximized? _____
_____
_____

Average? _____
_____
_____

Minimized? _____
_____
_____

What changes or enhancements could you make to the product of yourself that would cause its future value to be further maximized, and under what particular condition of need would each change create maximum value?

Change   Condition

_____   _____

_____   _____

_____   _____

Under what conditions might you give away the product of yourself in order to create future value? And how would doing so create future value?

Condition Value   Creation

_____   _____

_____   _____

_____   _____

And a final item. At the end of this book, we're going to ask you to brand yourself. For now, ponder this: How reliable is the core promise of your product, and how much latitude does that reliability give you in spot-pricing yourself? Think about that until the end of Part IV, and branding yourself should be easy.

Box 1
THE BRAND PROMISE

To maximize value, make it live in the moment.

◆ ◆ ◆ ◆ ◆ ◆ ◆ ◆ ◆ ◆ ◆ ◆ ◆ ◆ ◆ ◆

Every successful brand makes an implicit promise. The promise is at most two words but more often one word, and every successful promise is deeply embedded in the brand and its story. For Coke, the promise is refreshment; for Saturn, it's respect; for Disney, safety; and for Volvo, simply safe.

In effect, the reality of the product itself—the actual flavored carbonated water, the amusement park or animated movie, the internal-combustion-powered conveyance—is nothing more than an artifact of that promise. Stray from the promise, fail to provide respect to a Saturn buyer, fail to make a Disney patron feel a sense of safety in the park or the theater, and your artifact will always be punished, and you with it. Stick with the promise, and to the extent that it is a worthwhile promise that fulfills perceived need, you will create value.

Good enough; those examples are well known, but even the most successful companies need to renew their futures on an ongoing basis, and to do that, they have to continuously ask themselves (a) what is the implicit promise of our brand? (b) what is the operative value of that promise? and (c) is the future changing in such a way as to make the promise irrelevant?

How do you find those things out? How do you analyze brand promise? For starters, by not doing any of the traditional forms of market research.

Traditional market research is meaningless in brand-promise analysis because market research is a static measure, while brand promise is a moving target, and you have to capture it at its apogee to measure operative value. Yes, a brand has both a uniform and an elastic effect over all your products, but the promise of the brand changes continuously as it moves through different tiers of engagement with consumers, and each new tier creates an alteration in value. The promise of a bottle of Montrachet to deliver maximum pleasure matters far less in a wine store, where you have to fantasize the moment of satisfaction in some distant future, than it does on a wine list in a restaurant, where the moment of satisfaction is only minutes away. The promise also matters less in a three-star restaurant, where you bring fewer expectations to the total dining experience, than it does in a five-star restaurant, where the penalty for being wrong with your wine choice is greater. And it matters most of all in a five-star restaurant when you are about to propose marriage or celebrate a graduation or toast a new job or a new contract.

It's this tiering effect, between the different levels of encounter and different levels of expectation that accompany each encounter, that allows you to choose different price points: low in the wine store, higher in the three-star restaurant, higher still in the five-star restaurant, highest of all in a five-star restaurant that specializes in the celebration of special moments. In each case, the maximum pricing point is determined by the degree to which (a) the promise of your brand will be fulfilled immediately and (b) the relative service somebody has performed by having that brand for that fulfilled moment is like a tip. And to analyze your brand promise, these are the points to which you need to pay the most attention.

Are people willing to meet your price point at that moment when the brand promise will be immediately true and the fulfillment of the promise will fuse product and service into an offering? If they are, is your price point too low? If it is, then you can begin to zero in on the unrealized residual value of your brand promise. If people are not willing to meet your price point, is it set too high? If it is not set too high, if there is no reasonable pricing point at which consumers will choose your wine to maximize their experience, then (a) you have the wrong promise, (b) your promise is the right one but it is unclearly or ambiguously conceived, (c) you have strayed from the promise, or (d) the future has arrived, leaving you with the right brand promise in the wrong age. Whichever way the brand promise is missing, your goose is cooked, no matter what wine you serve with it.

2

• • • • • • • • • • • • • • •

THE PARADOX OF SIZE

*The bigger you are, the smaller
you need to be.*

S ome truths haven't changed since David and Goliath: The bigger you are, the harder you still fall. Nowadays, though, the bigger you are, the smaller you also need to be. To operate effectively in a world in which each individual is a microculture and to communicate effectively and directly to the interests of those microcultures, you have to, in effect, atomize your organization and miniaturize its units.

The opposite is just as true: The smaller you are, the bigger you need to appear. If your marketing unit does not have the personnel to assign segment-specific responsibilities and product-specific responsibilities and geographic-specific responsibilities, then each individual in the marketing unit is going to have to divide him- or herself three or six or nine ways until each of the functions is fulfilled, and fulfilled specifically. The microcultures are not going to go away, but if you don't recognize and service them, you might.

Like the great heavyweight boxing champion Muhammad Ali, companies today have to "float like a butterfly and sting like a bee," but they also need to remember that behind all that floating and stinging lay 220 pounds of rock-solid muscle. At his best, what made Ali great—like no other heavyweight champ before or since—was that there were always two bouts going in the ring whenever he fought: one between Ali and his opponent and the other between Ali and himself, between the dancer and the bone-crusher, the featherweight and the heavyweight. For corporate warfare at the start of the new millennium, there couldn't be a much better metaphor.

Global branding and global leadership are not elective courses these days because connectivity has created a global marketplace and neotribalism is creating highly segmented global bodies of opinion. You can't be seen as a market leader in, say, Europe and a market follower on the Pacific Rim: The two impressions don't compute, and you can't hide the one from the other because as the global population gets larger and larger, global opinion becomes more and more concentrated. Nor can you hide from the political heat and the political consequences of equalizing your assault over the entire planet.

As we write, Procter & Gamble's U.S. product lines absolutely dominate their markets. As we write, many of the same products are serious market laggards in Europe. The culture of the organization would say that the market managers of those products in the United States should be granted corporate kingships, while the managers of those products in the European market should be consigned to miserable local duchies, with almost none of the status and few of the rewards granted their U.S. counterparts. Yet to equalize itself globally and thus to maintain a favorable global opinion, Procter & Gamble needs to attack its European problems. To achieve its vision of being the world's greatest producer of consumer products, the company has to disproportionately invest in Europe at the expense of investing in the United States, and part of that means disproportionately extending rewards and the symbols of status to people who haven't earned them. And that in turn would go against not just organizational culture but the basic mores of social justice. To be what it wants to be, in short, Procter & Gamble has to be the impossible. It has to foment corporate injustice to achieve global domination. And thus the weird-ness of paradoxy compounds.

Once we lived in isolated tribes, then isolated families, then iso-lated communities. Opinion was as manyfold as there were sepa-rate social units to sustain it. Today we live more and more in neotribes that share and sustain a common body of highly idio-syncratic belief across the entire planet. Six degrees of separation have become five, five have become four, and three, and two, and one. If you are trailing the market in Melbourne and Tokyo and Bangkok, the fact that you are leading it in Zurich and Milan finally will mean nothing. Bad news inevitably overwhelms good in the marketplace of global opinion, in the segment you care about. Allow bad news to take root and grow in that segment, and you will spend years chasing the impression that you are a fol-lower everywhere.

The price of globalism, in short, is eternal vigilance. If you're not prepared to do battle on every front and do it simultaneously, stay home. But globalization has to coexist with decentralization, not just organizationally but attitudinally. To succeed as a global player today, you need to couple the predatory practices of a nine-teenth-century robber baron with the anything-for-the-customer attitude of a corner grocer: Jay Gould meets Dave Thomas. Once again (and it's worth saying again and again), you have to be your-self and not yourself, the thing and not the thing. There's no other way to move inside the steady collision of opposites.

And a second paradox of size: The larger you are and the more global your reach, the more you need to depend upon independent and isolated variables. Only then can you escape your own size, and unless you can escape your own size, you will become its pris-oner. Shell Oil recently began hiring consultants on twelve-month contracts—in some cases, at as much as $750,000 a year—to work on narrowly defined issues that the company considers critical to its future. In doing so, Shell's parent, Royal Dutch Petroleum, is trusting the fate of a 110-year-old global powerhouse at least in part to free-standing consultancies of one. Strange? Absolutely. Right? Absolutely, too. In effect, those consultancies are filling the

Fool Box. Unless that box is filled, there is no future, and unless the box is isolated, the present is intolerable.

Here's a bet worth making: One of those independent consultancies will come up with a tiny gem of an idea that eventually will overwhelm Royal Dutch Petroleum's core enterprises and redefine the organization. That's a third paradox of size: The more mass you have, the more density and weight, the more likely you are to be completely overthrown from the fringe—*and* the more you need to be. Great size is great power, but great size is also stasis. Insurgencies start on the edge and overwhelm the center. The center, meanwhile, has no choice but to march forward and conquer the world: Napoleon meets Che Guevara. The dance needs both—relentless forward momentum at the core, relentless insurgency at the fringe—because the dance would be incomplete without either. It's the waltz of the ballerina and the elephant. It's Muhammad Ali.

Big companies and small companies are different in degree, obviously. They operate on different scales. But big and small companies are no different in kind and no different in the problems they face.

Whether a company is big or small, it eventually will confront an emergency that will threaten to undermine years, maybe decades or even centuries, of work: a part that suddenly ceases to be available, a product with heretofore hidden side effects, a plane that falls out of the sky. Emergencies come in ways that can never be anticipated, in time frames that are never convenient, and unless they are managed well and immediately, they can erupt into irresolvable complexities from which organizations sometimes never recover. (See the box at the end of this chapter on complex emergencies.) Yet managing equivalent emergencies requires just as much energy, just as much attention, just as much manpower and human hours whether the company's market capitalization is measurable in the trillions or the millions. Disaster is equal opportunity.

So is going to the capital markets. Big and small organizations have different capital needs and different challenges to getting the money, but going after the money entails the same degree of labor whether the company is a lumbering industrial giant or a sleek new high-tech start-up. Both have to do the same accounting work, the same number and quality of press releases, the same courting of analysts and market opinion. Large companies have to convince the capital markets that they are small enough to control their borders. Small companies have to convince the same markets that they are large enough to sustain and maintain their boundaries. Both have to present identical faces to the capital holders even though they are utterly different in scale. How do they do that? How does a big company look small enough so that it's not seen as a Soviet Union on the verge of collapse? How does a small company make itself look large enough so that it's not a Kuwait, at the mercy of foreign powers to protect it from expansionist neighbors? By organizing in opposite directions to achieve the same end.

The larger the company, the more it needs to organize around what we call the Chicken McNugget model. Instead of meeting the world en masse, large organizations need to be broken down into bite-size pieces. Individual problems should be met by individual, Maoist-type cells of perhaps ten people maximum. Each cell needs to have its own mantra, and each mantra has to be tied to the larger mantra of the whole. Most important, each cell has to operate at the absolute edge of the organization. The cell is only that— one of many sealed units within the corporate whole. But to everyone and everything the cell encounters, it has to be not just a part of the organization but the organization itself.

Why? Because if you are GE or IBM or GM and you have a problem, the people with whom you have the problem can't afford to see you whole. Whole, you are bloated, immense, spilling out of your borders. Your size is inescapable, and because it is so, because you can never hope to get out of your own way, you're either in or on the verge of a state of collapse.

Maoist cells alleviate that. By operating at the edge of the organization, they escape the centrifugal forces that drag all thinking to the center. That's why they're the seed bed of insurgency. By being the manifest unit of the organization in whatever small arena they dominate—accounting, public relations, whatever—

Maoist cells allow you to appear very small in hundreds of different ways and from hundreds of different angles. Approach a Maoist-cell organization such as GE from the accounting facet, and GE will be ten people big. Approach it from the PR facet, and it will be ten people big again—a different pod, a different cell, a different ten people, but ten people all the same. Every encounter is manageable; no encounter betrays the massiveness beneath.

Because the cells control their very finite borders, the organization appears to control its almost infinite boundaries, and thus in ways large and small, the Chicken McNugget organizational model allows you to gain market control of your organization. The glory of a McNugget is that you never stop to ask yourself whether it came from the thigh, the breast, or the leg. Who knows? Who cares? Nor are you apt to think that the second McNugget was better than the fourth, or the third worse than the sixth. Every piece tastes good. Every piece smacks of equivalency. Every piece is both part of and stands for the whole.

One last irony of the Chicken McNugget model: The more you atomize and thus the smaller you make yourself, the bigger your brand has to be. The more successfully you break your organization up into tiny self-contained cells, the more you are dependent on your brand and its promise to provide the underlying aesthetic for all that simultaneous and disparate microactivity.

Small organizations, of course, suffer no such problems. Nor are they able to access any such opportunities. Small organizations have to practice the Roast Chicken model of organization because the Chicken McNugget model is not open to them. Instead of breaking itself up into identical bite-size pieces and letting the world encounter it only in the form of those pieces, a small organization has to make itself appear whole and complete no matter what angle you view it from. Set up Maoist cells at the fringe of a small organization, and you will have nothing left in the center to create forward momentum, and without forward movement the battle is lost. Set up the Maoist cells, and each one will have so few people that they will become autocracies engaging in continuous warfare. Still worse, the cells themselves will appear so frail that no one will be fooled in the first place. When the normal emergencies of corporate life arrive or when complex ones fall from the sky, a small organization has to throw the kitchen sink at them because in meeting the emergency it can never appear so small that it will be unable to protect its own turf.

What does the Roast Chicken organizational model require? That everyone in the organization better be versatile because today's crisis might be in accounting and tomorrow's in marketing and the next day's in production, and everyone who counts will have to fill a battle line in all three areas. If you don't know how to use the mortar, how to call in covering fire, how to lead a flanking attack, and how to just lie still and wait for the enemy to come to you, forget it—you're more harm than good. The Roast Chicken model also requires that everyone knows what page the hymnal is open to, and knows it all the time. Small organizations can't afford to "come up to speed"; they have to *be* at speed. Finally, the Roast Chicken model requires that everyone who counts within the organization be both insurgent and centrist at the same time. Every organization needs both, but small companies can't afford the luxury of specialization.

Versatility is tough. Life in small organizations can be a bitch. Being everything all the time—the thigh, the breast, the drumstick and giblets—is enervating. That's why the rewards can be so big.

Barnes & Noble and Amazon.com offer a case in point of the competing theories of organization. Barnes & Noble is America's largest bookstore chain, with over 1,000 outlets. In all, Barnes & Noble employs more than 15,000 people and moves in excess of 200 million books annually. Amazon, by contrast, is a teeny company with just a little over 2,000 employees.

Log on to the Internet, though, and go to either bookseller's site, and you will encounter almost exactly equivalent organizations: equivalent marketing, equivalent pricing, equivalent display, equivalent title lists, equivalent browsing system, equivalent everything.

Nothing about Barnes & Noble's site suggests that it is a very, very small part of a very large organization; nothing about Amazon's site suggests it is a very, very large part of a relatively small organization. Indeed, if someone who knew nothing about either parent company were to log on to both sites simultaneously and go to the same book-title subsite, he or she would probably assume Amazon was the larger enterprise: If nothing else, Amazon's reader reviews and hourly or daily rankings (hourly for the top ten thousand best-selling titles, weekly for the next one hundred thousand, and monthly beyond that) give each book's site slightly more heft.

Why such parity? Because Amazon throws the kitchen sink at on-line book sales. On-line book (and CD) sales *are* Amazon's business. Bn.com, meanwhile, is an insurgency within the larger bookseller, operated by people who eat, drink, and digest on-line book sales and in large part couldn't give less of a fig about how many books walk out the front door of the company's brick-and-mortar retail outlets. Or it was operated as an insurgency until Barnes & Noble decided to spin off its .com operation as an IPO.

A good move? We suspect so. Financial investment in the future always comes at the expense of political destabilization in the present, while financial investment in core competencies—making books and records walk out the door of those brick-and-mortar retail outlets—comes at the expense of all the future value that lies in the insurgencies out at the fringe of the organization. By spinning off its most unstable (and thus most potentially profitable) insurgency, Barnes & Noble protects its present—that tail *was* wagging the dog. By maintaining a significant interest in the spin-off, Barnes & Noble also protects its future. In effect, by taking a barely material entity selling books through the medium of its customers' computer screens and dematerializing it completely into a financial play, Barnes & Noble becomes the holding company of its own future. Therein lies the model for much more than the book business. Big is not only small, and small big; more and more, worth will be measured in negative mass.

Most of all, maybe, by spinning off bn.com, Barnes & Noble capitalizes on the accidental value its insurgency has created. A word, finally, on that.

* * *

Everything has accidental value, and by definition it always lies outside the core enterprise.

For centuries and centuries, the core competency of the people of Iceland was fishing: Iceland provided the world. But over all those centuries Iceland was also accruing an accidental value. Its very remoteness, its inbreeding, the cultural relentlessness that led it to store up fifty generations of family data, gave it a national genome unlike any other in the world—not just remarkably pure but remarkably chronicled. And today, as researchers pore through longitudinal genetic sequences to find the root causes of disease and to begin to fashion the interventions that might cure them, the "accidental" value of Iceland's genome is threatening to approach the "intentional" value of its core competency. In 1996, about 75 percent of Iceland's $1.8 billion in exports were fish-related, but the industry has been suffering from declining fish stocks for a number of years. Meanwhile, one pharmaceutical contract alone will provide the nation's people with $200 million for the right to develop products based on an analysis of their collective genome.

As is the case with Barnes & Noble and with Iceland, so it can and must be for other companies and social and political organizations as well. Big is small and small is big are not just paradoxes of size. As the present careens into the future, they also are survival skills. Nothing, no core competency, not lightbulbs (GE) or mainframes (IBM) or sweet rolls (Sara Lee), remains forever. The essence of survival is adaptation—from lightbulbs to finance, from mainframes to intellectual property, from sweet rolls to undergarments—and the essence of adaptation is weeding out vestigial skills and replacing them with new ones. The insurgency overwhelms the center. The present gives birth to the future. The parents shrinks; the child grows. And what seems new is often just an old truth, repeated time and time and time again.

One last thought before we leave size: It's in the eye of the beholder. By any external standard, Coca-Cola, which controls 50 percent of the global cola market, is huge. Yet Coke has only 2 percent of the global market in consumable beverages, and so long as the company organizes its affairs around expanding that 2 percent share instead of protecting its 50 percent share, it will be a small company struggling to be larger. That's how you stamp an attitude of insurgency throughout an organization.

◆ Future Exercise

Time to get out the pencil and paper again and answer the following three sets of questions.

1. How big is your organization?
   - ◆ How many people?
   - ◆ How many dollars?
   - ◆ How much growth capitalization?
   - ◆ How many organizational units?
2. How big would you like your organization to be in ten years?
   - ◆ What percentage of market share?
   - ◆ What market? (Remember the Coca-Cola example that we ended this chapter with.)
3. How small do you have to make your organization to achieve your growth goals?
   - ◆ How many microcultures do you want to market to?
   - ◆ How many units and how many people per unit will you need to create to reach each of those microcultures?
   - ◆ What kind of organizational social-justice system will best serve your microcultural marketing?
     - (i) Will you overvalue those who most effectively reach microcultures on the theory that past performance deserves present rewards?
     - (ii) Will you overvalue those who least effectively reach microcultures on the theory that future needs should determine present rewards?
   - ◆ How will you need to alter your brand promise to provide cohesiveness for an atomized organization?

Box 2

WHAT COLOR IS YOUR DISASTER?

Incident Management vs. Complex Emergencies

◆ ◆ ◆ ◆ ◆ ◆ ◆ ◆ ◆ ◆ ◆ ◆ ◆ ◆ ◆ ◆ ◆ ◆ ◆

From inside the belly of the beast, every disaster feels roughly the same: In ways big and small, the wheels come off. Lives are lost, or money. Businesses and careers are compromised, maybe beyond repair. Once there was a foundation to stand on, a safety net to catch you if the foundation failed. Now there is only free fall and the uncompromising laws of gravity. We've all been there in one way or another, helpless before forces we barely understand.

Externally, though, every disaster is different. No two planes crash for exactly the same set of reasons, even if they run into one another in midair. No two businesses fail from identical causes, either, no matter how similar the circumstances may appear. Disasters occur across a spectrum that ranges from isolated, single incidents to complex emergencies, and they occur at different pitches and resonances. The first step in managing one is to determine what kind of disaster you are facing and what its resonances are.

Single-incident disasters have a beginning and middle, and if they are managed correctly, they have an end as well. But to bring a disaster to an end, you have to understand what is at stake, and even single-incident disasters differ dramatically in that regard. Some change the story only in the short run that surrounds their occurrence because they are, at heart, uncomplicated events, however horrific they may initially seem. Others change the story almost forever.

Read contemporary newspaper accounts in the days immediately following the 1982 deaths of seven people in suburban Chicago from cyanide-tainted Extra-Strength Tylenol, and you'll become convinced that the very survival of Johnson & Johnson, Tylenol's maker, was at stake. That Johnson & Johnson didn't collapse is generally taken as a masterpiece of disaster management led by board chairman James E. Burke, and masterful it was. But the disaster management was also much simpler than it appeared. Yes, Johnson & Johnson had a colossal business crisis on its hands: Tylenol at the time controlled 37 percent of the total market in over-the-counter painkillers. If Tylenol couldn't be restored to market prominence or quickly replaced, J&J was going to bleed real blood.

But what makes Johnson & Johnson meaningful isn't the Band-Aids and swabs and aspirin-free pain pills it produces and sells; its meaningfulness lies in the faith customers have that they can entrust their cuts and sunburn and headaches to the company. And on the meaningfulness side, the company had almost a clean slate, even after the linkage between Tylenol and the deaths became public. If the company had produced a batch of baby shampoo laced with carbolic acid, all hell would have broken loose. That was a process over which it presumably had control. But no one reasonable could blame Johnson & Johnson for the fact that cyanide had been introduced into the tainted bottles. What could the company have done? Another nut was at work, in another nutty and deadly scheme, in a nation that was killing its presidents and civil rights leaders with almost wild abandon.

Swissair had a different sort of single-incident disaster on its hands when its Flight 111 caught fire and crashed off the coast of Nova Scotia in 1998 because suddenly it had to manage not just its business but its meaningfulness. To be sure, the European travel market is bitterly competitive, and no one rushes to book seats on an airline that has just had a plane fall out of the sky. That's the business side. But what gave Swissair its unique edge in the air-ticket wars was its reputation for precision and unflappability. This was the Swiss watch of airlines, the grace-under-pressure airline, the one that executives traveled, often at a premium, because it seemed to have the best chance of actually taking off and landing and defying all the horrible odds of travel at thirty thousand feet above sea level. When Swissair's pilots couldn't contain the fire, when they were captured on the flight recorder speaking to each other in one language and to the control tower in Moncton, New Brunswick, in another, when what appeared to be a containable crisis blossomed into an uncontainable disaster, what was lost were lives, but what was ultimately threatened was the airline's meaningfulness. And that can be a far harder hill to climb back up than the business side. Manage just the latter—just the business disaster of the crisis—and you will never regain control of your meaningfulness. Fail to do that, and you will not have managed the disaster at all.

Sometimes, of course, it doesn't matter what you do. Sometimes a single-incident disaster contains its own beginning, middle, *and* end, and all you can do is bury the dead and go on. Perhaps anxious to have word of his victory over the Sioux Nation delivered to delegates at the 1876 Democratic convention in St. Louis or perhaps just fatally overconfident, George Armstrong Custer led a pathetically undermanned force into unfavorable terrain along the Little Big Horn River against an overwhelmingly superior enemy, and the slaughter that ensued redefined not just the historical impression of Custer as a soldier and leader but the story of an entire organization—the United States Army—and eventually the whole nature of America's relationship with its native inhabitants. One man, one bad day, one horrible decision, and the results echo to this day.

Complex emergencies have a beginning, too, although it is inevitably deeply buried. They also have a middle—one that often seems to stretch forever. But if they have ends, the ends are nowhere in sight. Complex emergencies are just that—ongoing and complex emergencies—but the emergency often seems nonacute because the condition has existed so long. The origins of such emergencies are so deeply intertwined, and their consequences so complex, that whatever action you try to bring to bear will have so little long-term effect that you will assume it was the wrong action in the first place, even though it might have been entirely the right one.

Like the continuing food crisis in Somalia, complex emergencies tend to become routine in time. They institutionalize misery, and when they pop up in the news periodically—as they always do—their images of starving children almost always surprise us not because they are so frightening but because we thought that problem had been solved. Didn't we send troops? Hasn't the UN been on top of this?

Sometimes complex emergencies do worse than pop up: The tribal slaughter that descended on Rwanda in 1994 erupted not from a single cause but from a maze of breakdowns that made both an immediate and a long-term resolution virtually impossible. Months after the slaughter had ended, international advisers couldn't even begin to restore a judicial system to the once seemingly Edenic African nation. More often, though, complex emergencies resemble the fictional legal action from Charles Dickens's *Bleak House: Jarndyce v. Jarndyce*. A decade after the

Bank of Credit and Commerce International was first charged with help-ing to launder drug cartel profits, dozens of lawyers were still gathering almost monthly in Luxembourg to pick over BCCI's bones.

Complex emergencies stretch time to the breaking point, and because they do, they tend to recede into the white noise of an organiza-tion's background. The danger is still there, but the emergency begins to disappear because one of the things human beings do best is to adapt to their environments no matter how bad things get—Europe during World War II, America during the Great Depression. Put a frog into hot water, and it will hop right back out. Put it in a pot of water and slowly turn up the temperature, and, so the theory goes, the frog will just sit there until it boils to death. That's what complex emergencies do: They apply the boiling-frog theory to the corporate and political and social landscapes generally.

How do you handle complex emergencies? In truth, you almost can't. By their very nature, they resist management. Indeed, what appears to be management is often just containment—of suffering, of loss, of contami-nation. But complex emergencies begin as single incidents, and the trick to managing them is to never let them mutate in the first place. How do you do that? Four principles:

 ♦ **Admit it.** We did it. We're sorry. We're taking steps to assure it never happens again. And that's all we'll have to say. Imagine how the history of 1998 might have been rewritten if Bill Clinton had used words to that effect when news of his affair with Monica Lewinsky first surfaced. No one in business or politics likes to say they're wrong, and no legal department likes to hear you say it, but disasters have victims, victims deserve apologies, and a strikingly large percentage of single incidents that grow into complex emergencies do so because no one steps up to the mike and says, "Sorry." One added benefit to this approach: Once you've said you're sorry, the press has nothing to be vengeful about.

 ♦ **Watch your resonances.** Judged by the normal standards of legal maneuvering, Swiss bankers might seem to have been perfectly justified in initially offering to pay $39 million to settle claims relating to the dispo-sition of Jewish assets during and after World War II. After all, why start high when you know the bidding is going to go back and forth? But such reasoning assumes nothing else was at stake but the money when, in fact, the very heart and soul of Swiss banking lay in the balance. Make a preemptive offer of, say, $800 million, and you've protected the veil of secrecy that gives Swiss banking its meaningfulness. Nickle-and-dime the World Jewish Congress, as the Swiss tried to do, and you not only alienate Jews worldwide, you also give them both the legal and moral entrée to shred your privacy laws.

Let the best and brightest handle the negotiations. That's what they're there for, and everyone knows what has to be done. But have the gnomes in the Future Box divine the storyline, and make sure the best and brightest know what the storyline is going to be. When the veil of privacy is gone, how is a Basel bank different from one in Bayonne?

- **Go back to square one—and step outside it.** When U.S. Steel was stumbling toward financial disaster in the 1970s, the unchallenged assumption was that Japanese imports were destroying both the company and the American steel industry generally. Everybody said it, or everybody in the linear supply line that U.S. Steel sat at the top of said it, which was enough to make it true. Because it was true, the logical solution was to try to get more for every unit of steel sold, and because U.S. Steel raised its prices to try to do just that, what was a budding complex emergency became a full-blown one.

What was the reality of the crisis U.S. Steel was facing? Not that Japanese imports were destroying an industry, but that the industry itself was undergoing fundamental changes in its underlying structure and that the future lay not in continuing to view yourself as a construction-bolts industry and a container one but as a specialty steel manufacturer. Shout that from the rooftop of U.S. Steel's Pittsburgh headquarters in 1975, and the cry would have come back loud and clear: "Crackpot!" Walk out the front door of its factories, though, and walk into the plastics factory next door, and it would have been clear as day to anyone with eyes willing to see that plastic and other products were displacing steel throughout the primary industries of America.

It's an old saw by now, but it's still true: Get outside the box to get inside the problem.

- **Finally, when all else fails, fold your hand and go home.** When ValuJet's flight 592 crashed into the Florida Everglades in May 1996, the company didn't have the same options open to it that Swissair did when its Flight 111 crashed. ValuJet's meaningfulness lay in its name—it was the cheap airline, the one that cut corners to give you the best value up and down the East Coast. And now that cost-cutting had cost 110 lives.

What do you do when both your business and your meaningfulness are hopelessly compromised? Bail. Get out of the business. In ValuJet's case, lay low for several years and have yourself reborn as AirTran. Same cost-cutting. Same cheap fares. New name. Good move, and as smart as Daiwa Securities was dumb.

If Daiwa had been an American firm, it almost certainly could have survived the scandal that ensued when its traders were caught speculating under the table. But Japan is Japan, and once the firm had fallen into disgrace, what had begun as a single-incident disaster quickly mushroomed into a complex emergency complicated not just by cultural norms but by the national banking crisis. As we write, Daiwa is being absorbed piece by piece until finally there will be nothing left. What should the securities firm have done? Put itself up for sale the day after the scandal broke. Why didn't it? Because the need for activity in the present blinded it to the impossibility of solution in the future. In disaster management as in so much else, you've got to know when to hold them and know when to fold them, know when to walk away and know when to run.

3

• • • • • • • • • • • • • • • •

THE PARADOX OF TIME

At the speed of light, nothing happens.

For business, the paradox of time is, in part, the paradox of the visionary: To succeed in the short term, you need to think long term, yet the greater your vision and the longer the time interval over which you predict results, the greater the risk you will be unable to take the steps necessary in the short term to achieve long-range ends. Discoveries about the future tend to make actions in the present irrelevant, but only if you look at them in the context of future activity. Activities in the present tend to make discoveries about the future irrelevant, but only if you judge them by the standards of short-term success. By its very nature, the future destabilizes the present. By its very nature, the present resists the future. To survive, you need duality, but people and companies by their very nature tend to resist living in two tenses.

Cable TV didn't overwhelm the major television networks because it came out of the blue. The networks were examining the possibility that cable would be successful three decades ago. They understood all the basic principles and the technological potential. They even had a relatively clear (if paradoxical) path of operations open to them: to simultaneously oppose the development of cable TV in Congress while beginning to form the companies that would own cable once it happened. Doing so in the mid-1970s would have saved the networks billions of dollars in acquisition costs down the road. Instead, the networks' view of the short term overwhelmed their perspective about the long term, and thus they began a long slide into what threatens to become irrelevance.

Duality escaped the TV networks; the consequences of their inability to achieve duality didn't. But the networks are hardly alone in their inability to live in two time worlds. Just as ABC was studying cable thirty years ago, so GE was studying direct TV twenty years ago. As with the networks, GE understood the basic technology and even the basic potential. As with the networks, too, it was unable to make the connection between what it then did as a business and what might be a relevant field for the company to pursue in the future.

Virtually every company has a duality embedded within it, an essential time tension between what it is and what it needs to be. A television network is both an entertainment provider and a cable company, but only if it can escape living solely in the present. A computer component company is an entertainment company waiting to happen if it can just see itself that way—and if it can keep the vision of itself in the future from preventing success in the present. Today's entertainment company is an embryonic player in the soon-to-be-exploding career education business, but only if it can confront the issue of what its core business must do in the present to be successful in the future. The duality between present and future is maddening, but only if you resist it. Learn to sit on both sides of the table at the time, and the duality becomes what it should be: liberating.

Some companies can do just that. De Beers simultaneously advocates the growth of its diamond cartel and helps countries like Canada, where the cartel is illegal, exploit its native diamond resources. Soon De Beers will be free-floating Canadian diamonds on a market on the other side of the world that it dominates through its diamond cartel. In doing so, De Beers has stepped inside the duality; it has learned to function both in the past and present, where the diamond cartel gave it global dominance, and in the future, where it most likely will be without the protection of cartels.

More often, companies shrink from the contemplation of what lies ahead. Or they contemplate the future in a language and with an idea set so loose and broad that both can encompass virtually any possibility. And in doing so they all but assure that they will never take the actions in the short term that will allow them to get where they need to go in the long one.

Consider for a moment the opening words of the following "corporate mission" statement recently issued by Kodak:

> We will build a world-class, results-oriented diverse culture based on our five key values
>
> ◆ Respect for the Individual
> ◆ Uncompromising Integrity
> ◆ Trust
> ◆ Credibility
> ◆ Continuous Improvement and Personal Renewal

through which we will grow more rapidly than our competitors by providing customers and consumers with solutions they want to capture, store, process, output and communicate images to people and machines anywhere, anytime. . . .

All of which would be fine if Kodak's mission were to produce an empowered workforce or even to satisfy the spiritual needs of its stockholders. But Kodak is in the imaging business. Most of the people who work for Kodak do so because they love images and love to make them work. And the word *image*—in any form—doesn't appear until exactly 40 percent of the way through what is ultimately a 135-word mission statement.

What is Kodak's real mission? To increase the number of people who use images, to increase the relevance of images in their daily lives, maybe also to serve as a memory archivist for consumers overwhelmed by the presence of images in their lives, and to do anything necessary—from tearing the company apart and starting over again, to firing every existing worker, to superannuating core technologies—to achieve those goals in a future in which the only certainty is absolute uncertainty.

Say that, though, and you destabilize the present. Thus, the obfuscations and masking language such as "diverse culture," "respect for the individual," and "personal renewal." (It was George Orwell who first noted the tendency of propagandists to rely on Latinate words.) Fail to say what your real mission must be—fail to say, for instance, that Kodak must continue to own Christmas and its visual memories from now to doomsday—and you in effect deny what gives the company meaning to those who work for it. People crave certainty; companies thrive on certainty; yet the future denies certainty at every turn. And the surer you are about an outcome, the more certain you need to be that the outcome will never arrive.

It isn't just that the future destabilizes the present; the present destabilizes the future, as well. To succeed in the long term today, you need to micromanage every passing minute. Last week's marketing plan was made for a world that barely exists any longer. Last month's manufacturing budget involved components that have already become artifacts of a distant technological past. Change is constant, and constantly accelerating. Yet the more you micromanage, the greater the chance you and your company will simply cease to be. Concentrate solely on today, and you will never see what lies around the curve tomorrow. And there's always a truck passing just around the curve, and it's always coming in your direction, and it's always in your lane. That is the corollary of the duality of time: The future and present of any business or career are different, but they are always on a collision course.

If the decisions you make within an organization are binding out to the horizon, the immediate future of the business holds little or no interest: Fire fifty thousand workers and handling the human debris is someone else's problem; you're restructuring for the new century. If your decisions are binding over the short term, the long-term interests of the company inevitably become discounted in your reasoning. Who cares about restructuring? Fifty thousand displaced workers are waiting on your doorstep, all in a murderous rage.

Within organizations, this tension between present and future pits department against department. The 1998 strike at General Motors dragged on for two months not because GM's labor department and its employees' unions couldn't achieve a contract. It was in both their short-term interests to do so. The strike dragged on so long because the agreement reached between the labor department and the labor unions was not in the long-term interests of GM's logistics department, and the logistics department was able to foster an insurgency within the corporation that forestalled approval of a contract.

This same tension exists within individual workers as well, and in the relationship between companies and their employees. Most of us work like dogs to be successful within companies whose long-term plans almost certainly do not include us. Instead of collecting our compensation entirely in salary, we slave for stock options that require us to stay through vesting to get paid even though we know that at any moment the company can pull the plug and eliminate our ability to collect that incremental compensation. Most companies also work like dogs to educate and train workers who almost certainly will leave before they have reached their most productive years.

The U.S. Air Force spends a fortune to train its people, and trains them so well that it cannot afford to retain them once they've achieved their expertise and fulfilled their time-service requirements. Absent sufficient experienced hands, the air force has to relocate the hands it does retain more and more frequently around the world, and because relocation becomes less and less desirable as it infringes on the shrinking physical time available for personal relationships, the talent drain becomes greater still.

Faced with the same essential internal tensions, Arthur Andersen & Company uses luxury hoteling as a principal strategy to ease the pain of relocation and travel. More important, it trains its people with the expectation that many of them will be hired by Arthur Andersen clients and become future proponents of an Andersen-client relationship themselves. In effect, the company turns a present-future problem—the absence of partnership slots for many of its best young workers—into a future-present solution. It creates lifelong relationships at the same time that it puts itself on both sides of the table. By putting itself on both sides, it almost assures that bad news will flow in as readily as good news. And the former is just as important as the latter.

* * *

If you are in the oil business today, the most important question you should be asking yourself isn't how to maximize profits in the short term or what to do with excess revenues, but how to prepare for the absence of demand for your product in the long run. The internal combustion engine, to cite the most prevalent source of demand for petroleum by-products, is based on a technology far more than a century old. What's more, it's a technology that appears to be setting the world up for an increasingly bleak environmental future.

Honda is about to launch a car that runs on both gas and electrical power; other versions of a workable solution to the electric engine can't be far behind. There's also a critical time factor: People are no longer willing to sit on freeways, consuming petroleum as they inch their way to work or to the mall or the cineplex, especially when they can telecommute and cybershop and recreate by communing together rather than going out. What happens when all those factors converge?

Maybe the smartest play of all that an oil company, or oil executive, could make right now would be to get into the wind business or the solar business, or into cold fusion, but if that's what you are planning to do—if that's what the swamis behind the curtain are working on imagining—don't breathe a word of it. In the newly democratic workplace, maybe the most important thing a chief executive officer must do is keep from the bulk of his employees the information that is most likely to have the greatest impact on their lives. But avail him- or herself of that information, of the bad news, of counterviews and counteroptions, every CEO must, and must do constantly.

When the future constantly upends the present and the present struggles against letting the future ever arrive, the way to thrive is to move inside both. By nearly every standard of corporate warfare, petroleum companies and radical environmentalists are sworn enemies, yet John Brown, the CEO of British Petroleum, meets semiannually with the board of directors of Greenpeace to hear their concerns and get a sense of what's on the Greenpeace agenda. Thus, BP and Greenpeace live in each other's present and future, and Brown himself compresses both tenses by having his sworn enemies tell him what the newspapers eventually would tell him in any event.

We live today not in one tense, but in two—the present and the future—and we live in both tenses simultaneously, anxious to step forward into the future, certain we have to do so, and nostalgic for the present moment before we ever leave it. Once, deep ties held us in place—career, extended family, marriage. Today, we've sacrificed depth for breadth, and in so doing we have weakened nearly every link that ties us to the here and now. Think of life today as being lived in the pressure tense (*present* + *future*) because that's what it is, and that's where you are.

Too often, we live in the two tenses in parallel, but at the horizon even parallel lines converge. A little more than two decades ago, Corning was faced with a classic present-future dilemma. In kitchens across America, the company was thought of as the nation's preeminent maker of ovenproof casseroles and sturdy measuring cups—sold under the Corning Ware and Pyrex brands—but the company's R and D department had recently invented a new glass-based product called fiber-optic cable that might someday revolutionize the nascent telecommunications industry. How to resolve the problem? How to move into the future without destabilizing the present? In Corning's case, both wisely and humanely.

Eventually, nearly all of its consumer products division would be sold to Borden, but only on the condition that the headquarters remain in Corning, New York, so that lifetime employees of the company wouldn't find themselves and their families uprooted. Thus, the company kept its past alive in the present and future of its community, even while divesting itself of its own historical product line. Or rather, most of its historical product line. Corning retained its Steuben crystal-and-glassware line, and thus it kept its past alive in the present and future of the company as well, and in a critical fashion. It's only a short leap from legendary stemware to legendary fiber-optic cable.

Corning has never fully escaped the disastrous legal consequences of the silicon breast implants it manufactured jointly with Dow Chemical under the name Dow Corning, but the company today is one of the world's leading producers of fiber-optic cable. With a variety of joint-venture partners it controls about a 50 percent share of the U.S. market and a 35 percent share in the rest of the world, and its fiber-optic business is projected to grow by about 30 percent annually well into the next decade. By paying attention to its story, it made the present live in the future, and made the future a reality in the present. And by doing that—by working both sides of the pressure tense—Corning also moved inside the paradox of time.

Manage your time, junior executives are constantly counseled. But manage your tense might be better advice. Keep the story of your present alive in your future, make sure "to come" isn't held hostage to "now," and time will take care of itself.

Newspapers function in the pressure tense all the time, as author Bruce Feiler noted in an op-ed piece that appeared in the November 23, 1998, *New York Times*.

"For all the griping about the tabloidization of American news," Feiler wrote, "there's a subtler shift going on in news coverage that's arguably even more corrosive. Increasingly, stories no longer report on the past; they report on the future."

Feiler went on to cite numerous examples: news articles days in the advance of the event, reporting (or misreporting, as it turned out) that President Clinton "would appear irate" in his videotaped testimony in the Monica Lewinsky affair; business-section explanations that a company's stock had fallen or risen because its earnings had "failed to live up to" expectations or had "exceeded" them; *Entertainment Weekly's* Holiday Film Preview issue, which notes "not only what movies are opening but what will happen to them when they do—what reviewers will say and what the box office will show."

In fact, Feiler couldn't be more right. Take the front page of any major newspaper, read the first few paragraphs of the articles there, and it will seem as if the future already has occurred. Speculation gets treated as fact. Next week has become an element of history. Articles are based less on reportage than on predictions. Who, what, when, where, and how—the cornerstones of journalism as it was once practiced—have been largely replaced by a single question: What next? But the question seems always to be asked not in the interrogatory but in the declarative mode: Here's what's next.

But if Feiler is right about the phenomenon, he couldn't be more wrong when he attributes it to an "omnipresent (and omniscient) media insider" or to journalists succumbing to the temptation to "think they're seers." That's slaying the messenger. As is almost always the case, newspapers have simply gone where their readers already are. If more and more news stories commingle the present and future tenses, it is only because more and more the pressure tense is exactly where their consumers are living.

Yes, business pages do report that stocks have exceeded or failed to live up to expectations, but they have a good reason for doing so. Virtually every stock has embedded in its present price the estimated value of a company's earnings at least twelve months ahead. The present and even the near-term future have been discounted; the long-term future is what drives market capitalization. Stocks live in the pressure tense as much as people do.

Industry also lives in the pressure tense. The new practice of "anticipatory feedback" is built around telling employees in advance what mistakes they are going to make and then instructing them on how to avoid what would have been the inevitable. In effect, anticipatory feedback takes the lessons of the past, projects them into the future, and asks people to act on them in the present. Twenty years ago, it might have been a good concept for a science fiction movie or TV series. A little less than a decade ago, Bill Murray turned "anticipatory feedback" into the movie *Groundhog Day:* Do it over and over and over again until you get it right. Today, anticipatory feedback is becoming standard practice in employee continuing education.

Products live in the pressure tense, too. Once we talked about the concept of "planned obsolescence": Your Oldsmobile Delta 88 broke down after ninety thousand miles because that's when cars of that generation broke down, but the car's style broke down after fifty thousand because General Motors wanted to force you back to the showroom in three-year rather than five-year cycles. You continued to drive the old Delta 88 not at risk to your safety but at risk to your cool. Today, more and more, we have inherent obsolescence: Products become outdated not by any master plan but by their very nature, and the more futuristic they are—the more high technology goes into them—the less likely they are to survive beyond the present moment.

Apple's G-4 chip didn't just replace the older G-3 chip; it superseded it immediately and absolutely, especially for Mac users who are at the cutting edge of establishing taste in computer chips. With the highest technology and the highest technology users, there is no middle age, just very young and very old.

The Northstar system will allow your Cadillac to travel a hundred thousand miles before its first scheduled maintenance, but by the time your car reaches a hundred thousand miles, its technology will be three generations removed, already grandfatherly. Motorola's 1998 launch of the world's first digital, global communications system put the company at the bleeding edge of low-earth-orbit satellite technology, at the very moment that the technology already was becoming obsolete. Not long before the launch, Fermi Labs had fired a neutrino in the opposite direction—235 miles into the core of the planet—proving it was possible to send media messages through the earth.

Consumers also live in the pressure tense. We become nostalgic about our purchases almost at the moment we make them, knowing they won't last, knowing further that the best of them will last the least time. Gateway's "Your:)Ware" program is a time play and a risk play: By being guaranteed that they can trade in their old Gateway systems on new technology, consumers are protected against being overwhelmed by the future at the same time they have their risk of being played for a techno-sucker mitigated. But "Your:)Ware" is also an emotional play: It protects consumers against a sense of loss by assuring that the attachment to their computer equipment is never deep in the first place.

Not long ago, junior high school students in Utah staged a protest because they were being forced to learn their history from social studies textbooks printed in the mid-1980s that failed to anticipate the revolution in personal computers and still wrote about Ronald Reagan, the Berlin Wall, and the Soviet Union as if they were significant factors in the students' lives. Those junior-highers were caught in the pressure tense, too: trapped between having to learn a history that was only marginally true to them with respect to time and wanting to be prepared for a world for which their textbooks failed to lay even the foundation. And so damaged did they feel by the experience that they actually staged a strike against public authority in the most authority-conscious state in the union.

Caught between past and present, we spend half our time worrying that the long term won't turn out the way we wanted it to and the other half worrying that we are going to miss something in the present moment. And when we do miss something—a meeting, a plane, a game—our anger is absolute.

"Road rage" is a combination of many things, but it is at least partly "time rage." The car radio is filled with diversions. CD players, tape decks, and audio books can all distract us while we wait for the traffic to clear. And there's always the cell phone. But hours lost on the freeway are hours lost forever, and it's not just on the freeways that time rage and time confusion and time angst boil over. A study not long ago found that people standing in a line know pretty much how long they have been waiting up to the four-minute mark. After that, they move from real time to fantasy time, and the waiting time begins to grow exponentially, however long the clock says they have been in line. At five minutes, they might say they've been in line ten minutes; at eight minutes, the fantasy waiting time has grown to twenty minutes. Airlines can stretch the real-time sense of those waiting in ticket lines up to about ten minutes by sending attendants out to ask what flight people are waiting for, but even then, after about ten minutes, the pressure of lost time sets in and conceptions of waiting time mushroom.

Fantasy time also affects performance in the workplace. Require tasks that exceed reasonable real-time standards, and the excess time will grow exponentially in a worker's mind and convert inevitably into frustration. As a manager you can stretch that time just as airlines do, by walking the line and engaging employees in diversionary conversation. But you also can solve the problem by tailoring tasks to abiding assumptions about the periodicity of time. For the record, our best guess is that the length of time between two TV commercials is the unit of maximum concentration in America today.

The old saw is right: Time is money. In fact, Intel once figured out exactly how much money it was: Take the number of people in a meeting, multiply them by $50, multiply that number by every hour the meeting lasts, and then divide that figure by the average profit on the sale of a Pentium processor, which was calculated for this purpose at $100, figuring a margin of 40 percent. If you have twelve people in a room for two hours, you have consumed 12 Pentium processors, and the meeting better be worth that.

But time is more than money. Money can be made in the stock market in a few ticks. Time, though, is scarce, and irrecoverable. Unlike salary, it can't be deferred. Unlike assets, you can't invest time and make it grow. More and more, too, it is time, not money, that is the deal breaker in the workplace. Deny a senior vice president a raise or stock options, and he or she might take it in stride—there's always next quarter or next year. Require the same senior VP to travel to the Sydney office, and he or she might very well walk. After, say, age forty-five, crossing the international date line for business, not pleasure, becomes one of those experiences not really worth recovering from.

Busy people are busy absolutely. The more of the clock they fill, the more of the rest of the clock they need. And the more unsettled the clock becomes, the more they suffer. Psychic abuse can be endured. Financial abuse is unwelcome but bearable. It is time abuse that most strains loyalty to any organization.

Time is also respect, and it's disrespect. A number of years ago, we got stuck in a traffic jam on our way from downtown Los Angeles to the Disney studios in Burbank. The traffic jam was no more predictable or unpredictable than any L.A. traffic jam is—we would have needed to leave our hotel hours in advance of the meeting to have avoided altogether the possibility of being so delayed—and we were careful to call constantly from our car to alert Disney brass to our whereabouts and probable arrival time. And when we finally got to Burbank, we were met in the lobby by the assistant to the man we had traveled across the country to see and told: "He'd wait for Robert Redford, but he wouldn't wait for an asshole like you." True story. And $20 million down the drain.

So it is with time. How late you are for a meeting is no longer determined by any absolute standard. It's determined rather by how important the most important person in the room is. One minute late for a CEO who's time is being valued at $18 a minute is $18 late, and while you could presumably make that up out of pocket, you can't make up the reciprocal damage because time finally is status, too. By contrast, ten minutes late for a meeting with your colleagues is being on time, but being really on time for a meeting with your colleagues is showing them respect, and respect counts more than money. The act of abusing their time is the ultimate show of disrespect.

Never before in history has time been so finely calibrated, and never before have the calibrations of time been so commercially meaningful. We measure the clock not just in minutes or seconds but in nanoseconds. For not a whole lot of money, you can buy a clock that is connected, via radio, to the official U.S. atomic clock. You can have ticking watches and digital watches on the same face, watches that show you time zones all around the world. Baud rates make or break a modem brand; Internet portal sites are judged on download and upload times. Schoolchildren may not know their state capitals, but they can tell you with astounding precision whether Lycos or Excite makes a faster search engine. Time divisions are all around us, and never before in modern history have we been so certain that the calibrations of day time are exactly what they began as—sheer happenstance.

The Earth's rotation around the sun established the solar year, the Earth's rotation on its own axis gave us days, but when a day began or ended and how it was to be divided was anyone's guess. The ancient Egyptians reckoned days from sunrise to sunrise. The Saxons divided them into tides and gave us those beautiful words: *morningtide, noontide,* and *eventide.*

The first primitive efforts at calculating the day parts of time were probably sundials—from the Latin *dies*, for day—but sundials let the sun do their work for them: At night, or when the sky was overcast, time disappeared. Water clocks or clepsydra—another beautiful word, literally "water thief"—were the first real clocks, and for nearly a thousand years, especially in the Islamic and Chinese empires, they were the standard of timekeeping. On the outside, clepsydra put on beautiful shows, telling time with a pageant of sound and spectacle. One sent to the court of Charlemagne by the caliph of Baghdad became famous throughout Europe. Beneath and behind the spectacle, though, timekeeping was governed by a purely arbitrary measure: the size of the aperture through which the water flowed. The rate, in fact, didn't much matter as long as the reservoir replenished and emptied itself on daily cycles.

Neither clepsydra nor sundials were particularly practical for northern Europe, where the sun was spotty at best and water often froze in winter, and so in the second half of the thirteenth century, mechanical clocks began to appear, and time became calibrated, but only by the gears that drove the new clocks, not by any larger logic. It wasn't until the nineteenth century that American railroad companies introduced the concept of ante meridiem and post meridiem time—A.M. and P.M.—to accommodate their desire to schedule trains through two twelve-hour cycles each day.

Today, we're headed back where we began. The more clocks we surround ourselves with and the more divisions we create within each day and each hour and second, the less clocks really measure anything or tell us anything about time, and the fewer metrics of time we can agree upon. What do we mean when we say "a long time" or "a short time," "in a bit," or "later"? A second, an hour, a day, a week, a month, a year? Instantaneously? Never? Relationships used to be measurable in years. Today, the most important relationship you have in your life might last ten minutes but have the dimensionality of a relationship decades in the making.

Look far enough ahead, and time distorts again. Economists have begun talking about the "hyperbolic discounting of time" as an explanation for why Americans are so reluctant to save for retirement. For our parents, thirty years down the pike could be expressed by simple math: 1×30. The time frame could be imagined because it was a simple multiple of experience. Today, we don't see time as anywhere near so linear. The more we look thirty years down the road, the more time curves hyperbolically, and the more that happens, the more the math complexifies. Instead of 1×30, thirty years becomes 1×30 to the x power. Why save for what seems so fantastically in the distance?

Once not very long ago, nine to five was for working, nine to nine was for shopping, and eleven at night to seven the next morning was for rest. Today, e-commerce is constant, and e-mail arrives all the time. Videotaping lets us watch the Monday night game on Thursday morning if we choose. We can freeze a Brett Favre pass in midair and eat dinner, call our broker, or have sex before the ball ever comes back to earth again. Telephone meetings required everyone to agree to a specific moment in time and to commit to a place at that same moment; in effect, they shrunk the clock. The Internet, by contrast, allows us to communicate with anyone at any time and allows them to communicate back to us with no requirement that any party be synchronously available at the same time in any set place. The old metaphorical standard for dedication to the company used to be 168 because that is the number of hours in the week, and a 100 percent worker gave 100 percent of all time. Today, 168 has been replaced by 7×24, and it's no longer a metaphor at all. In effect, time has been stretched, the clock softened. The faster time goes, the softer the clock gets and the more fungible time becomes.

Time used to be continuous. Today, under the pressure of pressure-tense life, time changes from situation to situation. A minute of a workout session is not the same measure of time as a minute of childbirth or the minute after a space shuttle lifts off the launchpad or a minute of jail time. In the workplace, lengths of time can and should change dimension at different times of the year and according to the business a company is in. In March, a long advertising meeting for a retail company might be three days of brainstorming. Who's going anywhere? Two weeks before Christmas, a long meeting for the same company is five minutes. Who has time? Fail to realize this difference, and you will insult everyone present. Realize it, and you will show respect, and respect earns dividends.

Put an atomic clock on a starship and power it out of Earth's gravitational field, and each second of time will take longer to tick off as the starship accelerates. The length of a second, in short, grows in proportion to the speed that whatever you are using to measure that second travels at. Were it a human being that were being used to measure time, and assuming that the body could maintain its molecular integrity, human time would begin to disappear as energy turned into light, because here may be the ultimate paradox of time: At the speed of light, *nothing* happens. At maximum movement, time stands still.

All that, of course, is in theory, but suppose that we do find ourselves eventually living in a world in which we truly are connected by cyberspace—a world in which we are living at the speed of light. Will we age more slowly? Will more time be available to us for each moment we do live? Will we even be able to hoard time? To store it? To buy it and trade it on the open market or through black marketeers? And then ask yourself if we are not approaching that time now. What does the speed-of-light life of the Internet do but stretch each second for us? And when does the "speed-of-light" metaphor become a reality? In a hundred years? In fifty? In less?

One of the most highly touted benefits of connectivity and the computer age was that it would make information synchronously available universally. In stock transactions, the edge would no longer belong to those closest to the minute ebb and flow of the news because, with a $1,000 computer and a subscription to one of the electronic financial news services, anyone could have access instantaneously to what previously only a privileged few had known. Yet when information is universally available at the speed of light, there's no advantage to having it. Nothing happens. It's like taking a balloon ride on a mildly breezy day. Because you're traveling at the exact speed of the wind, there's no sense of movement.

* * *

What are the implications of softened clocks and fungible time for businesses and businesspeople today? One is to address the latent time stored in the organization.

Flat companies are flat for many reasons, but one of the main ones is that they are warehousing the excess time of their workers. Cut the workforce by 25 percent, say, and there will be virtually no effect on the operations of dead-in-the-water organizations because that much time has been sitting up in the rafters, gathering dust. Outsource, and your latent-time problems become your supplier's problems. Managing the risk of having excess time on your hands—and books—also underlies the astronomical growth of temporary and contract workers. When you work for yourself, no one pays for latent time. You either figure out how to turn latent into productive time or you go hungry.

But companies don't have to go outside the organization to manage their latent time. Unproductive workers warehouse time; productive ones use it up. To the extent that workers are granted dignity in the workplace, latent time disappears.

You also inevitably shift the balance of time within any organization by the budget decisions you render. Investment in research is investment in future time; investment in operations and production is investment in present time. Balance the scale one way or the other, and you create artificial time.

Most important, you need to refresh your business's sense of time, and you need to do so continuously. Officially, a business day lasts twenty-four hours and a business year 365 days. In reality, both a business day and a business year are elastic over the events they embrace. No matter how much they may need each other and how alike they are, no two businesses embrace events or calculate time in the same way.

AT&T would like you to embrace its vision of time, which is that you will make most of your long-distance calls between 11:00 A.M. and 4:00 P.M. in the normal workday. For embracing its vision, AT&T will charge you a maximum fee during that time span and allow you to make calls dirt cheap when you are least likely to do so. NEC also provides long-distance service, but it has a different sense of time based on the fact that, while its satellite is heavily used during the height of the Japanese workday, it is going largely unused during the height of the American workday. Use NEC during that time, let your calls bounce off a Japanese satellite rather than an American one, and you can cut what you pay for your prime-time long-distance calls by as much as 80 percent. But to do that, you have to know your own rhythms first.

What's the real calendar, the real clock your company lives by? Is it ten- and five- and one-year plans? Monthly and weekly planning sessions? Or are those only the patterns you're locked into? Is the real rhythm something else? And if so, what is it? Are you evaluating on an annual basis employees who fulfill their duties on a quarterly basis—account executives, let's say, in an advertising agency? If so, have you stopped to think how little sense that makes? How long is an average career? How long is the period between promotions? How long does it take your company to hire someone or fire someone? And can time be won back on any or all of those fronts? Industry averages will tell you a little something, but only a little. Studying your own rhythms will tell you far more, but even then, you can't apply time frames universally across a company.

As we noted earlier, different parts of any organization have different horizons—different time spans over which their actions and decisions hold sway—and those different horizons inevitably pit them against each other. But different parts of any organization also operate according to asymmetrical definitions of time that have to do with the nature of the clock each lives by, and those differing definitions of time pit them against each other as well.

What makes life meaningful for the logistics division? The golden screw—the one part in every product that is always in least supply and that therefore puts the greatest constraints on the purchasing cycle. It is the job of logistics, and operations working with logistics, to control the golden screw: to order it at the best possible price and in the minimum possible amounts. But the order cycle is always driven by everyone else in the industry seeking the same golden screw, all of whom want to order early and receive late according to the best dictates of "just-in-time" inventorying (which might more accurately be thought of as "almost-too-late" inventorying).

What's more, the order cycle is always asynchronous with salespeople who will never know until the end of the month how much product they need since their clock is driven by the unwillingness of customers to commit until they know their own inventory. And the logistics and sales departments are each in their own ways out of sync with the labor division, which needs to know at the beginning of each month how much labor to lay on through the end of the cycle.

Worse, all discontinuities in time ultimately become issues of self-worth because whenever separately calibrated clocks collide, someone gets hurt and someone gets yelled at, and the more self-worth is diminished within an organization, the less total productive time you have available.

Fail to discover the circadian rhythm by which your organization lives, and you will need to spend time defining time itself before any meaningful conversation can begin. Fail to establish organizational time metrics that take into account the asynchronous clocks by which your parts live, and you will find yourself engaging in a great deal of metacommunication about essentially nothing.

Find the rhythm, find a time metric into which all the separate clocks can be plugged, find a language that will allow you to talk about the present and future in the same breath—learn, in short, to live in the pressure tense, and you will move inside time itself. Because here is the final paradox of time: The more accurately we define it, the more time can be anything it needs to be, anything we make it.

◆ Future Exercise

In the column on the left, list all your activities in any sphere over the last seven days that were directly and solely related to life in the present tense. In the column on the right, list all the activities that were directly and solely related to life in the future tense.

Eating dinner, to cite one example, is a present-tense activity so long as you were eating for the enjoyment and sustenance of the moment only.

Eating on the fly because you were rushing out the door to a future activity doesn't count in either column. Eating dinner with a friend because you hope he will help get you on the board of the art museum is a future-tense activity. The same thing goes for meeting time at work: A conference call to deal solely with a crisis of the moment is a present-tense activity; a conference call to plan for a future meeting/product/crisis is a future-tense activity carried out in the present moment.

Now, the list:

Present	Future
_____	_____
_____	_____
_____	_____
_____	_____
_____	_____
_____	_____
_____	_____
_____	_____
_____	_____
_____	_____

Next, go back through each list and assign a value to each activity, based on its importance to your life during the last seven days. One equals minimally important; ten, maximally important. When you're through, add up the totals and fill them in below.

Present	Future
_____	_____

The closer the two figures are to being the same, the more you live in the pressure tense.

4

THE PARADOX OF
COMPETITION

*Your biggest competitor is your own
view of your future.*

Put yourself in the middle of a science fiction thriller, something
from the *Alien* series by way of *Star Trek*. You're stranded on a
distant planet, in a galaxy far away, but you're not alone. An
enemy, a force, a something that seems to live in three tenses—
past, present, and future—surrounds you, although "surround" is
not quite right because this enemy seems to exist both inside and
outside you. Sometimes it attacks in lightning strikes. Sometimes
it oozes toward you, or from you. The molecules around you grow
thick, and then your own molecular weight begins to double until
you can barely lift an arm or open an eye. Are you fighting an
external enemy that's trying to internalize itself in you? Or an
internal enemy that's trying to externalize itself from you? Or is
there no enemy at all—nothing other than your own self that
you're struggling against?

As with alien warfare, so it is with corporate warfare today.
Competition takes place in all three tenses for a variety of goals of
which market share and wallet share and the other traditional
shares are sometimes only the least battleground. What's more,
because competition takes place not just in one dimension but
three, it has to be viewed in terms of solid, not plane, geometry.

Just as important, competition needs to be viewed in both external and internal terms. The great works of fiction, William Faulkner said in his Nobel Prize acceptance speech, concern "the human heart in conflict with itself." So the great moments of business competition often concern the corporate heart in conflict with itself. "We have met the enemy," Walt Kelly's Pogo once memorably proclaimed. "And he is us."

Never before have we had better metrics to gauge our own performance, never before have we had better data available to tell just how we are doing against an almost infinite variety of market measures, and never before have we been less sure where our competition is coming from because, today, our competition comes from everywhere and nowhere, all at the same time.

Understandably, when companies evaluate their competition, they tend to look to other companies doing the same things they are doing in the present. Lateral competition in one dimension and in a single time frame—us versus them for sales this quarter—has always been and will always be a part of business life. Only so many minivans will be bought in any one sales period. Only so many Caribbean vacations will be taken in any season. Your share of those minivan sales is critical to success, as is the number of vacationers who choose the Caribbean, and the number choosing the Caribbean who come to your island, and the number coming to your island who stay at your inn and pay to eat your food. But the sale or the travel decision is the historical result of a whole series of other competitions, and if we fail to consider competition in all its dimensionality, we'll never get to the historical result we want.

What's more important? The company doing what you are doing now? Or the one that will be doing in the future the same thing you want to be doing in the future? The latter, if you want to survive much beyond today. But to compete in that dimension you need to expand the definition of your competitive set to embrace the nature of your business going down the road and how other businesses will drift in that direction if it proves profitable. Several years back, when Dave Coulter was chairman and

CEO of BankAmerica, we asked him who his biggest competitor was. His answer—not Citigroup, NationsBank, or some other financial conglomerate, but Microsoft—said volumes about how he and his company had organized their view of the future at the same time it told us what kind of future the company was likely to have, at least as viewed from that moment in the present. As always, too, you have to compete in the future dimension without destabilizing competition in the present and without subverting the core values that have sustained your business in the past. That's part of doing business in the three dimensions of time.

Companies also need to expand their sense of competitive venues well beyond the single dimension of sales or product. In the battle for capital, businesses are more likely to be grouped by performance category than they are by product category: Aircraft, electronics, biotechnology, and computer firms all might find themselves within the single family of companies whose estimated value is growing on an annual basis at 30 percent. How well you do relative to the others in the same family at attracting capital on the most advantageous terms will be determined less by market share than by, say, your real estate portfolio, your capital-acquisition activities, your supplier-management activities, or other comparisons that affect the perception of your success, whatever your categorical set. And how well you do at that will have a profound effect on your ability to compete within your product category on the most favorable terms.

Just as companies compete for capital outside of product category, so they compete for market attention broadly across the business landscape. Every business today tries to find as many different channels for reaching the market as possible: retail, direct, indirect, Internet, and so on. But how companies make money on any of those channels has almost nothing to do with the ways in which their traditional competitors use the channels and almost everything to do with how customers themselves use them. Focus on your immediate competition, and you'll end up imitating its possibilities. Focus on the consumer at the other end of the channel, and you'll immerse yourself in your own possibilities.

Channel competition gets to what is arguably the most important form of external competition today: not the competition for category share or wallet share, but the competition for share of mind. Enormous amounts of information today chase very minimal amounts of attention, and they chase those minimal amounts through every conceivable form of media and communication. Until you can crack through that—until you can create awareness, until you can entice someone at the other end of your message to choose to pay attention to it over all the other input heading that person's way—there is no sale.

How do you compete for share of consciousness? By advertising, through public relations, via the Internet, by any means that you can use to get your message out. But through the message itself as well, by effective storytelling. The message can't just celebrate the product—products are everywhere. To win consciousness share, the message has to tie the product to the experiences of the consumers you want to reach, so it can enter the full dimensionality of their lives.

To win consciousness share time and again, your message also needs such a powerful central tendency that you can shift the content as your business shifts without shifting the form. That means managing your brand in such a way that it allows you to simultaneously be both constantly different and constantly the same. Thus, GE the lightbulb maker and GE the diesel engine maker morph into GE the credit company as General Electric's vision of its future changes, and thus the company will change again and soon enough, all under the consistent umbrella of GE the brand. Fail to manage that consistency, by the way, and you'll find yourself a decade down the road in a business where the brand you've invested enormous assets in has a cash value approaching zero.

You also create consciousness share by never forgetting that all great consumers—the ones who set markets and launch new product lines—are acutely aware of themselves as markets of one. Fail to win a share of their attention by being innovative at the same time you are pursuing a share of the larger market consciousness, and you'll be sacrificing the future for the present. Nike, to cite one obvious example, has found itself attracting more and more market laggards while it loses its most loyal customers, and thus Nike in all likelihood is nearing the moment when it will attract the maximum number of people relative to the total market who will ever buy shoes from the company. Therein lies the paradox of success, which is really just a subset of the paradox of competition: The largest percentage of the market you are ever going to attract occurs at the very moment you begin to lose the customers who have made it happen.

One of the great fallacies of competition today is that marketing costs can be reduced to take advantage of "brand equity." In fact, marketing costs and communications costs generally need to rise as the category becomes populated, because to keep ahead of your own success you need to attend to more and more people in more and more ways. The more you have "leveraged" your brand, the more you need to invest in the brand, and the more market share you accumulate, the more you have the dollars to do so.

What is true of companies and competition is equally true of the people who work for companies. Think for a moment about who your real competition is. Is it the person down the hall with an office the same size as yours, a secretary paid the same as yours, a title and salary package identical to your own? Or is it the woman a floor below you and ten years your junior, with an office half the size of yours but an ambition as big as all outdoors? Is competition measurable in current or future time?

Literally, the word *competition* comes from the Latin *competitio*, which has its roots in *com* (together) and *petere* (to seek). "Competition"? It means to "seek together for." The "for" is very important. Something is at stake; something hangs in the balance of the seeking. There's a striving for, toward a goal. But that's the broadest usage. In ecology, the word gets narrowed to a more exact meaning: Ecological "competition," according to the *Webster's New World Dictionary,* is "a struggle among individual organisms for food, water, space, etc., when the available supply is limited." Maybe that's how we should think about the subject: "Competition" in business is a struggle among limited resources for sales, reputation, share, salary, and the like, and thus our biggest competitor is the one who stands between us and our share of the limited supply.

But maybe, too, we need to make a final distinction. The law of the jungle says that competition is lateral and horizontal: Eat or be eaten. Get the water or don't get the water. Control the space or don't control the space. The paradox of competition says something different: Whether we are an individual or a corporation, or even a society, the battles that count most are often the ones against ourselves: ourselves in the present and ourselves in the future, and ourselves in both dimensions doing battle against one another.

An example of what we're talking about:

Two decades ago, in the early 1980s, John Hendricks had just left his job as director of corporate relations for the University of Maryland at College Park and was running a small consulting company specializing in educational television programs when an idea struck him: The world was awash in nature documentaries, yet in the then-fledgling industry of cable TV, no one had yet gotten around to starting a channel built around such documentaries. Why not, Hendricks thought, himself?

By 1985, with the help of Walter Cronkite, whom he had written to on a whim, Hendricks had raised $5 million and bought a hundred hours of programming from the British Broadcasting Company (for $100,000) and other documentaries from Canadian and additional foreign sources. In June of that year, his Discovery Channel aired its first show, "Iceberg Alley," about ice floes in the North Atlantic. But the battle was far from over. A year later, Hendricks had maxed out three different credit cards and taken a second mortgage on his house when a coalition of national cable operators agreed to take a stake in his company. By early 1999, the Discovery Channel was reaching seventy-six million homes, which made it the third largest cable channel in the United States and the fastest-growing one. The Learning Channel, which Discovery Communications bought for a song in 1991, was going into sixty-nine million households, and the company's Animal Planet Channel, launched in the fall of 1996, had already found its way into forty-eight million homes via cable. Revenues for the company, which had crept over the $300 million mark in 1994, topped

$1 billion in 1998, and Discovery Communications was valued at about $10 billion. Hendricks had had to give up virtually all the equity in the company he founded to secure the backing of the cable operators, but his 1.4 percent stake in Discovery was still worth about $140 million.

That's one side of the story. Here's the other, which took place at the same time in downtown Washington, D.C., less than ten miles away from Discovery's Bethesda, Maryland, headquarters:

Two decades ago, also in the early 1980s, the National Geographic Society was among the world's largest nonprofit publishers, and maybe its richest. Its flagship magazine was reaching more than ten million "members," as subscribers are known at the Society. The Society also enjoyed a flawless pedigree that by the mid-1980s was nearing the century mark, and it was not just a player in the world of nature photography and documentary making. It was *the* player, *the* brand, very nearly *the* trademark, the eight-hundred-pound gorilla of the business.

Practically every top nature photographer in America, and many of the top photographers from around the world, were either under contract to the Society or had a working relationship with it. The Society published book after book showcasing the best in nature photography. Its televised National Geographic Specials set the standard for nature documentaries, too, and the Society didn't just film adventures; it backed them and arranged them and lived them. The *National Geographic* had had a hand in the discovery of the ancient Incan ruins at Machu Picchu and in the polar expeditions of both Richard Byrd and Robert Peary. It also had backed the first American team to conquer Mount Everest as well as ape experts Jane Goodall and Dian Fossey. And always *National Geographic* cameras were there recording the historic moments.

That much by way of background because in the mid-1980s, just about the time John Hendricks was maxing out his credit cards, Tim Kelly had an idea, too. Kelly had come to the National Geographic Society in 1983 to expand its television division—he'd previously worked for a company that produced cable TV programming—and now he thought he saw where the future lay: cable TV, a National Geographic channel that would take advantage of the society's vast archives of still and live film, while also capitalizing on and enriching its brand. Inflamed by his idea, Kelly drew up a business plan and took it to Gilbert Grosvenor, the fifth in his family line to serve as the Society's president. Alarmed by the cost and wary of straying from the group's mission, Grosvenor said no, and in the dynastic realm of the National Geographic Society, Grosvenor's "no" was the end of the matter.

A decade and a half later, by the start of 1999, Grosvenor had turned over day-to-day direction of the National Geographic Society, and Kelly's television division had come under the aegis of a new for-profit section of the Society: National Geographic Ventures. The biggest project on Venture's books? Launching a National Geographic cable channel that would be built around the society's archives; with luck, Kelly hoped to have the channel in place sometime during the year 2000. The biggest impediment to launching the channel? John Hendricks's Discovery Communications, the eight-hundred-pound gorilla of the business.

"If National Geographic had done the cable channel years ago, [Hendricks] never would have gotten Discovery off the ground," Chuck Ross, the media editor for *Advertising Age*, told journalist Linda Killian for an article that appeared in *Washingtonian* magazine.

But does that make Discovery Communications the biggest competitor of the National Geographic Society in the TV business? If competition is both external and lateral, the answer is undoubtedly yes: In the jungle of cable television, ad dollars and homes penetrated are the equivalent of food, water, and space. They are what count, and they are all that count. But we think the answer is just the opposite. We think National Geographic's biggest competition in cable TV was and is both internal and vertical: its own failure of imagination, its inability to look around the corner in the mid-1980s and understand where it might be, and where it ought to be, by century's end. That won't necessarily change, by the way, if and when the Society does succeed in launching a nature channel: The more the National Geographic cable entry defines itself by the Discovery Channel, the more certain of failure it is. Imitation is death by a thousand wounds.

* * *

The only way to succeed in the marketplace today—the market-place of individuals or products or services or ideas—is to know your own story and to follow it into the future. Define yourself by someone else's benchmarks, immerse yourself in someone else's possibilities, and you become the thing you define yourself by and immerse yourself in. Measure yourself against your own rate of change and you stay inside your own story. That way, when the other side ceases to exist, you still have a reason to go on.

For more than four decades after the end of World War II the United States was involved in a cold war arms race against the Soviet Union. Then in 1989, the Soviet Union shut down, simply ceased to exist any longer, and . . . the arms race went on. Hundreds of billions of dollars continued to be spent annually on weapons systems. Troop levels, which had been falling before the Soviet Union went under, dipped a bit more, then held steady. The bilateral world had been replaced by a unilateral world. Two superpowers had become one. And from an accounting perspective, it was virtually impossible to tell the difference.

The arms race, it turned out, had been only tangentially about the Soviet Union, or maybe more accurately, the communists were the objective correlative for an arms race that would have existed with or without them. The benchmarks were never Soviet production or Soviet technology. The benchmarks were U.S. production and U.S. technology; the measure that mattered was American, not Soviet, rate of change. The Soviet Union shut down and the competition went on unabated because all along America was in an arms race with itself. Just as it should have been.

The external, lateral model of competition says that Democrats compete against Republicans in American politics. The internal, vertical model says that Democrats are still competing against their own 1972 rules changes, engineered by Gary Hart on behalf of George McGovern, that turned the party of the Big Tent into a party of fiercely protective Little Tent orthodoxies. Which model explains the Democratic losses in the 1980, 1984, and 1988 presidential races? We don't think it's even close: It wasn't the Republicans that drove the rank and file screaming out of the Democratic

Party. Nor do we think there's any question whom the Republican Party competes against in American politics. Until the GOP solves its own internal schism between those party members who define politics in terms of fiscal conservatism and those who see politics as a battleground for the nation's soul, Democrats or Ross Perot or the Clinton impeachment trial will be nothing more than a sideshow.

External and lateral competition is the distraction. Internal and vertical competition is the game. The person on the other side of the line is the one you have to get past or block or knock to kingdom come, but *The Karate Kid* and every high school football coach who ever called his team together for the Big Talk before the whistle blew had it right: The real battle is against yourself.

The Denver Broncos didn't beat the Green Bay Packers in Super Bowl XXXII. The Packers were the distraction. The Bronco's beat their own past, a history of failure in the crunch that included John Elway's sometimes miserable performances in two previous Super Bowl losses. Nor did the Broncos beat the Atlanta Falcons in Super Bowl XXXIII, except in the most superficial sense. In that game, the Broncos were competing against their future, against the promise that with a repeat win they could join the elite teams of NFL history. Compared to that, the Falcons might as well not have even taken the field.

We have met the enemy, and he is us.

The external model of competition says that you never give away information that might create value for your opponent. The internal, paradoxical model of competition says that creating value for a mythical opponent is never the point in any event. The more you give away the house secrets, the more you create value for yourself.

By definition, practically, the accounting profession operates in the past tense, with an almost priestlike secrecy. While acolytes light the candles and vergers guard the door, historical numbers get toted up to arrive at bottom lines that have almost instant archeological significance. Why, then, has PriceWaterhouse been modeling for its clients the exact optimum amount of information to give away to increase shareholder value? Because the CNBC squawk box isn't reading from annual reports or even quarterly ones, and in a world of near-complete connectivity, market players aren't reacting to them, either. Hoard information, and you'll be seen as a little evolutionary siding unwilling to play in the larger ecology of the marketplace. Make a gift of your information, and you'll be seen as part of the larger network of a connected economy. Be seen as the latter, and you'll create real value for your share price. And it is your share price, not anyone else's— your value, not anyone else's—that has to be the benchmark by which that decision is made.

Look at competition as external and lateral and existing in a single dimension of time, and a bright young man or woman coming out of college today with an interest in making a bundle in industry and rising to the top of the corporate heap would appear to have just one route open to pursue: an MBA, and the higher the reputation of the school it comes from the better. See competition as vertical and internal and existing in multiple dimensions of time, and the options look a little different: Competition can never be imitative, and the question can never be what will best prepare you to do battle in the business world today because the business world today will cease to exist tomorrow.

What's our advice to such a person? What sort of degree program should he or she be pursuing? Maybe one that combines management theory with enough math and science to be technologically literate and a thorough enough grounding in literature to be able to find the story and appreciate a good tale for what it is. Indeed, the fact that we can foresee the need for such a degree program may say that it's already true.

Look at competition as external and lateral, and you also can never stop defining yourself by the present moment. Do that and you can never escape from the present into the future. Fail to make that leap, and the changes you are required to make will always be both reactive and degrading.

It wasn't Microsoft that invented double-click technology. Nor was it Apple Computer, although that's a lot closer. The wizards of Xerox PARC were the first to hit upon the algorithmic principles that led to double-click technology. Why, then, isn't it the Xerox logo and not the Apple or Dell or Compaq one that's plastered all over our desktops? Because Xerox essentially gave Windows away. And why did it do that? Because Xerox was and is the Document Company and personal computers didn't fit into its story line.

Was that the wrong decision? Yes, if the decision was at heart a failure to look beyond the epic battles over internal resources that always define the present moment and see a Xerox that was successfully both the document and the PC company, and we can see plenty of synergies between the two. No, if the decision represented just the opposite: a decision that pursuing PCs would destroy core competencies and carry both the company's story line and its brand where neither could go. And we see plenty of reasons why that might have happened, too.

Failure in the future is sometimes just lousy chance: An avalanche, figuratively or literally, thunders down the mountainside and obliterates everything in its path. More often, though, failure in the future is the result of inadequate imagination in the present. The present tense is historic: Today is over practically before it begins, and all technology is transient in any event, dead before it can be fully depreciated. What counts is tomorrow. Envision that, envision the business your business will be in then and whom you will be competing against for market share, and you're using the chimera of external competition to drive an internal process of change. If you're in the consulting business, will you be "competing" with another consulting firm or with Mattel, which wants to make "play theory" a vital part of the corporate decision-making kit? Whichever choice you make for either question posits a very different world that you will have to begin to deal with and plan for now, even though you can have no real idea whether the choice you made was right: That's why it's the future, not the present.

Storytelling has always been an exercise in imagination. You have to imagine your own future in order to get there. At the same time, you have to realize that the only certain thing in business or in life is that when you get to the future, the field of battle won't look at all like it looks now.

Billions of dollars are placed every day on stock-market risk bets about the future of the infrastructure of the Internet, but the greatest challenge of Internet competition today has nothing to do with its infrastructure. Search engines, portals, anything related to the endoskeleton of the Net bring in the dollars, but the dollars chase the distraction. The eight-hundred-pound gorilla of the Internet today is both much more simple and much more complex: It's the exoskeleton. If the Net is going to be the cutting room of life, if all that cybertime is going to be filled up with the detritus and minutiae of existence, then who owns the intellectual property rights to content that is steadily accelerating in value? How can content producers control their property? How can they capture and protect its value? Will the Net eventually evolve a system like the National Football League of "franchise" content providers—ones who are paid for each minute of cyber-airtime because they attract the greatest number of clients to the site, just as Brett Favre attracts the greatest number of Green Bay Packer fans to Lambeau Field? Are we headed toward what will essentially be the Internet equivalent of closed-circuit TV specials?

We don't know the answers, but until such issues are resolved, there are no winners or losers on the Net—there's only mystery. And until the mystery is solved, there's no competition on the Net either, or there is only side competition against the abstraction of the central battle. Lycos? Well, maybe. Netscape or Yahoo!? Who knows? More to the point, who cares? An Internet without content is random atoms in search of meaning. And if an Internet infrastructure company is not taking the issue of intellectual property control and writing it into its own story line, then all the competitive fervor and stock options in the world won't make a dime's worth of difference because eventually the endoskeleton and exoskeleton of the Internet are going to merge, and if you are not prepared when they do, then your screen is going to freeze and your hard drive turn to dust.

And that leads us to the final paradox of competition: There may not be any. Seagram, Sony, Bertelsmann, Viacom, News Corp., Walt Disney, and Time Warner effectively surround the entertainment industry. They circle the same pool and attack at the same time when the same blood meat is thrown into the water. They also have innumerable joint ventures between the seven of them. Does their community of interests make them competitors or cooperators? Are they seven companies doing battle for the same pieces of the pie, or are they one big company splitting the pie among themselves?

Conventional economic theory holds that the seven companies are all competitors: They vie with one another for sales, for brand preeminence, for market value. All ahead full speed; no quarter given or expected. But as the world moves beyond mere communications connectivity to something deeper, as internal and external borders disappear, the model of the economy shifts, too, from pure competition to something far closer to biology. And in biology, competition is only one part of a larger symbiosis of all existence.

Steel provides another example. By traditional standards, all the major steel manufacturers compete with one another for market share, yet all the major manufacturers also collaborate with one another on the definition of standards for the industry, and it is in their profound economic interest to make everything within the industry definable to the same few "standards" instead of to thousands of different ones. Is the steel industry in competition? Or is it in collusion? And what definition of competition do we need to embrace to include the steel industry and the communications companies we cited just above?

As the U.S. confrontation with Saddam Hussein limped toward the end of its first decade, the joke was going around the defense establishment in Washington, D.C., that every time Iraq "painted" another American plane with radar and thus provoked another missile attack on one of its radar installations, Raytheon threw a cocktail party. And why not? Raytheon was selling the missiles, at about $2 million a pop, that the air force was using, and a $2 million order is worth a cocktail party. But does that mean that Iraq's President Hussein and Raytheon chairman Dennis Picard are competitors or allies? Is the destruction the point, or is the point a symbiotic relationship that produces economic value for

Raytheon at the same time that it produces political value for Hussein in his increasingly narrow slice of the Arab world?

Another example of ecosystem economics: The classic model of competition holds that your distributor is your best partner, but the truth is that the typical distributor today takes a significant margin and puts the burden of demand generation on the producer. Rather than being a partner, your distributor is your competitor for market access to the total economic product of your product. Yet without your distributor you are sunk, and without your product to distribute, your distributor is sunk. And it's not just the manufacturer-distributor chain we are talking about here: Rockwell and Honeywell compete bitterly for market share in manufacturing automation, but 100 percent of the actuators in Honeywell technology are built by Rockwell. That's what life in an ecosystem is like.

General Electric and Rolls-Royce both build jet engines; they both compete for market share in one of the most fiercely competitive industries in the world; and they both supply both sides of the table, which should make them prime examples of free-market competition, except that they also collaborate in the development of jet-engine technology and industry safety standards. That, too, is life in an economic ecosystem.

Then there's the competition that is, when you strip away all competing reasons, competition with yourself. In the mid-1990s Procter & Gamble found itself concerned about declining market share. Typically, such concerns would be addressed by adding new products and "re-ing" old ones: repackaging, renewing, refreshing, and rebranding. Instead, P&G did a study that showed their biggest deterrent to effective merchandising was excess choice: In essence, they were battling themselves for consumer attention and product focus. Rather than add and refresh, Procter & Gamble withdrew brands and simplified the choices within brands, and the company gained five full points of market share in hair care and related products.

McDonald's had a similar experience, but for different reasons. The excess choice on its menu board was competing with its own brand promise, which is speed and efficiency in the purchasing process. The answer: simplify the choices by grouping options into "value meals." A West Coast chain, In-N-Out Burger, carries that lesson still further. If the promise is speed and efficiency, then the most reasonable way to avoid competing against your own brand promise is to offer only one choice. In-N-Out doesn't do quite that, but it limits the options to hamburgers, French fries, milkshakes, and other beverages, and the chain has been a howling success.

It's all in how you look at competition, of course: as the battle for market share or the battle for market access to the economic value of your own product, as rivalry between collaborators or rivalry with self and with your own self-promise, as the battle for sales or the battle for awareness, as the struggle with the company that is producing today the product you are selling today or as the struggle with the company that will be producing tomorrow the product you want to sell tomorrow. But how you look at the competition changes everything.

◆ Future Exercise

At the upper left of a fresh sheet of paper write down the business you are now in. Across from it, at the upper right, write down your chief competitor. Now go to the bottom left and write down the three businesses that you think it is most likely will be driving your company in ten years. Across from that, at the bottom right, note the three companies that you think might be your chief competitors then, depending on which business you are in. ("Anonymous" is okay.) Now draw three columns in the space between the top and bottom of the page, and in those columns list all the changes your company will have to make, depending on which vision of the future holds and thus which company you are most likely to be competing against.

Finally, take a clean sheet of paper and do the same thing with your job: What is your career now? Who is your chief competitor? What are the three most likely careers you will be in a decade down the pike? Who will your three most likely competitors be then? ("Anonymous" is still okay.) What changes will you have to make in the way you do business and conduct your professional life, depending on which vision of the future holds?

This is how you see yourself in your own story.

Box 3
GLOBAL METAPHORS AND GLOBAL BRANDS

You can't have one without the other—and you need both.

◆ ◆ ◆ ◆ ◆ ◆ ◆ ◆ ◆ ◆ ◆ ◆ ◆ ◆ ◆ ◆ ◆ ◆ ◆

Globalism and penetrating global markets are the goals of virtually every company today, and with good reason. The world has turned into a single bazaar, and a sale in Buenos Aires counts every bit as much as a sale in Boston or Bangkok. But if global sales are the goal, the truth is that global brands—for all the attention paid to them—are still precious few in number: Coca-Cola, certainly; Sony, too; maybe British Airways and McDonald's as well; maybe soon Mercedes and Ford.

What makes a truly global brand? Well, market penetration counts, as does market awareness, but both those are little more than aftereffects. A brand can be truly global only when it means the same thing in every marketplace around the world, no matter how different the context and culture might be, at the same time that it means something unique in each of those cultures and contexts. To do that, brands have to tap into global metaphors—into those emotions, those qualities, those colors, those whatevers that say the same thing universally and that appeal in the same way to people all around the world in equal measure, whatever the race, creed, color, nationality, sex, or age involved.

What are the global metaphors? We confess we don't know all of them—it's a study we'd love to have the time to do—but some we can name. Truth, goodness, beauty, liberty, fairness, justice, equality, the meaning of the universe, the place of humankind in the universe: They all appeal to and occupy people across the globe in the same fashion. In some senses, life never gets beyond the issues that fill our hearts in sixth grade. Jokes have universal appeal, too; virtually everyone honors the need to have laughter stimulated. The dark side is a global metaphor as well; Darth Vader (literally, "dark father") needed no explanation in any nation where the *Star Wars* series was shown, and it was shown everywhere. Colors, too, we suspect, have metaphorical qualities that girdle the planet, and the more sophisticated the nation, the more sophisticated the metaphorical palette.

Tie your brand to those global metaphors, and you give it a meaning and a translatability that destroy distance both figuratively and culturally.

Coke is refreshment, and everyone, from Mali to Manitoba to Maui, wants to be refreshed and knows in approximate terms exactly what that entails even if they have unique expectations of how and where and when refreshment might be delivered. Everyone also wants reliability. Everyone wants the TV or portable CD player they bought yesterday to work as well today as it did then and as well in five years as it did in its first year. That's the global metaphor Sony has tied itself to, and it's why Sony survives and prospers while virtually every other key element of the Japanese economy seems ready to sink into the western sky.

Tie your brand to those global metaphors and you also do one other thing we talked about earlier in this book: You provide the comprehensiveness that allows you to atomize your organization to the nth degree. The larger you are, the smaller you have to become, but the smaller you become, the more you need the overarching connection that tying your brand to a global metaphor provides. Divide and conquer at the same time you unite and conquer: Those are the extremes, and global metaphors are your way to move inside them.

5

• • • • • • • • • • • • • • • • • •

THE PARADOX OF ACTION

You've got to go for what you can't expect to get.

Yyou're standing over your golf ball on the toughest green on the hardest course you have ever played. For thirty feet in front of you, the green runs uphill to a ridge. Beyond that it drops away sharply to the right. The cup lies another eighteen feet down the slope.

The reality of the putt is entirely yours to control—it's your ball, your putter, your nerves that are being put to the test—but every decision you make, every tic in your backswing or follow-through, will effectively change the location of the hole and the chance of your ball finding it. Send the putt too far out to the left as you head up the ridge, and the ball will never swing back far enough to the right to find the hole. Cut the putt too close to the right, and you'll end up below the hole. Stroke the ball too hard, and unless your aim is dead on and the cup forgiving, you'll end up off the green on the far side, maybe in the trap beyond the fringe. Stroke the ball too soft, fail to clear the ridge, and you'll have to make the same miserable putt all over again.

Now take that golf ball and make it yourself or your business. The ball sits where you are today. Forty-eight feet away is the hole where you need to be in ten years, and every decision you make now will change the effective location of the hole when the ball finally arrives there. In between the two, between now and then, lie events you can only begin to predict—cleat marks, product failures, caprices of history—and each event will affect where you are going and what you will find when you arrive. And there you have the paradox of action: *Nothing will turn out exactly as it is supposed to.* No path can take you safely with assurance to where you want to be. Where you want to go today is almost certainly not where you will get to when you arrive. And yet if you fail to act, you will cease to exist in any meaningful professional or business sense. You've got to go for what you can't expect to get.

Wait for the future to happen, and you will have no future. That's a given. Rush out to meet the future, and your action will automatically begin changing the future that you are headed to. That also is a given. Between the two givens, though, lies a world of difference. Yahoo! didn't invent the global economic powerhouse that it is today: No one could have possibly predicted when Yahoo! was created in 1994 that within half a decade, the company would have a market capitalization in the range of $50 billion. What Yahoo! invented instead, and more importantly, was change. It rushed out and embraced the future, and in so doing, it opened itself to its own potential. The world in short order would conspire to make the company a far bigger deal than anyone could have expected, but the world could do that only because Yahoo! had from the very beginning immersed itself in possibility.

So can you. Let's say for argument's sake that your goal—the hole you are putting for—is to write a best-selling novel in the year 2010. How do you get there?

- First, by making sure the goal is authentic because in a culture built on inauthentic events, inauthentic aspirations, and inauthentic language, the real thing is riveting. Ask yourself not so much if your goal is realistic: Reality is up to you to make. Ask yourself, instead, if it is what you really want or what you think you should want. If the latter is the case, go back to square one.

- Second, by going in your own mind where you want to be and then imagining how you got there. What will have to be in place for you to be the best-selling author of the year 2010? You'll have to learn to write a good novel, of course, and all the literary tricks that go into that. But you'll also need a good agent, and you'll have to build that close relationship over the decade between now and then. It also wouldn't hurt to cultivate a publisher who will get behind your novel and give you the advance that will allow you the time to write the book well. What can you do now to water that association? And what can you do between now and the year 2010 to increase your visibility and reputation among book editors of the most influential magazines and newspapers? More and more, the inability to succeed in the future will be a failure of imagination in the present, just as the inability of AT&T to become AOL is an expression in the present tense of a failure of imagination in the past.

◆ Third, by being as prepared not to achieve your goal as you are to achieve it. Face facts: Many are called to write best-sellers, but each week only one author wins. Don't pursue the goal, and you'll neither succeed nor fail. Pursue it, and you will at least open yourself to the chance of success. Do that, and your goal might change as you go along. Maybe in the course of pursuing best-sellerhood you'll find that you really want to be an agent or a book editor—we're told both are honorable work. Even if your goal doesn't change, though, you will have begun to manipulate the circumstances that favor your ambition and the ones that oppose it, and more than that, it is almost impossible to ask for.

The great lesson of Alcoholics Anonymous is really not much different than the great lesson of baseball: Just because we have no control over own destiny doesn't mean we shouldn't take responsibility for our own behavior and try to affect outcomes on our behalf. If the bases are loaded and the stats say the next hitter bats .232 against lefties with runners in scoring position and .350 against righties, bring the southpaw in. Unless, that is, your intuition says otherwise, because that, too, is part of the equation of action in a paradoxical age. Set false goals, and every decision will require a balancing of all the accumulated lies; you can't be intuitive about what you don't really believe. Make your goal authentic, and intuition (and, just as important, counterintuition) can take over, just as it must in a world in which there is no time for action to be married to reason.

Times don't change as much as we like to think they do. Even in the Dark Ages, people—nobles and commoners, priests and pagans—had the same basic roster of wants that we do. They yearned for the same things we yearn for; they were governed by the same set of emotions, for good or ill. One person's joy was another's sorrow, then as now.

What is different today is the accelerating speed at which the human drama is played out. Every action still has an equal and opposite reaction, but the two—action and reaction, the thing and its opposite—arrive not sequentially but simultaneously. The future already exists in every moment of the present, and the two—present and future—tug at us as if they would like to rip us in half. Act in the present with an eye to the future, and you will warp the very place you are intending to arrive at. Act in the present with an eye only to the here and now, and you will fail to prepare for a future the very nature of which is utterly uncertain.

Trapped between colliding opposites, buffeted by competing claims, we have to learn to act as if we contained two opposites within ourselves. We have to be and not be, do and not do, exist in the now and exist in the then, start in the future and work back to the present at the same time we start in the present and create the circumstances that allow the future to unfold in our favor. What's more, we have to do all that within the framework of every individual moment, and we have to recognize that every decision we make in one moment will destabilize the next moment.

Is learning to live in such a world and time easy? No. Can doing so be learned? Yes, with effort. Can your company be structured so that it acts both intuitively and counterintuitively, so that it is both itself and not itself, so that it acts in the present and the future at the same time? Yes, that, too, and we'll get to how later in this chapter. First, though, a game that we call the Scenario Plan. Play it with your whole family, or your housemates, or your action team. It's an exercise in negotiating your way through life's little (and continuous) collisions of competing claims.

Have everyone sit around a table—breakfast or conference, or barroom booth—and write down one thing that they would like to be true about their personal future or the future of their career or business. Insist that whatever they write down be authentic, and then have them slap a date on it:

- ◆ I will stop smoking on March 25, 2003.
- ◆ By August 2007, the price for a key component in my business will be exactly half of what the price is today.
- ◆ I will watch my daughter graduate from Stanford University in the spring of 2009.
- ◆ By the year 2012, I will be married to someone else.
- ◆ By the year 2036, my company will dominate space propulsion systems.
- ◆ I will celebrate my one-hundredth birthday on November 25, 2047.

Those are the goals, what they want to be headed for, the future they would like to unfold for themselves. Now have each player go there in his or her own head and ask three questions:

- ◆ What are the things that had to happen for me to realize my ambition?
- ◆ What are the things I needed to keep from happening?
- ◆ What are the things I did nothing about?

In business, for example, you absolutely need to manage capital in accord with your ambition for the future, and you also need to manage propaganda so well that the critical mass of those involved becomes convinced that the direction you are taking the company in is the right direction. At the same time, you absolutely need to avoid the sort of political entanglements that change always brings.

You also need to adjust the things you need to happen and need to avoid to account for the fact that they will be taking place in a different time frame than the one you are now living in. Today, the Stanford admissions department may reward deep commitment to extracurriculars or community service along with an exceptional performance on the Scholastic Aptitude Test, but will the admissions department still be rewarding that by the end of the decade? Or will the critical difference between two applicants be the capacity to solve intuitive problems? And if that is the case, and you have been booking your daughter year after year into ballet lessons and soccer teams and the usual panoply of tutors, all with an eye toward the Stanford commencement in the year 2009, have you been doing exactly the wrong thing? That's why planning backward from the future is so helpful. It's also how you destabilize the future you are headed for by the simple act of heading there. Every move you make changes where you are going.

And you need to ignore some things as well. The state of the Russian economy may be crucial to the future of the globe, but unless you're George Soros or aspiring to be him, give it a good leaving alone. We've said it earlier: When you finally get where you are going, the prize isn't likely to be what you now think it will be, but unless you keep your eye on the prize from day one, you'll never get where you are probably not going to end up. The most important characteristic of people who survive into the future isn't brains, although brains are nice. It isn't money, or physical strength, or beauty, although all those can be admirable, too. The most important characteristic is faith—faith in where you want to go, faith that you will get there, faith that even if the future you arrive at isn't what you envision, the journey will have been worthwhile.

Now, back to the Scenario Plan game. Pick one of the scenarios—"I will celebrate my one-hundredth birthday on November 25, 2047"—and let's begin playing. What are the implications of your goal? What must you do? What must you think about? What must you avoid? What can you ignore? How are you likely to change your future by pursuing it? And what have you learned from the perspective of that one-hundredth birthday? Have everyone join in. These are the questions for which there can be no real answers because they are about a time that is yet to be, which is why they are the most important questions you can ask. And welcome once again to the Fool Box.

If your ambition is to celebrate your one-hundredth birthday in November 2047—not an unrealistic goal given the current exponential growth in the number of centenarians—will you be in good health, mobile enough to spend a significant amount of time out of bed and off the sofa, acute enough to know where you are and what you want to do today? And if you are going to be in good health, what should you do now to pursue the future you foresee?

How about money? If you've been to see a retirement planner, you're likely to have come up with a savings plan that will assure your affluence into, say, your mid-eighties. But what about the extra decade and a half, and whatever time might follow after that? (If 100, why not 110?) What do you need to begin saving now to assure a satisfactory level of affluence into and beyond your one-hundredth year?

How about the nature of the family you will still be around and healthy enough to enjoy? If you have two children and they have two or three children apiece and they have two or three children a piece, your extended family could eventually number into the mid-twenties. Do you want them to be able to continue to visit you en masse at holidays? If so, how large a house or condo or apartment will you need? If you intend to visit your children and grandchildren and great-grandchildren—and great-great, most likely, by the time you clear one hundred—how much should you be budgeting now for travel expenses then? (Remember, the failure to achieve any particular future is in large part the failure to imagine yourself in it.)

How are you going to keep up with the family, share in the interests of all those grandchildren, have the remotest idea what's going on in the heads of all the great-grandchildren? You will have grown up at the leading edge—in years only—of the computer age; they're likely to have grown out of the other side of it.

You also will have grown up in an era when young men and women were still fined and thrown in jail for the possession of relatively minute amounts of mood-altering and mind-altering drugs. They'll be living in the middle of an era in which virtually every imaginable form of mood- and mind-related pharmaceutical will be legally available and widely utilized. Tell them about a time when South American drug lords held governments hostage and a staggering percentage of the African Americans doing prison time were incarcerated for drug-related crimes, and your grandchildren and great-grandchildren will have no frame of reference for understanding what you are saying. You might as well be talking about how your own grandfather hand-cranked his Model A to get it started. They did *what? Why?*

How can you begin to prepare yourself now to cope with that world then—cope with it so that, when it arrives and you are living in it, you don't feel like a museum piece? Should you learn now all you can about low-earth-orbit satellite transmissions? Take a course in algorithms? Begin popping recreational amounts of PCP? Plan to get a master's degree at seventy? A Ph.D. at eighty?

And how proactive should you be in assuring that your health, mental and physical, at age one hundred is as good as it can be? Should you be taking antioxidants? The recommended amounts or far more or less? And what sources can you trust for such information? Your neighborhood health store? *Lancet?* How about synthetic human growth hormones—DHEAs? They're edgier, but they could be more meaningful in the long run. Or less meaningful. Or just plain dangerous, given the absence of longitudinal studies.

If learning a foreign language really does grow dendrites in the elderly and improve circulation throughout the brain—and studies seem to indicate such is the case—should you be planning to spend your ninetieth year in Barcelona, your ninety-fifth at an *école française* in Provence? Learning to play a musical instrument seems to have the same effect. Maybe you should be pointing toward the famed Julliard School of Music instead, and maybe the best future play Julliard could make right now is to begin planning for an adjunct school that would offer instruction to seniors.

For that matter, what should you be prepared to sacrifice now for maximum health then—because action is just like time: The more you act with an eye to the future, the more you destabilize the present, and the more you act in the present, the less uncertain—even unlikely—your future becomes. Should you avoid sunlight now so that your skin will remain soft and elastic into your hundreds? Or is it not worth looking like a beached whale in midsummer in your early fifties to achieve such a goal almost double your life span hence? Should you get yourself to a plastic surgeon today on the assumption that no one wants to turn a hundred and be ugly? Or would the bruising and scarring now be a greater punishment than the reward of a tight jawline in that distant tomorrow? Action is choice between future and present.

Back to money: Maybe you can put aside an adequate amount today to be almost certain of affluence decades down the road, but how mean will you have to live in the present to live much better than meanly in the future? Should you begin to prepay your health insurance now, as a hedge against inflation? And if you feel strongly enough about inflation, should you be investing in property and minerals as well? Dump Intel and load up on Newmont Mining?

We know the givens of the future: We will all need money. We will all need food. We will all need shelter. What we don't know are the critical uncertainties of the givens: Money in what form? Real assets or financial ones? Stocks or bonds or hard cash buried deep in the backyard? Food for pleasure or food for survival—a basement full of bottled water, canned goods to see you through a nuclear winter? Shelter from Arctic blasts or from tropical storms?

If you believe that energy sources are going to be in short supply fifty years down the road, you could ignore the possibility, figuring that another fifty years down the road your energy is going to be in short supply, too. But you also could invest now in the cheapest industrial resource in the world today: coal. Sure, the Chinese are dumping it on the world marketplace and driving the cost of a ton of anthracite toward zero, but that also means that places like Utah are filled with coal ghost towns—not because the supply ran out but because the market ran out. Buy such a town now, and the coal pit that created it, and half a century from now you could be sitting on a gold mine, not a coal one.

Or maybe you believe that the earth is going to run out of fossil fuel altogether over the next century. If you intend to be around in those dying days of coal and oil—or if you intend to so comport yourself now that your children and children's children can benefit from the end of fossil fuels—wouldn't the play in the present be to buy acres and acres of real estate in Mississippi or Louisiana or someplace where land is still relatively cheap, the rule of law is likely to prevail over the long term, and the temperature rarely drops below thirty-two degrees Fahrenheit? If the world is going to be running out of heating oil and coal, Americans are going to be running out of Boston and New York and Philadelphia and Cleveland and Chicago as fast as their stubby little frozen legs will carry them, and the more money they have, the faster they will run. Why not be in Mississippi to greet them with building lots when they arrive?

Action is choice between present and future, yes, but it is also choice on the fly because the present disappears, the future becomes the present in the blink of an eye, and the only thing in life you can be certain of is that the things you thought of as terribly uncertain are almost certain to arrive. Yet the more you plan for the certainty of uncertainty, the more you destabilize your sense of place in the certain but transitory present.

Example: You love your spouse. Your spouse loves you. You are certain you will be married forever, but the odds say otherwise, and so maybe you should begin to think about the possibility of divorce, just as an intellectual exercise. What lawyer will you use if that possibility were to arise? And what grounds will the divorce be based on? Your spouse's grounds or yours? If your grounds—and the best defense is a good offense—what will they be and where will you find them? Well, follow the money, they always say, so you begin studying your spouse's credit card usage, and you find charges for flowers you never received and four-star restaurants you never visited, and perhaps it's all explicable: flowers for Secretary's Week, four-star restaurants for business dinners that your spouse forgot to mention. But maybe it's not so explicable. And either way—explicable or not—by acting in the future, you've destabilized the present and perhaps caused the terrible uncertainty of a divorce to terribly arrive. Thank goodness, you've also assured that when the terrible certainty does arrive, you'll be ready.

Or what if the "terrible uncertainty" of actuarial averageness were to arrive unbidden. You want to live to age one hundred. You've planned to live to age one hundred. But you are a white male in his early fifties, in average health although slightly over-weight with elevated cholesterol and no genetic disposition toward longevity. About you, MetLife has tables it has bet the bank on. Those tables say that you'll be lucky to make it to eighty and that your last years could be costly ones. What then?

Do you join the Hemlock Society? Start smoking again? Get close to Dr. Kevorkian instead of a divorce lawyer? Make up with your children so that when you are institutionalized, *someone* will come to visit? Or just seize the upside of a shorter life span? A retirement plan meant to fund thirty-five good postwork years calls for sacrifices that one meant to see you just a decade-plus out of the traces doesn't require. Instead of heading to Costco for discount olive oil, why not bail out to Bali? Maybe you should even be taking out one of those reverse mortgages that drains the asset utterly in the very year MetLife says you will perish. (But if you do, you better perish that year and no later because there will be no net to catch you if you don't.)

Life is a balancing act. Skew your actions so much that you become trapped in the future, and you won't be able to perform well enough in the present to be a part of the future when it arrives. The present can be cruel to those who don't embrace it. Skew your actions so much that you become trapped in the present and ignore the future, and you'll miss the enormous upsides waiting to be exploited. The future is equally cruel to those who refuse to dream about it.

Dream as far out as you can—predict the future over the farthest horizon you can imagine—and you will be called a crackpot, and the bigger the crackpot you are, the greater your reward stands to be because the only "certain" predictions are ones that are statements about what already is becoming true. The farther out a prediction goes, the more uncertain it becomes; and the more uncertain it becomes, the greater the chance it will outperform every other prediction competing with it.

Had you predicted fifty years ago that the average school-teacher today would be as much social worker as instructor, that rudeness would be commonplace in the halls of even the most upscale public schools, that litigation would hang over the average classroom like a black cloud of doom, and that every teacher would go to school every day aware of the possibility of violence on a massive scale, what would you have been called? A crackpot! You would have been called a crackpot, too, if you had even dared to suggest that by the year 2000, after two great wars that washed the continent with blood, Europe would have adopted an almost universal currency or that you could drive a car from London to France. Ze car? It swims? *Sacrebleu!* And the people who called you a crackpot would have been right, in the short term. More important, you would have been right, too—and right in the long term, where being right really counts.

How about if you had predicted even as recently as 1980 that by the century's turn the United States would have weapons of war that would require no physical engagement with the enemy? That a company with almost no physical assets such as Microsoft would have one of the highest market capitalizations of any company in the world? That Fuji would be scrambling for cash to make its payroll? That the human genome would be nearly mapped in its entirety and DNA evidence would far outweigh any other form of testimony in courts of law? That, for heaven's sake, individual trading, not brokerage-house trading, would be poised to drive the stock market? Individual trading? With all those complicated investment algorithms that only a math Ph.D. could possibly understand? Crackpot! And crackpot! crackpot! crackpot! crackpot on all the other predictions, too. Out of the gene pool! Take a shower! Except, of course, that the United States has now waged multiple military actions that entailed virtually no physical engagement with the enemy, and Microsoft could liquidate its tangible property almost overnight, and Fuji is hurting, hurting, hurting, while DNA has become the evidentiary behemoth of the courtroom, and on-line trading has gotten so cheap that your broker better be an awful lot smarter than you are if she wants to charge you ten times what an e-trade would cost. In short, crackpot that you are, you would have been right all along.

Or how about if you had predicted in 1980 that by 2000 cold fusion would have solved the global environmental dangers posed by fission-based nuclear power generation? Crackpot! And they would have been right. That's another thing about acting in the future in the present: You've got to be willing to be very wrong, too.

Every business wants to own the future because every business knows that if it can be waiting there with a product or service when the future arrives, commerce will beat a path to its door, but publicly traded businesses want to own the future for a more practical purpose that plays out in the present every day: The future is what the market values.

For most American investors—institutional or individual—the price-earnings ratio, the gold standard of investment decisions a generation ago, has simply disappeared as a meaningful market measure. Earnings are reported in the present, but they are past-tense news. Share price occurs in the present, but it is a transitory measure, and in the P/E ratio, it is set against an artifact of history. Market capitalization, by contrast, is in the future-present tense: It's what the business is worth today based on the expectation of where it will be tomorrow, next month, next year, or next decade.

To own the future, though, businesses and individuals alike need to avoid the activity traps that can lock them into the present. We eat lunch within the same hour most days because the clock tells us it is time to eat lunch, call staff meetings because it's Wednesday morning, issue quarterly earnings reports according to a calendar that may have nothing to do with the internal calendar of our profit and loss, and know we're doing a good job if every day a media spending plan, a product distribution mix, and a sales forecast are filtered through our office. The repetitive actions become the metric for our individual and corporate progress through life—even though we know that our life and our business's life change every day in ways large and small. Indeed, the more unsure we become about the future, the more repetitive we are likely to become in the present.

How do you break out of such traps? One way is to ask yourself what would happen if you "didn't." If you didn't eat lunch according to the clock, would you suffer blood-sugar problems or migraines? Become irritable or irregular? Or would you have one of those minor senses of liberation that might allow you to see past the fog of the moment? Or what would happen if you didn't call the staff meeting? Would paranoia sweep through your division? Would key personnel you depend upon feel devalued? It's certainly possible, but it's also possible that somewhere along the corporate food chain not calling the meeting might set off a small epiphany that would begin to unlock a puzzle of long standing.

Don't mistake: Breaking out of activity traps is delicate work. Each individual has to handle his or her own sense of order very carefully, and has to be very careful about destabilizing those above and below and lateral to him in the pecking order. A sense of order is like a gyroscope: Once it goes out of whack, all hell can break loose. But some activities have to be done; some don't. Distinguishing between them is the beginning of wisdom.

Here's another way of breaking out of the activity trap, related to the first: Instead of making a "to do" list, make a "why to do" list. Think about how each action is connected to outcome; reacquaint yourself with the model that underlies the way you are spending your time. Don't know just your actions. Know why you are taking them and what business you are in, why you are in that business and where you want to go with it.

You also need to find your comfort zones and attack them. If you are a scientist, your preoccupying question is likely to be something like: What is the nature of knowing? Instead, ask yourself something far more interesting: What is the nature of not knowing? If your company specializes in the movement of people from Point A to Point B—Amtrak, an airline, a steamship company—all your energies are likely to go into the issue of when a person feels comfortable traveling via your routes. Try asking instead what it is like when a person is comfortable with not traveling. Project yourself into that reality, and you will learn a lot about yourself. When is a magazine a drug? When is an automobile a bedroom? When is the cartoon real? In your comfort zone, the answers are obvious: never, never, and never. Comfort zones reinforce conventional thought—that's why they're comfortable. Outside of comfort zones, though, almost anything can become possible.

Not long ago we recommended to Saturn that it make Mackinac Island its "sacred site"—the place it goes when it needs to escape itself and think clearly about its future. Why? Because there are no cars on Mackinac Island, and cars make life meaningful for Saturn and its senior management. By the same token, Delta Airlines might run a manager retreat on a submarine, or Newmont Mining might run one on a converted C-135 with in-flight refueling. We also recommended to British Airways that it consider renaming its business class the "bitter class." Why? Because instead of pretending they can make businessmen comfortable in an inherently uncomfortable environment, airlines need to help businessmen learn how to manage their discomfort—the bitterness of flight, even in the expensive seats. But whether British Airways buys our reasoning or not, the very act of considering the proposition changes the question of air travel by forcing it to embrace its troubling (and authentic) opposite. Changing the question is another way of attacking comfort zones and upsetting assumptions. Do that, and you expand your possibilities exponentially. And it is only by immersing yourself in all your possibilities that you can prepare for a future in which every possibility is uncertain and every uncertainty is a possibility.

How can you run a business in both the present and future tenses? How can you break out of the box of either one? Here's a paradox: by compartmentalizing. By segmenting the organization and its efforts. And in particular, by pulling the curtain around your Fool Box so tightly shut that not a single beam of light shines through to the rest of the organization.

You may be by nature a nurturing chief executive who wants to empower everyone throughout the organization by involving them in the work of the Future Box, but if your fools are any good, they are likely to create a discussion that is deeply at odds with the story of the organization, and no end of instability can flow from that once it bleeds beyond the curtain.

One way to pull the curtain is to outsource the work. It's easier to protect the future that way from the political infighting common to any organizational structure, and the work is also less likely to be deeply tied to the so-called common cost tax basis by which most companies levy costs of divisions in proportion to their revenues. But if outsourcing can help move futuring onto the organizational equivalent of the CIA's black budget, it also raises issues of intellectual property rights that companies ignore at great peril. Who owns what? In the CIA, it's easy: The agency owns intellectual property, and *you* go to jail if you try to take it. In the corporate world, outsourcing the future can entail a lot of lawyering.

Other companies outsource the future by moving it onto corporate campuses: Arthur Andersen and Xerox have done so, and with great success. But you need to be certain that the campus is a real one, not an adjunct of the CEO's ego. Does flattery abound? Is sycophancy palpable among the ranks when the corporate brass arrives? If so, the campus is being run for some purpose other than unfettered inquiry, and whatever vision emerges from it will be far more about present power than future direction.

A third and maybe most practical way is to simply get very close to an existing academic institution and let it be your Fool Box. The very qualities that tend to make academia look so silly from the outside—its distance from the real world, the weight of intellectual and academic tradition, the intense, almost theological jealousies that characterize campus life—also have allowed universities to do an extraordinarily good job of inventing the future.

"For here we are not afraid to follow truth wherever it may lead." The words are Thomas Jefferson's, much quoted at the institution he founded in 1819, the University of Virginia, but Jefferson's words capture the spirit you want your Fool Box to operate in, wherever it is located.

Which university you want to get close to depends both on what business you are now in and what business you might want to be in, and a university that's right today as a partner might be wrong tomorrow. That's why you have to follow the truth—or at least the futurist's version of it, which is often closer to fiction— wherever it might lead, even if it leads right out the front gate. Just as important, you have to be prepared for that "truth" to enrage you, and you should become enraged yourself if it doesn't.

Whether your fools are located inside or outside your wall,

you're using them to institutionalize insurgency within your organization. Their job isn't to ask nice questions or to observe the politics of corporate correctness. Their job is to ask the questions that upset your equilibrium and force you to confront a tomorrow where all your actions of today will be of no avail.

What, for example, will be the impact of aging on the spot-buying practices in your principal market? The question has no bearing today. Don't trouble your organization broadly with it. But it means everything for tomorrow because tomorrow there will be two enormous age groups—old people and young people—and almost no one in between. Average the buying behavior of both groups and you will be sure to describe no one: the famous human being with slightly more than one breast and slightly less than one testicle.

How about severe constraints on natural resources? Again, the question is likely to have little relevance in the present for any company. Products have to be gotten out; manufacturing and marketing need to be done. To contemplate environmental disaster organization-wide is to invite discontent on every front. But the growing aggressiveness of bacteria, the growing shortage of sterile water, the dramatic shrinkage in world phosphate reserves—all have resonance far beyond themselves. How do you begin to plan now for then? How do you immerse yourself in the possibilities of that future and still be true to your story? Because finally nothing may be more important than this: When you fill your Future Box, be sure to fill it with people who understand not just your business but your meaningfulness. Remember: The former is what you do; the latter is what you *are*.

Should General Electric be General Electric or General Electron? The latter, if electricity is irrelevant, and it needs to be positioning itself to be General Electron today, although it has to continue to be General Electric in the present. Will the future of the credit business—GE's real cash engine—continue to revolve around consumer loans? Or if gaming is going to be the dominant recreational activity of the future, should GE be getting into the gaming business now—inventing a system that manages casinos and does moment-to-moment sweeps of net profit into investment accounts run by GE Capital?

Doing so would seem to make sense. The casinos, in theory, would get the float on the house take that now lies dormant until the next day's deposit, and GE—again in theory—would get a big enough percentage of that float to make its shareholders happy for decades to come. But if the company is going to do that it will have to get in bed with the University of Nevada at Las Vegas, which is the only university in the world that offers a curriculum based on the theory of gaming. It will have to get close to state gaming commissions as well because the commissions have a long history of needing to be courted to the edge of legality and sometimes beyond. And if GE were to do all that, it will have taken an extraordinary leap from its beginnings in New York State—and maybe not a very large step at all from the core of its own myth, its meaningfulness. Thomas Edison was the father of electrical invention, yes, but he was also a great gambler who started the company by betting everything on the success of electrifying a square block of lower Manhattan. Between rolling the dice on a primitive generator and rolling them on a craps table is a space that is both wide as an ocean and thin as a horizon.

Right action is true to the story. And because it's true, it unites past and future. Right action allows you to be yourself and not yourself. It simultaneously explores both intuition and counterintuition. And at the end of the day, it always brings you back where you began, which is always the same place and never the same place at all.

◆ Future Exercise 1

On the right-hand side of your pad, write down one thing that you think is likely to be true about your company in ten years. On the left-hand side of the pad, write down exactly the opposite of what you wrote down on the right side. Now, beneath each of those extremes write down all the implications you can think of for that "truth" and opposite "truth" about your company a decade from now, and all the actions that you think might flow from those implications. Leave a little corridor of space down the middle of the page, between the two lists, and try to project yourself into that space. The corridor is the central tendency of your business. The extremes on either side of the page are where you must act and live in order to keep that central tendency clear and focused.

◆ Future Exercise 2

Complete the following four propositions, but before you do, consider these three rules:

◆ Your answers must be stated as absolutes. No gray areas, no fence-straddling, no wishy-washiness allowed. If an answer sounds like the beginning of an editorial, start over.

◆ The answers must be conceivable in your own mind and authentic to your own reality. If you can't imagine yourself in the future you describe, you've got the wrong future in mind.

◆ For each answer, there needs to be a set of activities within your span of control that will (a) increase the probability that the future the answer describes could come true and (b) decrease the likelihood that it won't come true. Always being positive without removing the negative is never enough. You have to attack the negative and increase the vector force on the positive at the same time.

Now, the propositions:

◆ In order to be successful in the year 2003, I must _____.

◆ To be happy in the year 2007, I must _____.

◆ To feel that I have made a difference by the year 2016, I must _____.

◆ On my one-hundredth birthday, I will _____.

6

◆ | ◆ ◆ ◆ ◆ ◆ ◆ ◆ ◆ ◆ ◆ ◆ ◆ ◆ ◆

THE PARADOX OF
LEADERSHIP

*To lead from the front, you have
to stay inside the story.*

A December 1998 political cartoon by Steve Kelley that first appeared in the *San Diego Union-Tribune* captures almost perfectly the paradox of leadership in the postinformation world. Drawn as the Clinton impeachment proceedings languished between House and Senate, the cartoon shows a political pollster, clipboard and pen at the ready, interviewing three presumably average Americans. The question the pollster has asked is only implied, but the answers ring crystal clear:

"Keep the creep," answers a middle-age woman.

"Don't fire the liar," an older white man chimes in.

"Why dump the chump?" an African American male asks.

Substitute Bill Gates as the implicit subject of the pollster's question, or George Steinbrenner, Rupert Murdoch, Tony Blair, even China's Jiang Zemin. Find the right sample group to poll— the computerati, baseball fans, mediaphiles, Brits in the street, or Sino-American businessmen—and we suspect the answers would be pretty much the same: Keep the creep. Don't fire the liar. Don't dump the chump.

Why? Because each of the people we have just cited contains within himself his own paradox; each has a remarkable capacity to be both reasonable and unreasonable in his activities; most important, each has moved inside and absorbed his own set of contradictions.

Bill Gates? He's a duplicitous, monopoly-craving monster, ready to crush any competition under his heel; reams of Justice Department documents will show you just how he has done it. Gates also pursues monopolistic control because a monopoly is in the best interest of consumers, and there's plenty of evidence to support that as well. What's more, Gates is entirely comfortable crushing competition and looking out for consumers, and doing both at the same time. And thus we both admire and despise him—and look to him for global leadership in the software sector.

As the principal owner of the New York Yankees, George Steinbrenner became such a nationally recognized caricature of the capricious, ego-obsessed team owner that an actor playing him could become a near-regular on the nation's highest-rated TV comedy series. At the same time audiences were laughing at the fictional Steinbrenner on the *Seinfeld* show, the real Steinbrenner was assembling the pieces that would produce one of the best teams and best seasons in the history of baseball. Either role would have been sufficient to make Steinbrenner a celebrity, but the ability to live simultaneously inside the skin both of a buffoon and of a shrewd manipulator of baseball talent is what makes him admired, and a leader in sports ownership and administration.

And thus the examples go. So effective is Rupert Murdoch at controlling every side of a media market that he can be a champion of the First Amendment rights of free speech at the same time that he closes out any possibility of serious debate. So staunch a conservative is Murdoch, too, that his tabloid newspapers and Fox TV network have consistently led the way in pushing forward the frontiers of bad taste. Externally, the contradictions can seem baffling; internally—and this is the point—they make perfect sense.

Jiang Zemin is the last staunch communist leader who truly matters in the world at the same time that he is a wild-eyed advocate of free-market capitalism, even if it has to be imposed by ruthlessly authoritarian practices that include kangaroo-court trials and long prison sentences for prominent democratic intellectuals. A paradox? In fact, a multiple one, and so near as anyone can tell, Jiang Zemin seems entirely comfortable living inside it, just as the Labour Party leader Tony Blair seems perfectly comfortable being one of the most effective conservative prime ministers Great Britain has ever had.

South Africa's Nelson Mandela is admirable on many fronts: for the stoicism with which he seems to have endured twenty-eight years of imprisonment, for the quiet depth of his revolutionary fervor, and for the ease with which he dons a suit after all his experiences and moves easily among the world's political and economic elite. All that qualifies him for sainthood. What makes Mandela a global leader, though, is his ability to be not one thing or one person, but so many things and so many people at once: the revolutionary in the suit, the symbol simultaneously of suffering and of forgiveness, the emblem of both his nation's bitter racial past and its uncertain racial future.

So, too, Bill Clinton and, for that matter, Hillary Rodham Clinton. What we admire about him—and Americans were giving him record approval ratings even as the sordid details of his private life filled the evening news—is exactly this capacity to be moral and immoral simultaneously, to be right about the budget and wrong about his wife, to be good at so many things and bad at so many things and to remain calm in the midst of his own storm. What we admire about her is her ability to stay calm in the midst of that same storm, too: to be wife, mother, politician, and author at the same time; to be the wronged woman and the faithful spouse and to be both without going nuts with the contradictions that circumstances have forced her to live with.

In a world that prided itself on its consistency, we found virtue in the constancy of our leaders and punished their deviations from whatever single reality we embraced. Thus, in the dying decades of the Age of Reason, John F. Kennedy was lauded for his New Frontier policies even as we refused to confront his paradoxical behavior—mob connections, ballot-box stuffing, a parade of women in and out of the White House such as to make Bill Clinton look almost monogamous—because doing so would have upset our sense of structure and righteousness. Thus, too, we punished Richard Nixon for his role in the Watergate break-in and cover-up, even as we refused to confront the paradox that this Red-baiting demon of the political left had produced one of the great centrist legislative records of the century.

That was then, though; this is now. And in an inherently inconsistent world, consistency is no longer the virtue that it once was in our leaders. Clinging to a single reality—whether it's an orthodoxy of the right, left, or center—makes no sense in an age in which multiple realities are everywhere and everywhere apparent. And therein lies the first principle of leadership in a paradoxical world: What people most resonate to in leaders today is a high comfort level with their own inconsistencies and a high capacity to inhabit multiple realities simultaneously. The more our leaders manifest the absorption of paradox in both the ways they conduct their business life and the ways they work and live as human beings, the higher our own comfort level with them grows and the more we are willing to listen to and follow them as better examples of the selves we know we must become.

The social power of a Bill Gates or a Bill Clinton or even a Warren Buffett arises not from the fact that each can be explained away by his actions but by the fact that none of them can be explained away by his actions. All three men live their own paradoxes, and because they do so and live their paradoxes so publicly, we are drawn to them like moths to a flame.

The second principle of leadership flows from the first: Just as great leaders have to live inside inconsistency and inhabit multiple realities, so they have to manage day to day based on fact, while at the same time leading day to day by the light of a vision that's based not on fact but on an ideal.

Ask any great leader—Jack Welsh at GE, Duke University basketball coach Mike Krzyzewski, Tina Brown at the new *Talk* magazine, Bill Clinton for that matter—for the stats, and he or she will give them to you until the cows come home. It's not just that fact-based management is the rage, although it is. Day to day, any company or team or magazine or any other organization has to be run on the basis of its hard data. What's the margin? What did you sell yesterday? How many broken-product (broken diesel engines, lost recruits, outraged readers, broken social policy) calls came in? A leader who doesn't know those things doesn't know his organization. But a leader who knows only the facts also doesn't know where his organization is going or why.

As much as it is about facts, great leadership is also about concretizing ideas and about having the vision that feeds those ideas, and it's about tending and managing both the facts and the vision simultaneously. What's the margin, yes. But also, how can we relax the margins long term so that we can take more share? And how can we increase quality in the long term so we have fewer broken-product calls? And what do we need to do in the long term to assure that the fact-set we are operating from then is different from the fact-set we are operating from today because every business, from the business of running a country to the business of waging war to the business of crushing software competition, represents a dimming reality. And if a leader is a custodian of one thing above everything else, it is just that: that dimming reality, that sense of the fact-based present disappearing into an obscured future where probability tells us everything we know will be turned on its head. The simple fact is that without a vision based on an ideal, a leader will never get us there.

In 1995, Pierre Omidyar was just another twenty-something Silicon Valley software developer. But Omidyar had a girlfriend, the girlfriend had a collection of Pez dispensers that she was trying to expand, and therein lay a challenge that Omidyar set out to convert to an opportunity. He started by opening up a Website where Pez-dispenser collectors could trade their wares. The Pezzers, in turn, showed up in such record numbers that Omidyar thought, if dispensers, why not lamps and if lamps, why not, oh, rugs, and so on. The result is eBay, cyberspace's largest on-line auction house and the source of a $3 billion fortune (on paper, at least) that has made Omidyar one of the most admired businesspeople in the world. What did he do? He paid attention to the facts at the same time that he concretized an idea, won his girlfriend's heart (they were engaged as of the start of 1999), and made a vision come true. Going once, going twice, sold! And great leadership.

Ted Turner will always be half a Satan to the political right.

That's part of the dowry of marrying "Hanoi Jane" Fonda, and partly because he seems to have an uncontrollably loose mouth of his own. But Turner saw before almost anyone else did both the potential synergy of TV superstations and sports teams and the incipient global appetite for a common body of news. By paying attention to the facts on both fronts, he was able to concretize the two ideas and turn them into a communications empire. By paying attention to the facts of his communications empire, he was able to turn the Atlanta Braves into the National League's version of an empire. And by paying attention to the facts of all his empires—from the Braves to Time Warner, where he serves as vice chairman—Turner has earned sufficient discretionary wealth to donate $1 billion toward concretizing his vision of a kind of one-world federalism. That's leadership, too.

To the relatives and friends of those who died or were injured in the 1998 bombings of the U.S. embassies in Kenya and Tanzania, Osama Bin Laden is more than half a Satan. It was Bin Laden, presumably, who financed the operations from what was then his mountain stronghold in Afghanistan. But by paying attention to the facts, Bin Laden was able to make a fortune off of trading oil contracts with Western petroleum firms, and by embracing the logic of paradox, he has been able to use that fortune to concretize the idea of waging a terrorist guerrilla war against the industrialized Western nations that had helped make him rich. And thus Bin Laden is admired and revered as a leader by those with whom he shares common goals.

The more effectively leaders manage the facts day to day, the more ready they are to move beyond facts to vision. The more they lead in the service not of facts but of ideals, the more we are likely to see, applaud, and revere them as people who can provide us with guidance and direction. Once again, we recognize in them the capabilities that we know we need in ourselves. By following them, they fulfill us as all great leaders ultimately do.

A third principle of paradoxical leadership flows as well from the first two: Great leadership today requires us to recognize and separate short- and long-term value, and to make both of them live in each other.

When the Houston Astros traded several minor league prospects to the Seattle Mariners for pitcher Randy Johnson during the middle of the 1998 baseball season, the team did so knowing that it would never be able to hold on to Johnson's services for longer than the few months left to play that year. They also knew that picking up Johnson was likely to upset all the social equities of the organization and turn the rational rules of management on their ear. The Astros built from the inside, and because they did, the team had one of the lowest payrolls in baseball. Players, coaches, and even the manager were living on short salary rations. When he was free to negotiate his own terms at season's end, Johnson was certain to command a contract worth almost a third of the Astros' entire salary budget. (Johnson ultimately would sign a $52.4 million, four-year contract with the Arizona Diamondbacks.)

Why, then, sign him at such risk to the mores of a poor but successful franchise? Because the team's long-term interests required that it generate enough fan and civic interest to make a financial success of a soon-to-be-opened new stadium that voters had approved two years earlier, and that long-term goal could be met only by winning in the short term. Short- and long-term values collided, and by breaking the mold and violating the team's own canons of justice, general manager Gerry Hunsicker and the rest of the Astros management group made both sets of values live in one another, and thus they took the team inside its paradox. That's good leadership, too. It's also the sort of solution that takes pure guts. Most to the point, it worked: The Astros made the playoffs, and the team's fans bought the new skyboxes.

And that gets to another element of leadership today: Never before, perhaps, have companies and governments been more enveloped in the language of values and the demand for "correctness"—whether it's political, environmental, or some other orthodoxy. And maybe never before has the bottom line of leadership been so clear and mercilessly drawn: promised performance, delivered performance, accepted performance—the hard numbers. The question that any CEO has to ask first thing in the morning and last thing at night isn't "How are my values doing?" but "How is my stock doing?"

The greater the value orientation of the world, the greater the tendency to judge leaders by performance alone, because in a world of splintered realities, there's really no other choice. No single exercise of values can satisfy all the value systems a business or a government today has to operate in, whether it's a multinational enterprise (Islamic values vs. Hindu values vs. Orthodox Jewish values vs. Christian values) or purely national or local (feminist values vs. family values vs. various ethnic values vs. radical-environmentalist values). A few simple numbers, though, can fill the bill just fine: projected quarterly earnings, market share, share price. The more deeply in thrall we are to values and political correctness, the more performance is the only thing that stands out.

Leaders need to remember that they lead in a world in which virtually everyone perceives themselves as someone else's leader, and thus they lead in a world of selective followership.

"Early adopters"—the people who buy the first new cut of Levis, the first new RAM storage system, the first new theory on health care reform—set the market for products and ideas. Lose them, lose the people who perceive themselves as leaders in the subcategories of your field, and you will find yourself leading a shell enterprise—whether its purpose is to sell computers, fashion accessories, or a consumption-based tax. Lose the people who follow the people who lead the subcategories, and you'll be no better off in the long run.

Leaders get the big bucks, the big press, but leadership doesn't take place just at the top. In a world driven by disparate realities, leadership is a continuum that has to take place and be managed at every relevant new tier of understanding and across every relevant new strata of values—"relevant" because you may not care if a Hindu or a survivalist buys your product or theory, but if you do, you'd better manage leadership specifically at that level of reality.

Leaders need to remember, too, that what they ultimately will be judged on is part their own performance and part the performance of the leaders they create, because leadership is a continuum in that sense as well. When history finally gets around to softening its stance on "Tricky Dick" Nixon, it will note not only his legislative record and his efforts to open up China but the fact that he brought into government a generation of men who continued to serve with distinction long after he had disappeared in disgrace from the public scene—among them, Caspar Weinberger, George Shultz, Frank Carlucci, and Daniel Patrick Moynihan.

Despite the tendency of the public to wrap leaders in mythic qualities and worship at the gobs of money they often make, those atop the worship pile also need to understand that in America today there is nothing more revered than a hero and nothing more quickly discounted if he or she forgets to show the necessary humility at the moment of triumph.

The successful prosecution and conclusion of the 1991 Gulf War gave America what it had so long lacked: two fresh military heroes in the person of Norman Schwartzkopf and Colin Powell. If anything, Schwartzkopf, who had led the fighting in the field, had the greater stature. Today, Schwartzkopf has nearly disappeared from the public radar screen, while Powell remains a tantalizing political possibility. What made the difference? The Saudi desert had barely stopped smoking before Schwartzkopf was out of uniform and signing contracts for his memoirs and other services. In the public eye, he'd shown a lack of humility by going for the gold, while Colin Powell soldiered on.

In the National Football League, the 1998 summer training camps seemed to herald a rookie quarterback rivalry worthy of the first days of John Elway and Dan Marino. Would Peyton Manning, fresh out of the University of Tennessee, or Washington State's Ryan Leaf win rookie-of-the-year honors? By the end of the 1998 season, the statistics weren't even close: Manning had a distinguished rookie season, while Leaf spent the last part of his deep on the San Diego Chargers bench. But what must have hurt Ryan Leaf far more was how few people cared. Simply put, he'd acted like a jerk from training camp forward. Leaf didn't seem to have humility in him, while Manning almost oozed it. Bottom line: no contest.

Nowhere perhaps has the hero-humility axiom been more surely put to the test than in the 1998 baseball season. Mark

McGwire and Sammy Sosa captured the headlines with their home run race, but they were made lovable by the humility they showed toward the game's fans and toward each other. By season's end, they not only had obliterated Babe Ruth's single-season homer record and set new standards for personal conduct in the face of overwhelming fame; they also had almost single-handedly saved a game that only a few seasons earlier had seemed intent on self-destruction. (Or perhaps more accurately, Sosa and McGwire had finished the work that another paragon of humility, the Baltimore Orioles' Cal Ripken, had begun a season earlier when he obliterated Lou Gehrig's mark for consecutive baseball games played.)

Heroism is for the moment, and leadership today is no guarantee of anything tomorrow. But humility can help stretch the moment far beyond its natural life span.

One more thing leaders need to remember: While their brand reputation drives market share, their own reputation in the corporate world may have nearly as profound an effect on the bottom lines by which performance is judged. The brand carries your company's value proposition to your consumers, but the corporate reputation of a leader—how other leaders judge you—carries the company's value proposition to capital suppliers.

Manage your reputation well—let it be known that you are around for the long haul, that your word has meaning, that you understand what business you are in—and money will be looser. Other leaders will be more ready to recommend that people go to work for you, that suppliers equip you at advantageous prices, that key institutional investors buy your stock. Manage your reputation poorly as a leader, and the suffering will stretch down through the pipeline to the widows and orphans who buy your stock and pray for a little light at the end of the tunnel.

Last and most important, leaders need to understand that while they always will be judged by the numbers in the short term, the story they have to tell and their capacity to make listeners live inside the story of their company or organization or country will determine in the long run how the numbers go. The model for today's leader isn't "Chainsaw" Al Dunlap; Dunlap is all about numbers, nothing more. The model for leadership today is Homer, because Homer could both create the myth and take you inside it to a time and place where people were required to survive the paradoxes and inconsistencies of an unnatural world—a world, that is, very much like our own.

Everything we've just written about—the strength to live inside inconsistency and embrace multiple realities, the wisdom to let short- and long-term values live inside each other, the ability to appeal to subleaders across the spectrum of splintered realities, the capacity to mentor and spawn new leadership to succeed you, the need to practice humility at the moment of maximum triumph, the reputation you yourself enjoy in the corporate world— all of this is finally tied up in the story you have to tell. If you don't get that right, if you don't manage the story effectively and make it your benchmark in every relevant decision, the numbers will always let you down in the end.

Two rules:

- One, no leader has to be able to deliver a great speech. But every leader has to have a great speech to deliver.
- While a good storyteller tells a good story, a great storyteller helps you find yourself in the story.

What goes into a great story? Five things:

- It must be told in the future tense. If your story is about the past of your enterprise, you're leading in the past tense, and if you are leading in the past tense today, you and your organization are officially dead. If the story is about the present, you're dying. The story must be about where the company is going; it must be about discovery, not history. And the leader must be certain that his story is communicated so thoroughly throughout the organization that it creates a future metric toward which every employee can strive.
- While the story is about what lies ahead, it must embody mythic figures from the past who have shaped the present and will shape the future: the Harvard dropout who borrowed $50,000 and turned it into a $275 million contract and from there into a $60

billion personal fortune (Bill Gates), the candy maker who saved the orphans (Milton Hershey), the two keepers of the secret drink formula who can never be allowed to fly on the same plane together (Coca-Cola). Does it matter if the myth is true? Not really. Does it matter if the myth is pervasive through and beyond the organization? Absolutely. Whatever the literal truth of a great story, it makes the past live through the present into the future.

• The story also needs to embody the truth of your organization, contained if possible in a single word, and that truth—that single word—cannot be jury-rigged or otherwise constructed.

Here's an exercise for CEOs: Take the people who are responsible for communicating your organization's story, put them in a room, and get them to write down the words they are most likely to use in describing what gives your business meaning. Next, get your senior executives to look over the words the communications people have come up with, and have them pick the ones that express the qualities in which they take the greatest pride. Last, as CEO, pick the single word from those your senior executives have culled that you personally like the most—the one in which you take the greatest pride—and see if it plugs into this sentence: "The meaningfulness of [my company] is . . . ," as in "The meaningfulness of GE is excellence," "The meaningfulness of Coke is refreshment," "The meaningfulness of Disney is safety," "The meaningfulness of Saturn is respect." If the word doesn't fit—if it fails to ring absolutely true—start over again, and again, and again, until you find the single word to build your story around, because the word that encapsulates your meaningfulness is your promise. The story of every great enterprise begins with the delivery of a promise, and every product a great enterprise makes is nothing but an artifact of the truth of that promise.

Once you've found that word, make sure everyone in the organization knows what it is. The business of the Walt Disney Company is entertainment, but the promise of Disney, as we noted above, is safety—from among other things vile language and pornography in their films and sexual predators in their amusement parks. It's the promise, not the business, that allows parents to park their children unattended in front of a Disney film at home or to take a birthday party of kids to a Disney film at a theater without fear of offending other parents or to abandon their children (sometimes literally) at Disney's entertainment parks. Commit a crime against the business you are in—a film that flops at the box office, a toy tie-in that fails to fly—and time is likely to forgive you. Commit a crime against the meaningfulness of the business you are in, and there will be no hiding.

* The performance of a leader may be measured by statistics, but the story a leader tells must be anecdotal. That Berkshire Hathaway's stock collectively is worth something on the order of 2.4 times the liquidation value of the shares Berkshire Hathaway holds in its fund may be yet another sign of wholesale madness on Wall Street, but the premium is largely explained by Berkshire Hathaway's annual report, which is written by Warren Buffett himself in everyday, anecdotal language that draws heavily on his own experience and that of his managers. That report *is* the story of Berkshire Hathaway, and while the stocks and economic conditions mentioned in it vary from year to year, the story at heart is always the same because the investment stratagems and decisions Buffett reports on always go back to the same two or three fundamental investment principles.

That, too, is part of the story: It needs to be the same every time it is told because the story is the bedrock of your company. If the story cannot resist the winds of change, it's the wrong story, and if you cannot resist the winds of change in telling it, you are the wrong leader, the wrong person to be delivering it. The story is more than a tale; it's your proof: The more things change, the more they stay the same.

* The story needs a hero and a villain. It should have some melodrama; some action; climax and resolution; a plot that turns toward the good at the end on the strength of a key virtue; a beginning, middle, and end—all the things that were taught in Literature 101 because in the last analysis a great story must be just that: a great *story*. The story has to have its own fictive truth, its own logic and internal consistency, and it needs to grab listeners not just by the ears and brain but by the bones and deep organs. The more you can practice what Keats said Shakespeare had in such great abundance—"negative capability," the capacity to exist in mystery and doubt without irritable searching after fact and

reason—the more your story will absorb paradox in its own right, and the more that happens, the easier it will be for listeners to find themselves inside your tale.

And a last caveat: The story needs not just the ring of fictive truth; it needs the ring of your own truth, too. It has to come from the heart, not the division of public affairs.

What does the story matter? What difference can it make in leadership? What difference can it make for companies being led and for their stakeholders? Two examples, by way of conclusion:

The first, Michael Eisner and the Walt Disney Company. Few American executives have pocketed more money in recent years than Eisner has as CEO of Disney, and almost none has had a better payday than Eisner had on December 3, 1997, when he cashed stock options worth $565 million. Yet just a month before Eisner cashed his options, *Business Week* had named Disney America's worst-governed corporation, and the company spent much of 1998 lagging behind the market in both earnings and share value. Its stock was down 3 percent for the year; its total return to shareholders fell off 9.1 percent for the year. Why? Part of the problem undoubtedly is cyclical forces affecting movies, theme parks, TV, and publishing. The larger part, though, we suspect, is Eisner himself. And the larger part of that is that he never got inside the Disney story in the first place.

Yes, Michael Eisner will swear, he serves as CEO because of his affinity for Walt Disney's vision. Yes, he'll claim, he's been true all along to the core value propositions of the company, true to its promise, true to the mythology that lies behind the promise. But the facts say otherwise, and not just the financials. Mentoring at the company is virtually nonexistent: The top executive ranks of the company are vacated on a near-turnstile basis. Eisner's story and the company's have become asynchronous. Instead of being in the CEO's slot for the company, he appears to be in it for the money. And while he has been enormously successful in the latter regard, the stock has paid the consequence. Performance is the measure of leadership, but the story drives the numbers that create the metrics by which performance is judged.

The second example involves Roy Vagelos and Merck & Company. As Michael Useem recounts the tale in his book *The Leadership Moment*, Vagelos was a laboratory director for Merck back in 1978 when a Merck research scientist named William Campbell happened to notice that a drug the company had developed to treat parasitic worms in livestock might also be effective against a biological cousin of the parasite, one that causes human river blindness, a devastating disease that affects some twenty million mostly impoverished people worldwide. In his capacity as lab director, Vagelos gave Campbell the go-ahead to develop a strand of the drug suitable for humans. Nine years later, though, Vagelos had ascended to the CEO's office, and by then he had a far harder decision to make. Yes, the drug appeared to be extraordinarily effective in combating river blindness, but it would likely cost more than $3 a tablet to produce and distribute, and it was destined for a market that had no resources whatsoever to meet the expenses, much less show a profit for Merck.

What to do? Vagelos went to the story of the company, which traced its roots back more than three centuries to Germany and which had long preached to its scientists that their job was less to produce drugs and chemicals that would fill an immediate market niche than it was to conduct bench research that would benefit humanity. Approve manufacture of the drug, and Vagelos would be true to the core myths of Merck; disapprove it and he would be true to the short-term interests of the bottom line. For Vagelos, as it turned out, the choice was easy.

Another ten years later, by 1997, Merck had "lost" $200 million on the manufacture and distribution of the drug, dubbed Mectizan. But what it had gained was immeasurable. Vagelos had been true to Merck's promise and true to its value proposition. He had moved inside the inherent paradox of funding at great expense a nonproductive asset. By doing so, he had made short-term and long-term values live in one another, and the world had taken notice. One business writer noted Merck's "light and airy genius" and its "streak of idealism." Just as important, investors had noticed, too. In 1998, Merck's stock beat the Dow Jones industrial average by 2.5 to 1, rising 41.5 percent and increasing the company's total return to investors by almost 40 percent for the year.

How much of that is again attributable to cyclical forces—Bristol-Myers Squibb posted almost identical increases for the year—and how much is due to the residual affects of enlightened leadership is impossible to say. What does seem certain, though, is that the $200 million-plus Merck has thus far committed to Mectizan couldn't have been kinder to the bottom line. Have the right story as a leader, stay within it, live the inconsistencies as they arise, and the performance by which you are judged will take care of itself.

♦ Future Exercise

At the top of your pad, write down the name of a leader you have greatly admired, from any field of endeavor (but not your own CEO).

Below the name, list the attributes that have most caused you to admire this leader.

Now, think about how the application of those attributes would pave the way for the future success of your company or organization and list those ways.

Do this for as many leaders, from as many different fields, as you want. When you're through, compare your "pave the way to future success" lists to the following. We looked at three hundred companies globally that have been in business for at least 100 years, looking for common criteria of success. We found that the companies studied shared four qualities:

♦ All had access to capital.

♦ All were extraordinarily sensitive to their stakeholders.

♦ All had a high tolerance for ambiguity in their thinking.

♦ And none of them still made their money from what they started at.

Finally, ask yourself how your list of great leadership attributes stacks up against our attributes of great and enduring global companies. Where the two lists seem incongruent, ask yourself these four questions:

♦ Are you celebrating the wrong qualities in leaders?

♦ Are you celebrating the right qualities for today but the wrong ones for tomorrow?

* Are you reaching too low in the leaders you might aspire to emulate in the future?

* Or we are inhabiting a sufficiently different reality from your own that both our lists are correct for each of us?

Box 4
GOVERNANCE, PATRIOTISM, AND LOYALTY
Good-bye and hello.

◆ ◆   ◆ ◆ ◆ ◆ ◆ ◆ ◆ ◆ ◆ ◆ ◆ ◆ ◆ ◆ ◆   ◆

An odd little fact that may not be so odd: Over the course of the last decade, the percentage of foreign news in American newspapers and on American radio and TV newscasts has declined by about 40 percent, according to a study reported on in the August 30, 1998, edition of the *Denver Post*. Does that mean that Americans have become disengaged from the world even as they have become the world's sole superpower? Does it suggest that because so many of us live today in both the present and the future, any "news," even including news about our own country, is foreign to us? Or does it say that the very use of the word "foreign" has changed for many of us—that if we live in, say, Seattle, New York and London are equally foreign to us, and equally familiar?

In truth, we think it's some combination of all three. We've become globally connected only to become globally disconnected from old understandings of nationhood and patriotism. The closer we get to one world, the more we split up into billions of them, and each of those worlds exists in such a tension between present and future that what happened yesterday or even the last hour is already history. The more global we get, too, the more we come to new understandings of borders and allegiances. People are still patriotic, but the "patri"—the "father" of patriotism—refers less and less to a fatherland.

U.S. high-tech firms have no trouble recruiting globally—a third of all NASA employees were born on the Indian subcontinent—but it can be far harder to recruit locally. Many Silicon Valley workers are wedded not to their occupations or their companies but to their turf. You can offer them almost anything by way of work so long as they don't have to move away, and you can offer them almost nothing that will get them to go. Silicon Valley has become their brand, in the same way San Francisco becomes a brand for many of those who live there, and Paris and Sydney and New York become brands, too. As the world comes more and more to congregate into city-states, specific places reach such a critical mass in meaning that they are what people define themselves as: A Valleyite or a San Franciscan, not a Californian, and not an American. Their "patri" is where they live, not what they live in.

As mass reality atomizes into individual realities, nations atomize, too. Workers who were once loyal to their flag and their company find themselves loyal instead to their neotribes—feminist neotribes, Harley-Davidson neotribes, Martha Stewart neotribes—and their new loyalty is often measurable in direct proportion to how poorly they feel their former loyalty was rewarded. The depth of commitment of the Tribe of White Supremacists lies in the depth of the disappointment of its members in what they thought had been the promise of a white America. Instead of a nation segmented by political party or even by economic class, the United States has become a nation segmented by reality groups, and where America goes, the world follows.

Companies, too, have come to interpret loyalty and even patriotism differently than they once did. Instead of loyalty to workers, businesses more and more have a loyalty to growth that in theory benefits all their stakeholders, not just the stakeholder employees. As they spill outside the borders of their nations of birth, companies also become global citizens. Is IBM an American company, or a global company with headquarters in America? Can you even call Royal Dutch Petroleum a European company anymore, or is it a world company with a slight continental accent? Is Ford's "citizenry" the 272 million inhabitants of the United States of America, where Ford was born, or the holders of more than a billion shares of Ford stock, scattered broadly around the globe?

Inevitably, government has to change its role as the people and businesses who are governed migrate in their understanding of what they owe allegiance to. Once, government was like the opposing team in a baseball game: Business hit, and government was in the field. Business fielded while government took a turn at the plate. Out of the rivalry between the two—antitrust suits, vertical monopolies—the economy was molded. With the advent of the Great Depression, government in the

United States came more to resemble an alternative team: When the starters got battered, government was sent in for them to stimulate the nation through make-work programs, bank holidays, and other forms of rescue operations, all in the name of an activist Keynesian approach to the economy.

With the end of World War II, the United States controlled half the world's gross domestic product, business took off (as an old ad pro once told us, in 1950 you could market dog poop in a paper bag if you had half a brain), and government left the playing field and went behind the plate to umpire the economy and make sure everyone was playing fair. AT&T was broken up. Regulations mounted, especially during the Nixon years, until they formed a mountain, and the mountain of rules began to slow the game down so much that it threatened to grind to a halt.

As that happened—and in part because that happened—people and companies began to disengage from their government and their sense of nationhood. Globalism was launched. The Japanese model of private-public collusion and long-term planning proved infinitely inferior to models that stressed laissez-faire approaches to business, because laissez-faire meant speed and flexibility, and as the mid-nineties approached, speed and the ability to turn on a dime were exactly what the economy began to most reward.

What do we want most from government today? That it gets out from behind the plate. That it goes up to the press box and starts keeping score, *really* keeping score, because in a denationalized, dematerialized economy, scorekeeping is what businesses most need—the statistics to understand the environment they operate in—and also what they least get. Census data aside, more than three-quarters of all U.S. government statistics today concern agriculture.

Government, in short, still does have a role to play. The more it gathers and disseminates the right information, the more it can be the enabler that helps companies make the smartest possible decisions. Instead of interfering with what businesses do, government needs to give them what they need to do business better. By doing that, by taking on that enabler role and making it its primary role in the economy, the American government could also begin to move inside its own paradox: that the more powerful it gets, the less anyone cares.

7

$$\blacklozenge \quad \blacklozenge \quad \blacklozenge \quad \blacklozenge \quad \blacklozenge \quad \blacklozenge \quad \blacklozenge \quad \blacklozenge \quad \blacklozenge \quad \blacklozenge \quad \blacklozenge \quad \blacklozenge \quad \blacklozenge \quad \blacklozenge \quad \blacklozenge \quad \blacklozenge$$

THE PARADOX OF LEISURE

Relax, dammit: Play is hard work.

For all of history that we know of, work and play were like the two sides of a seesaw: When the amount of play was driven down by economic or social necessity or by the sheer need to survive, the amount of work rose. Similarly, when prosperity or favorable natural conditions brought a reduction in work, play went up. Today, even that basic principle of leverage no longer applies. The amount of time devoted to work and the amount devoted to play are both rising. As they rise, they converge, and sleep falls out of the equation. The more time we have to do absolutely anything, the less absolutely we do. The less time we have to do anything, the more we work and play simultaneously so that we can do everything, and the more we do that, the more indivisible the work and leisure worlds become.

Draw on your pad or just imagine two balls—one very large, the other very small—that intersect at just one tiny point along their arcs. The very large ball is work in the middle of the nineteenth century, the very small one is play, and the point of intersection is a country fair, one of the very few places where people worked and played at the same time. By the middle of the twentieth century people were working so they could recreate—a week off with pay, plus ten days personal leave to add to national holidays—and the play ball was growing larger. Today, the play ball is almost as large as the work ball. More important, the play ball has moved inside the work one almost entirely. Moments that were once clearly one or the other more and more carry the properties of both.

Think of your own work and play lives. Are you recreating if you go to see a professional basketball game? Is it still recreation if you take a client? How about if you play basketball at lunchtime in the company gym? Or softball on the company team? If you spend a half hour first thing in the morning reading reports or watching the financial news while you work the stationary bike, do you credit that time to your work or play account? Golf is play, but is it play if you are working to improve your game because your new divisional president values golf above all other forms of recreation? And is golf play if you play with a customer? How about the three-day sales meeting in Maui? Do work times and play times follow the printed schedule? Or do the two segments bleed all over the page into each other? How about if you spend time at the office following on-line scouting reports for your favorite sports teams? Or time at home—the stereo is on, you've got a glass of wine by your side—downloading a file you'll need for the office the next day?

Baking is your hobby. You make extraordinary breads. Thanks to the speakerphone in your kitchen, you also can handle a three-way conference call as effectively while you knead dough as you can from your home office or your downtown one. Tape the call, use voice-recognition software, and you can have a full transcript ready before the loaves are finished baking. Were you working as you recreated? Or recreating as you worked? In fact, the distinction grows meaningless. Were you a more effective participant in the conference call because while you talked, you kneaded, and thus your mind was floating free, out of the box? Quite possibly so, which brings up another issue of leisure. Not long back, it was dangerous to your career to be seen as too play-oriented. Good-time Charlies still suffer if they have too good a time, but nowadays organizations also discriminate against people who are said to be workaholics or otherwise unable to recreate effectively.

Evolution is the process of natural selection, and natural selection today favors those capable of doing two things—work *and* play—simultaneously. But natural selection doesn't happen whimsically. It needs a root cause, and the root cause in this case is strikingly simple: In contemporary culture, there is never enough time, ever.

The rise of the cell phone is explained in part by the sheer novelty. A tiny little phone we can carry with us, anywhere! But cell phones also point to a larger issue. In the accelerating pressure of modern life, virtually every moment is being not just asked but forced to do double duty. Once airplanes were a place to escape the office: Now, we carry the office to our seats in the form of laptops and use the GTE Airfone to call our clients from thirty-five thousand feet. Automobile commuters listen to books as they drive to work; subway and commuter-line riders read *and* listen to symphonies or motivational tapes or the Wallflowers on their headphones (or to the cell phone calls of their car mates). And even home is no refuge: In the door, pop a microbrew, log on to AOL, check the e-mail, check the portfolio, e-trade, fax, scan. When you are ready to relax—finally relax—you can watch two television shows simultaneously on your window-within-a-window TV. Years ago, parents screamed at their children to turn the radio off when they did homework. Who could do algebra and listen to godless rock 'n' roll at the same time? Turns out, it's a good thing most of us didn't pay a bit of attention to Mom and Pop. Processing simultaneous input is no longer a parlor trick; it's another survival skill. It may even be *the* survival skill.

At the same time the work and the nonwork worlds have become indivisible, they've also become invisible to one another.

If our grandfathers were white-collar, they went off to work in exactly that: a white collar and a tie and suit in all likelihood and a hat. At the end of the day they would come home, take off the hat, hang up the suit coat and loosen the tie or take it off, and maybe even substitute slippers for wing tips. If you were their child or grandchild or even their wife, you knew then that the workday was over. Like a good story, work had a beginning, middle, and end. Ride the USAir commuter flights from Washington to Boston on any random midweek workday, and more than half the passengers look as if they're dressed for a campus party or a long weekend—and that's on the East Coast, where American propriety was born. Even white-shoe law firms in places like Washington and Boston have dress-down Fridays, and if they are distinctly uncomfortable moments for many of the senior partners, a point is nonetheless being made and it goes well beyond simple dress: Increasingly, there are no divisions, not even stylistic ones, between work and nonwork.

To encourage more work hours and to make employees who pursued longer workdays more comfortable, Silicon Valley firms brought the health club to the corporate campus and upgraded the corporate cafeteria to near-restaurant quality. To meet feminist demands and satisfy their own manpower needs, other companies moved day-care centers into the corporate headquarters. The latest fêng shui theories of office arrangement combined with coffee-break yoga classes and after-lunch meditation to bring psychic health and New Age thinking into what was once the grim bastion of nine-to-fivers. What is work anymore? What's home? What's the place you went to escape both? It becomes harder and harder to tell.

Separated from their roots, from the towns of their birth, from extended families, the corporate warriors of America find their friendships and leisurely moments not at bars or church socials but at the place where corporate warriors spend the most time and feel most at home: work. Even the sports that are in greatest ascendancy today are the ones that allow for the greatest interplay between commerce and play, between work and leisure. Whether or not jogging is done solo, it's still a breathless activity. Tennis puts competitors on opposite sides of a net, in an adversarial relation. Golf, by contrast, requires two to four people to stand and sit side by side for three to four hours in an isolated environment where the only distractions are side bets and the 70 to 120 swings that each participant takes at his or her ball. Tiger Woods may have put golf over the top with the broad public, but the game needed no boost with the executive set: Golf is the sport of the deal.

Play also is how new regimes announce themselves. If golf is the obsession of your CEO, chances are company meetings are built around golfing resorts. If the new CEO favors entertainment, pack up the golf clubs because your next company meeting will be in New York or Las Vegas. His (or her) leisure determines your work environment; the work environment determines the leisure you pursue.

How much time do you create at work for play? How do you hold people accountable and yet encourage leisure? And how do you do so in a work world where a Saturday-afternoon company picnic might offend Orthodox Jews and Seventh-Day Adventists, a weeknight company barbecue with beer and wine might offend Muslims and Southern Baptists, and any company event however carefully planned might draw the wrath of any one of dozens of groups restlessly prowling the corporate landscape for a reason to express their anger, their dispossession, their marginality?

In today's work world, these are not abstract questions. Indeed, they are questions with very specific and very large dollar signs attached. Get the percentage of work and play wrong for a corporate sales meeting at some distant resort—fail to carefully and wisely consider the ratio of golf to party to meeting—and you will have wasted tens of thousands of dollars: Sales managers who are golfing when they need to be meeting learn no more, and tell you no more, than sales managers who are hung over or ones who have had their interest levels ground into dust by a relentless parade of seminars. Get the physical structure of your headquarters wrong, miscalculate the feel, fail to create a lightness both in structure and in accessory, and the glumness will be palpable. People need fun, and the harder they work, the more fun they need where they work.

Workplace play can be annoying—there's an indefinably thin line between creative leisure and plain old goofing. It's often perplexing as well. From a corporate time-management point of view, one of the great problems of contemporary life is the degree to which the Internet and in-office Internet access encourages play—and not just play at electronic forms of solitaire or even play at pornographic Websites, both of which are at heart boredom relievers. Interactive sites go well beyond that by providing environments that engage not just the attention but intellects for which the company is paying a premium.

Install pop-ups to warn workers when they have wandered into Internet sites that are too playful for company tastes, and you may win the employee's time back, but you also risk sending a message to workers that you are not interested in that side of them that knows it must play in order to thrive. What's more, you risk defining Internet playfulness as an insurgent activity, like dope smoking, and in so doing you also create insurgent heroes, because no matter how many Big Brother eyes you install in the workplace, someone will always be one step ahead of your surveillance.

Take more Draconian steps—GE is said to be on the verge of making personal use of the Internet a cause for dismissal—and you may win your workers' time back as well. But unless the denial of fun is built deeply into your corporate value system and inculcated into workers from day one of their employee relationship, you win that time back in the present at the risk of telling your workers and other stakeholders that you fundamentally misunderstand the future.

But if play can be perplexing and even alarming, it also can move mountains. Build play and leisure into your corporate culture—make a play ethic as integral a part of the office building as a work ethic—and the problems begin to disappear, and even become opportunities. One of the many charms of Southwest Airlines, and one increasingly copied by other airlines such as Frontier and even American, is that it encourages its pilots to be playful in their communications with passengers, and thus an environment of inherent discomfort is made a little more comfortable. The best prison wardens also know that they can make a bad product more desirable by allowing a reasonable amount of playfulness within the confines of a secure environment.

In the pursuit of a balance between work and play—and as further proof of the indivisible merger of the two—Mattel Toys built a stage, an actual one, in the cafeteria. Management uses it to make in-house presentations about company affairs and policies in the form of plays. UMB Financial took a different route to the same end: Recognizing that the absence of playfulness in a banking environment suppressed the creative instincts of its technologists, the company built playrooms for staff meetings in a new technology center. One room has a western theme, another has an aquarium, a third has an open environmental feel, a fourth has an almost shrinelike effect. Other companies are building nap centers for their employees—the office as kindergarten—and non-stimulus chambers such as those at Texas Instruments.

At Avis, good acts are rewarded with time—fifteen-minute blocks that you can piece together into a vacation or to make time to coach your daughter's softball team, a direct conversion of successful work into the potential for successful play. Years and years ago, Standard Oil of California (Chevron, today) used to run a summer camp and country club for its employees. Eventually, size overwhelmed capacity, but in the club's heyday, facilities included swimming pools, hiking trails, a golf course, and tennis courts. Collectively the club married play to the family nature of the company. The latter is probably no longer possible—too many tribes move through companies today to create a family—but the deep sense of play, and the deep respect for it, is where the future is arriving. The more generous you are in managing the work-play paradox, the more you stand to be rewarded with employees who are willing to stay for the long haul, whatever directions the constantly changing vision of the future might carry you in and, as Apple found out, however low you might sink in your fortunes along the way.

Then there's IBM and its resolution of the Internet issue. Instead of threatening dismissal or installing pop-ups, IBM so encourages Internet playfulness that its thirty thousand scientists have created something on the order of two million Websites. Thus, Big Blue slakes the thirst for play, and thus, we would bet, will IBM discover, way out on the fringes of its playfulness, the next business it will be in.

Lou Gerstner deserves credit for many things at IBM, not the least of which is raising the company's share price eightfold, adjusted for splits, in his first six years as Big Blue's CEO. But maybe what

Gerstner most deserves credit for is making the dour old mothership of the computer age a fun place to work.

The story gets told in Armonk, New York, and elsewhere that shortly after Gerstner took over as IBM chief in April 1973 he decided he wanted to meet as many employees as possible so that he could ask why everybody up and down the line was so pissed off. To that end, Gerstner had his people schedule a meeting with all the employees at IBM's data-acquisition and storage-device facility in San Jose, California. Shortly after the corporate jet took off, headed for the San Jose get-together, Gerstner summoned the stewardess and asked for a martini.

"Oh, Mr. Gerstner," she responded, "we never serve alcohol on IBM aircraft!"

"Fine," Gerstner is said to have replied, "land the plane at the next available site and have me delivered a bottle of gin and another of dry vermouth."

"But it's against the policy of the company," the stewardess persisted. "We don't do that."

"Read my lips," the new CEO told her: "Land. Now. And. Have. Them. Delivered. Olives. Too."

Is the story true? We don't have any idea, but we do know that the tale went through IBM like waste matter through a goose. And we know, too, that even if the tale is apocryphal, it changed the corporate culture of Big Blue. For decades IBM had been a company where presenting a new concept—any new concept—to senior management was like addressing the United Nations Security Council. Not surprisingly, IBM also had been about as effective as the UN Security Council at seizing the cutting edge of new issues and ideas. Now Gerstner's tale had given people throughout the company the promise that change was not only possible but just down the hall in the CEO's suite.

Finally, we had the pleasure of seeing the change in action not all that long ago when we were asked to talk to several hundred of the company's top scientists at a gala dinner. As if to test our mettle, the front row was taken up with the best of IBM's scientific best, a lineup of laureates that would have been even more intimidating had several of them not been noticeably tipsy.

If the time had been midday and the place corporate headquarters, we would have been alarmed, maybe even horrified. Bombed at Big Blue? What next? But this wasn't work, and it wasn't midday. This was work-plus, a fete. Leisure and the workplace had flowed into one another, and whiskey and wine were being served in celebration of the marriage. Decades of prudery had been reversed. Play and fun had been allowed through the front door, and Big Blue's best minds were behaving as human minds always do in the presence of the fermented beverages that humans have craved since the dawn of humanity.

My God, we thought, the company has become human! Instead of clucking our tongue in disapproval, we almost pulled out a cell phone and gave our broker a buy order on the spot.

Maybe most important, a corporate sense of play is one of the most useful variables going for measuring the validity of the corporate value system.

Visit the McDonald's corporate headquarters in San Diego, and while it's not exactly like a McDonald's Funland, you can't help but be struck by an overwhelming sense of play. For starters, company doodads pop up in nearly every spare corner of every workspace, and all along the employee food chain. Happy Meal trinkets, Beanie Babies, drink glasses and key chains and every other weird thing McDonald's has dreamed up to give away as a promotional or a movie tie-in—they're all there and they're everywhere. And not only the trinkets. The halls of the headquarters complex are lined with the world's most extensive collection of McPaintings: works by world-famous artists such as Robert Rauschenberg, paintings by realists and nonrealists and antirealists, memory paintings and paintings by people no one will ever hear of or see displayed again in any other place on the face of the earth. And all the paintings have one thing in common: In some form or another, they all make a reference to McDonald's. Maybe it's Ronald McDonald flying a kite; maybe it's just the barest hint of a golden arch or a half-eaten Big Mac. But McD's is the price of admission to hanging in this gallery.

Fly directly from McDonald's in San Diego to the corporate headquarters of the 180-year-old private banking firm of Brown

Brothers Harriman & Co., on Wall Street in Lower Manhattan, and you are likely to think not just that you have come to a different part of the country but to a different country altogether and maybe a different planet and solar system. The myth of Brown Brothers is that it is the only investment bank to operate entirely independent of the Federal Reserve Bank. That means that Brown Brothers sets its own rules, and it means that the bank operates without the sort of safety net that other investment banks enjoy, and it means further and most important that operating as it does, without a net, Brown Brothers better not be wrong, about anything. There is no room for error, in short, and in such an environment, play as we normally perceive it is the devil's workshop.

Instead of Happy Meal trinkets and McPaintings, Brown Brothers takes its leisure from an overwhelming sense of order and structure so pervasive and so total that it carries over to the weekends as well. To be sure, the partners of Brown Brothers have large houses in the Hamptons to repair to when the markets are closed, and large boats waiting for them as well. But the boats are spotless when they arrive, they are spotless while in operation, and they are spotless very soon after their owners go back to the city to make more millions of dollars. And if you are invited to sail or cruise on one, heaven help you if you show up in a wife-beater undershirt and Air Jordans.

Is McDonald's right and Brown Brothers wrong? No, because with corporate culture and leisure, right and wrong can never be seperated from mission.

Would you want to take your daughter and her six best friends to the board dining room at Brown Brothers to celebrate her sixth birthday? Not unless you were particularly twisted. That's for McDonald's, where the sense of play at each outlet and at corporate headquarters is wholly consistent with the company's value structure and with the brand itself. Yes, the food is important—or at least it shouldn't kill you—but fun, a sense of lightness, and a devotion to speed the minute you walk inside the door are what we really want McD's to deliver.

By contrast, would you ever think of asking your McDonald's order taker for stock advice—"Two fries, a shake, and what do you think about shorting Doubleclick?" Obviously, not that, either. As with McDonald's, so with Brown Brothers: Its sense of play becomes the reflection of the moral virtue of the organization. You might hate working at that particular investment house; we might, too. But ultimately such a place will attract employees for whom the sense of play is just right—employees for whom order and structure are not only a form of leisure but also liberating—and it is to such people ultimately that we would prefer to trust our money, though not our daughter's birthday party.

Get the sense of play right, align it with the business you are in and with the promise of that business, and you energize not just your business and your product but the workers who must deliver on it. Get the sense of play wrong, and you enervate promise, business, worker, product, and mission.

We don't like to pick on anyone and we promise not to pick on Kodak again after this, but we have to tell about a trip we made to Eastman Kodak's corporate headquarters in Rochester, New York. We had gone there to immerse ourselves for a brief while in the corporation, to do in essence an audit of the company culture. What was Kodak's mission, we kept asking workers? What did the workers there, at all levels, understand Kodak's business to be? One phrase kept coming back at us time and again: We want to be the company that produces Kodak moments for everyone, including our own people. For consistency, we had to give Kodak an A+: The message had been gotten out, and it had been spread up and down the line. But what struck us far more than the consistency of the mission was the consistent sterility of the culture that surrounded it: sterility in structure, in design, in thought, in ambience, in almost every measurable and immeasurable way. If Kodak moments aren't about fun, if they're not about joy, if they're not about love and laughter and tears, what are they about? And if that is the case, we kept asking ourselves, how could this possibly be the home of such moments? Play had been sucked out of the building.

Like Kodak, government at all levels but especially at the federal level has much to learn about this intersection of work and play. Build 'em big, build 'em drab, build 'em lifeless, and give the employees enough federal holidays off each year to recover from the experience of working for their government: That seems to be the operative motto, and we happen to agree about the number of days off. Grave diggers should get long vacations, too. But perhaps if government were to try another approach—if it were to build structures that breathed life into the work environment instead of damping the life out of it, if it were to spend at least as much time introducing play into the workday as it spends calculating each worker's GS rating—government might find itself with employees who want to come to work and would be more productive each hour they spent on the job. Compared to what we have, it's got to be worth a try.

Even the long, dank corridors of government, though, are almost an amusement park compared to the historical work culture of Japan. So antileisure and antifun is the Samurai work ethic there—and so long has it been that way—that many Japanese companies have had to build so-called play zones into the work lives of their executives. The play zones are, in fact, bars, and the "play" that takes place there is most often corporate-sponsored drinking binges of epic proportions: drunkenness as teamwork, humiliation as fun, with no consequences for drunken social deviancy, even being drunk in front of your boss, a sin of high proportions in the United States. Not surprisingly, and certainly not unrelatedly, Japan is increasingly facing a very serious alcoholism problem among its upper echelon of executives. Cultures can and do survive fire, famine, plague, and pestilence. Conquered by an outside power, a culture can go dormant for centuries without losing its core values. But over the long haul no culture can survive an absence of fun.

One more word on bringing work and play into harmony: Doing so can give you a whole new metric for rewarding your best people. We were taking part in another immersion in corporate culture a number of years back in St. Louis, at the headquarters of what was then McDonnell Douglas (before the Boeing merger), when it suddenly dawned on us that what the executives we were talking with really liked was not making tons of money on federal contracts—that was incidental. What they really liked wasn't cheating on those contracts either, although that was sometimes required. What they really, really liked to do was to make things that go boom! The company understood that, too. When McDonnell Douglas wanted to reward someone for special performance, it didn't hand him a check; it sent him to Edwards Air Force Base for test flights. Thus, the schema of play within the organization was consistent with the organization's mission—to make the best things-that-go-boom in the world—and thus, too, McDonnell Douglas's most rewarding moments of play were inextricably tied to its value structure. Genius.

This tendency to merge work and leisure—and to make each moment of both do double duty—is not confined to the workplace or to work-related activity. We play when we work at the everyday stuff of life, too, and we do so just as fervently and out of just as great a necessity.

Not surprisingly, some of the earliest enterprises to attempt to merge the two activities sprouted up on the edges of college campuses, where play and work have always been deeply intertwined. Were the combination Laundromats and bars (they always had names like "Suds & Duds") that grew like a mushroom flush in the mid-1970s taprooms with a row of washers and dryers attached? Or were they self-service laundries with several beer taps and a row of stools to occupy patrons during the rinse cycle? Suddenly, what had been two distinct activities in two distinct realms—what might be called the "life-work" of washing clothes and the leisure play of pushing back a beer—became one blurred activity in one merging realm. The distinctions between everyday work and everyday leisure began to grow invisible to one another, and they haven't stopped doing so in the decades since.

Shopping malls today routinely open their doors an hour early so that exercise groups can power-walk their long corridors before settling in for a double latte and the business of finding shoes to match a new purse. To be sure, it's a trade that benefits both teams: The walkers get the climate protection and safety of the mall; the mall has an audience waiting the moment stores open.

But it's also a merger of life-work and play, just as the televisions tuned to CNN on the wall above the exercise machines at the health spa and the TVs suspended from the ceiling above the checkout lines at the supermarket are a merger of life-work and leisure: keep fit and keep informed, shop for the groceries and learn about reunification woes in Germany while you wait to pay. Go to Costco, and there are enough snacks being prepared and given away in the aisles that you might momentarily think you have stumbled into a particularly strange alcohol-free cocktail party. Go to Nordstrom, and you're likely to find someone on the second floor wearing a tuxedo and playing classical airs on a grand piano for your enjoyment. Come-ons? Sure. Costco wants you to taste and buy. Nordstrom wants to put you in an expansive mood so you won't mind those steadily climbing prices as you ascend from floor to floor. But leisure and work are also being integrated. Time is doing double duty.

Investment clubs and book clubs—maybe the two "leisure" activities in America with the greatest growth rates during the 1990s—serve the same purpose. At the beginning of the 1990s there were just a few more than seven thousand investment clubs registered with the National Association of Investors; by the end of the decade, that number had climbed past thirty-seven thousand clubs. Who can even begin to count the number of book clubs that came into existence during the same ten years? There's not a Barnes & Noble outlet in America today that doesn't sponsor at least one such club. Many Barnes & Nobles and Borders and other bookstores sponsor clubs every night of the week, and those are only the tip of an iceberg that has found its way into living rooms all over America.

Did the stock market bubble of the 1990s drive Americans crazy for the camaraderie of fellow investors? Maybe. Is one of the unintended consequences of the Internet that it has led people back to the printed page? Maybe that, too, and it's a subject that could be worth a book someday. But investment-club and book-club booms are also part and parcel of this compulsion to make work out of play, and play out of work. Why else would they so often be so bitterly competitive, so full of alpha wolves and growling she-bears?

Even away from the workplace, we take our leisure in activities that resemble work, and the more they resemble it—stock reports, book reports, investment decisions, the search for subterranean meaning—the more we flock to them.

Leisure isn't just leisure anymore. Leisure is work and play, but it's also identification and communication. An official National Football League jacket bearing the logo of the San Francisco 49ers says that we take our leisure, in part, by watching football on television or in the stadium, but it also says that we belong to the neotribe of those who identify themselves through their devotion to football and particularly to the 49ers and their West Coast brand of offense. The same is true of Harley-Davidson gear, yachting caps and deck shoes, golf shirts, baseball caps (whether they are real or one of the designer versions favored by Monica Lewinsky and others speaks volumes), the Nike "swoosh" in general, Air Jordans in particular, Ralph Lauren's pocket-patch "Polo" pony, and much, much more. Like everything else, our leisure-wear logos are made to do double duty, too. They speak *of* us and *for* us. They introduce us and identify us. They tribalize us, and they tell us what tribes others belong to.

Work isn't just work, either. We play at our work, and we work at our play. And no one does the latter any harder today than children.

Not all that long ago parents who relentlessly drove their sons and daughters to excel at a sport or activity were considered warped at best and monsters at worst. While it was inaccurate as biography, the movie *Shine* portrayed a standard of the type: a father so obsessed with producing a piano prodigy that he produced a piano freak instead. But we don't have to go to the movies to see the phenomenon in action. In Canada, promising hockey players are sent off at the beginning of their teen years to distant provincial cities in the hope that they eventually can make it through the junior leagues to the NHL, and fame and fortune. Girls who show almost no signs of puberty travel hundreds, sometimes thousands of miles to work with gymnastic coaches, part of whose challenge will be to strengthen the girls' bodies while assuring that the outward manifestations of puberty stay as muted as possible. Nick Bollettieri's Tennis Academy in Bradenton, Florida, has a huge waiting list of boys and girls sometimes still in, sometimes barely out of middle school. Talk with the top tier of high school basketball recruits—the ones headed to Kentucky and Kansas, Arizona and UNC—and you'll learn that most of them have been recruited for one team or another since they were in sixth or seventh or eighth grade and that nearly all of them have been playing throughout high school in summer leagues that can involve as many as sixty games and weeks on the road. No wonder so many of them look so tired so much of the time. Any soccer field on any Saturday, it seems, has at least one parent and sometimes whole sidelines of them for whom the game is anything but a game—and the higher the level of competition, the more fierce the sideline parents are likely to be. No wonder so many of the children running up and down the field seem to have forgotten how to smile.

The why of such frantic activity is obvious enough: Kobe Bryant had just graduated from Lower Merion High School, outside Philadelphia, when he signed a three-year, $3.5 million contract with the Los Angeles Lakers, later extended to a six-year, $71 million contract. Martina Hingis won a new Porsche in a German tennis tournament before she could legally drive a car. Leisure at a high enough level has a clearly convertible cash value. But the downside is obvious enough, too: sexual predators preying on the lonely, confused boys of the Canadian junior hockey leagues; the seventeen-year-old gymnast Dominique Moceanu winning an order from a Houston court requiring her father to stay at least five hundred feet away from her.

Not long ago, the professional Turino soccer club in Italy spent the equivalent of $75,000 to secure the eventual playing services of a Naples boy, Vincenzo Sarno, who had scored many dozens of goals in youth soccer leagues and showed astounding skills. At the time the deal was arranged, Vincenzo was ten years old. Is he a pro or an amateur? A little economic unit or a little boy?

What is work these days? And what is play? What happens to adolescents who haven't been allowed to have an adolescence? And if enforcing a sense of play in the workplace is hard today, what will it be like in twenty years when the children of such joyless drive begin to bubble up through the executive ranks?

Relax, dammit! It might just sound comforting to them.

◆ Future Exercise

List all the activities you can think of that might be considered either work or play. (Golf with the boss, for example, or dinner with a client.) When you are through, write a capital W beside those activities that your company would consider work and a small w beside the ones you personally consider work. Now do the same thing for play: Put a capital P beside the items your company would consider play and a small p beside the ones you consider play. No wishy-washy choices, either. Every entry has to go one way or the other. Now, add up the Ws and Ps.

The winning capital letter will tell you whether your company has a bias toward work or play; the winning small letter will say the same thing about you. And the difference between the two scores will tell how out of whack or in alignment your own values are with the company you work for.

Now, answer two more questions:

◆ How should you manage work and play so that your employees can stay a part of your universe?

◆ How should you manage work and play so that you can stay a part of your employer's universe?

◆ Second-Term Exam

If possible, wait until the end of the day to complete.

Divide your pad into four columns and label them, from left to right: Same, Different, Event, and Moment. In the left-hand column, list everything in your life (personal, professional, or both) that did not change from yesterday. In the next space list everything that did change. Beside that, list all the precipitating events that caused the changes in the column marked "Different." If a precipitating event is responsible for multiple changes, draw lines from each change to the event. Now study your list of precipitating events and decide which ones have the potential to be seminal moments—ones that might make not just yesterday but all other days different. Write these under "Moment."

Finally, run all the items you listed in the far left-hand column through the screen of each potential seminal moment you identified in the far right-hand column. How might the moment cause each of those items to be shifted from "Same" to "Different"?

III

THE SERIAL FUTURE

Our reality is yours alone.

In Part I, we gave you the tools that would help make you your own futurist. In Part II, we introduced a series of everyday paradoxes that you could test your tools out on as a new member of the Future Council. Now we want to show you the tools we have used to hone our own understanding of the future. Before we begin, though, here's a hard fact about the work you are preparing to undertake: The future is a tale that needs constant retelling.

Because every significant change in the facts of the present or in the understanding of the past invalidates the future, and because the facts of the present and our understanding of the past are always in flux, the future itself is in constant flux as well. Every moment of every life—individual and corporate—is lived in a tension between past, present, and future, and the variables between and among the three tenses are always changing. Thus, being a visionary means that you have to reinvent your vision time and time and time again, and that you have to accept the near certainty that every one of your visions will ultimately be proved wrong.

An example: In our 1997 book *The 500-Year Delta*, we predicted that within five hundred weeks Yale University would be bankrupt and out of business. Our prediction at the time was based on the convergence of several factors, including Yale's unfavorable location in downtown New Haven, its then moribund endowment and stratospherically rising costs, a history of labor problems, and the rising pattern of free education being supported by the Internet. What we did not know at the time, though, was that the factors of Yale's present were changing. Through its endowment, Yale had become one of the lead investors in venture funds associated with a vast number of start-up Internet companies such as eBay. Overnight, it seemed, the net value of the university's portfolio rose by well over a billion dollars, and as that happened Yale reinvented its future—and reinvented our view of its future as well.

Circumstances change, in short; knowledge changes; and the future changes with them. Experience also changes, and as it changes, we have to change with it and reinvent and retell what our previous experience had led us to believe.

An example of that, too: In June 1998 we went to Japan, and there we encountered a country far different than our expectations had led us to believe. Instead of an economic powerhouse, we found a very fragile country and a people who perceived themselves as having no particular future at all. Everywhere, Japan seemed to be stalled in the past—in a bubble economy on the very edge of extinction. Our driver told us that the problem was that Japan had no natural resources. Failing them, he said, the country eventually would be swallowed up—by China, by the Arabs, he didn't know who would do the swallowing; he knew only that his homeland was doomed.

As we flew back to the States with that experience colliding around in our head, we came to a decision. We would get out of the market immediately, sell everything—and not just everything that gave us an exposure in the Pacific. We'd put our money in CDs, in money markets, in short-term T-bills, and we would wait, because if our trip to Japan had taught us one thing, it was that a major market correction lay ahead. Too many banks and manufacturers and much else were riding for a fall in the Land of the Rising Sun and throughout the Japanese-led Asian economy. The next day, we set out to do all that . . . and our future collided with other futures. Our experience ran up against other experiences.

Sell everything in a rising market? Our wives thought we were nuts. Sell everything when everything is going up, up, up? Our brokers thought we were wacky, too. Instead of getting out of the market, we held on, and by August 31, 1998, when the Dow Jones industrial average fell nearly 513 points to complete an 1,800-point slide from its peak of the month before, we had missed a chance to increase our net worth by almost 30 percent.

And the moral? Our reality wasn't anyone else's reality. Our experience wasn't anyone else's experience. Thus, our future wasn't going to be anyone else's future, and the more accurate we were in predicting our own future, the more fine-grained we saw it, the less accurate and binding our vision would be for anyone else.

From that realization flowed one more: If each future is unique, if every reality is different, then predictions aren't the point of futuring in any event. Predictions, after all, are answers to questions about the future. It's the questions that count, and each of us has to answer them separately according to our separate journey through the world and according to the separate choices we make that form our individual realities.

The role of the visionary—the role you will soon assume—we came to understand wasn't to be a seer but to be the provocateur: to present a series of visions of the future against which those who want to prepare for the future can react. Nobody, after all, knows what the future holds; all you can really know is what frames of mind, what receptivities, what structures you need to have in place to meet whatever does eventually come down the pike. And no one is less ready for tomorrow than the person who holds the most rigid beliefs about what tomorrow will contain.

Thus it was that we decided to start this book with a new notion: not of the continuous future but of the serial future. Think for a moment of serial murder, and think of it from three perspectives. From the point of view of the victims, each new act of murder is a random collision with the forces of evil. Similarly, each of our serial visions of the future is a random collision with the forces of possibility from the reader's point of view. But that's only from the victims' perspective. From the murderer's point of view, each new act of violence is a systematic collision with criminal opportunity, and so, too, we mean for our serial visions to be connected in time and space by a larger logic: that the only way to approach the "truth" of the future is to systematically break down and rebuild the "truths" you have created.

Finally, look at serial murder from the detective's point of view. Each new murder fills up a new piece of the puzzle, and thus the more murders, the better the chance that the murderer will identify himself (or very rarely herself) to such a degree of certainty that he will be caught. What does the detective want? For the murders to stop? Or for the murders to go on? At one level, the detective is the insurgent at the crime scene, alienated from all his comfort zones because his duty is to suspect everyone and to resuspect them every time the facts of the present or his understanding of the past change. At the second level, he's the crime archeologist, looking for the seminal moments that will unlock the puzzle he has set for himself. At the third and deepest level, he's also caught between the extremes of desire—for cessation of the murders without resolution and for continuation of the horror until apprehension—and it is only by absorbing and moving inside this paradoxical state that he can go on.

Think of yourself as that detective, because that, too, is the role of the visionary.

Now on to our own tools. It was with this new concept of the serial future in mind that we set out to unlearn—*unlearn,* not *discard*—everything we had learned in *The 500 Year Delta.* It wasn't a matter of correcting what had been wrong in our previous vision but of embracing a new set of determinants so we could be right again.

Instead of parsing the future in sweeping five-hundred-year blocks as we had done in our previous book, we would parse it in something far larger: the great macrocultures that have divided the human experience, from the earliest hunter-gatherer culture to the Age of Uncertainty that is emerging out of the ambient chaos of our own times. But then we'd do something else: We would take those macrocultures and divide them by the microissues that both shape each separate culture and are common to all of human experience.

Our goal was to find the penetrating changes that affect everyone in the culture, on an ongoing basis, in hundreds of different ways. By tracking them laterally across history, we could create individual snapshots of the cultures as we passed through them, but we could also establish the momentum that was carrying each of the microissues into the future. Collectively, the microissues would begin to create the picture of the new macroculture they are spawning and being spawned by. By parsing the future at both the macro and micro levels, we wanted to create a story both large enough that anyone could walk into it and small enough that anyone who entered the story could find themselves inside it.

Maybe most important, the right-hand column of the chart that follows on these pages was blank when we began tracking each of these microissues through each of the macrocultures. We didn't work backward from assumptions about today. We worked forward from what we knew and were able to learn about the past, and as we did so, we let the vectors and trend lines speak to us, rather than our speaking to them.

A last story by way of illustration before we get to the chart:

Back in the mid-1990s, we gave a keynote address at the annual convention of the Securities Industry. Our job that day was to talk about how the affluent customer was responding to the chaotic conditions in securities markets that began with the market crash of 1987. The theme of this meeting was customer service, but the subtext had to do with the declining confidence in institutional advice, the growing confidence in investor self-management, and the resulting risk to the traditional brokerage and investment-banking model.

Not long before the convention, we had come across data showing that something like fifteen million people would turn fifty in the years after 1996, and we used that data as the basis of our talk. It seemed to us reasonable, we said, to assume that beginning in 1996 there would be a generalized increase in interest in wealth creation—fifty being an age at which people begin to look seriously at retirement—and thus we built a demand model that asked a very simple question: If people weren't adding to their real estate portfolios, where would they put their money to grow? To answer that question, we put the entire demand bubble from fifty-year-old boomers into the equity market, and on that day we forecast a 10,000-point Dow Jones Industrial Average.

This forecast received not one compliment at the time, but now that it has come to pass, we have been asked how we did it. And this is the key to becoming a futurist: We didn't ask what if the market went to 10,000 and then hunt for variables to support the hypothesis. We said what would happen if everybody started preparing at the same time for the inevitable end of their earning years, and then we started following the variables: Where would the savings come from? Would consumption be lower? Attention to self higher? Planning more of a big deal? As each variable cropped up, we had to test its weight against other variables, and then we had to ask what its effect would be on the DJIA: Going up? Going down? And if going up, is there compelling evidence that this variable helps create shared confidence circulating at high volumes within the economy?

Force the variables to answer questions, and you'll always get the answer you expect. Let the variables speak to you, and something wonderful happens. That's what we want to do in this section of the book: show you our variables so that you can use them (or so that they will provoke you) to find your own and then let those variables speak to you. That way, something wonderful can happen to you, too. Now, on to the chart:

We'll begin to explicate this chart in a few pages, and we'll invite you into the process then. Before we do, though, we need to define the terms used in the chart, and we need to introduce you to how to use it. Let's start with the terms, and let's begin with the biggest of them all.

Macroculture: a collision of ideology and civilization that produces for those living within it distinct ways of dwelling together and organizing ideas into belief patterns. Thus far, there have been five macrocultures in the long history of the human species. They are:

• The *Hunter-Gatherer Epoch*, which carried us from the dawn of mankind through eons of survival-driven nomadism to the first rough practice of both the cultivation of crops and domestication of animals. Archeological evidence suggests the epoch of

MACROCULTURE →

MICROISSUE →

	HUNTER-GATHERER	AGRICULTURE	CONSUMER	KNOWLEDGE	UNCERTAINTY
Philosophy	Holism	Pantheism	Mechanical Causality	Complexity	Absorption of Paradox
Mission	Survive	Structure	Power	Well-being	Omnireality
Preoccupation	Survival	Reason for Being	Ascension	Quality	Immortality
Work	Group	Personal Labor	Service	Knowledge	Spiritual
Ritual	Hunt	Seasons	Day	Access	Singularity & Uniqueness
Travel	Foot	Natural Effects	Mechanical Propulsion	Jet Propulsion	Media
Weapons	Personal Strength	Eye to Eye	Remote	Mass Destruction	Surgical
Status Symbol	Offspring	Land	Possessions	Awareness	Events
Defining Activity	Hunting	Growing	Buying	Understanding	Dreaming
Recreation	Storytelling	Socializing	Belonging	Viewing	Being
Membership	Tribe	Family	Hierarchy	Networks	Neotribes
Physical Structure	Tent	Farm	Factory	Office	Theme Park
Dominant Resource	Territory	Fertilizer	Raw Material	Process	Intellectual Property
Dominant Person	Chief	Head of Household	Owners	Celebrity	Storyteller
Learning	Instincts	Cycles	Interactions	Scientific Method	Probability
Intelligence	Language	Literacy	Education	Creativity	Intuition
Visionary	Shaman	Priest	Ideologue	Economist	Futurist

the hunter-gatherers lasted from roughly 4 million B.C. to 2 million B.C.

* The *Agricultural Epoch*, which extended from 2 million B.C. to about 1850, when in advanced Western nations the balance between farm and factory finally tipped in favor of the latter. The agricultural epoch began with people learning to plant and ended with the perfection of the concept of tool.

* The *Consumer Age*, inappropriately thought of as the Industrial Age, which had its first origins in the beginning of the Age of Reason, became firmly established during the mid-1800s, and survived until the end of World War II. It was during the Consumer Age that we learned how to merchandise and how to trade. As that happened, the production and consumption of goods on a massive scale became the defining economic activity for the first time in human history. The process of manufacturing ultimately would be perfected to fulfill that goal, but it was the desire to own—and a liberation from a time when only nobility and a few priests truly owned—that spawned the epoch. The defining innovation of the Consumer Age? The invention of the bureau, in the late seventeenth century. Without places to store things and keep them well, the ownership of more than a single pair of pants made no sense.

* The *Knowledge Epoch*, which took root after World War I, gained momentum with the introduction of the IBM 603 ENIAC calculator in 1946, and extended for half a century past that. Before the Knowledge Epoch, graduating from high school had been deemed sufficient to most tasks and overly sufficient for many. By the time the epoch reached full flower, a college degree was becoming the great divide of American life, and knowledge had become the driving force discriminating the strong from the weak, the rich from the poor.

* And the *Age of Uncertainty*. Presaged by the atomic attacks on Hiroshima and Nagasaki with their implicit promise that the entire human species had an uncertain future, the age was given further shape and direction as quarks and black holes began to challenge the notion of fundamental stability. The Epoch of Knowledge taught us *how* to discover and disseminate scientific information. *What* was discovered—quantum mechanics—spelled the epoch's end. The Age of Uncertainty was officially launched in

the mid-1990s, by which time the World Wide Web had reached critical mass, and it had become apparent that what the Web was connecting were billions of separate realities.

Matrices, of course, lie, and ours is no exception. By imposing clean lines between macrocultures, we imply an exclusivity that does not and that cannot exist. The hunter-gatherer culture doesn't simply end with the rise of agriculture. Rather, the experience of the hunter-gatherers becomes the base that the agriculturists build on, and the cumulative experience of the hunter-gatherers and agriculturists becomes, in turn, the base of the Consumer Epoch. Macrocultures don't go away. They get compounded, and while the compounding changes their nature, each macroculture is still present in every macroculture that follows.

◆ Future Exercise

Many writers have thought of different ways to organize the seasons of our lives and the epochs of our businesses and of history. Like their "stage theories," our five epochs are at best a shorthand summary of a great deal of pluck, luck, complexity, contamination, and uncontrolled factors. But our model does allow us to concentrate on the ideas and technologies that frame our vision of futuring, and we think that building your own model will allow you to do the same. (Talk about a paradox: We're suggesting you create a subjective list for an objective analytical process!)

To build your model, take your life, your business, your relationship, or any fragment of your experience that you want to forecast the future for, break its present, past, and future history into the smallest imaginable number of transitional stages (or epochs), and list those across the top of your pad. For example, a relationship might be divided into an ingratiation stage, early intimacy, formalization (marriage), maturation, and so on.

Below and between each stage or epoch, list all the variables you can think of that either have affected or will affect the transition from one stage to the next. (The role of children, role of friends, role of work, health of spouse, etc.) These are your signposts to the nature of change.

Finally, write down a goal for this fragment of your experience. ("A life-long marriage," say, for the example we've been using.) To measure how likely your goal is to be realized, monitor the variables. If they change precipitously, you may have to adjust your goal, or the variables you think are important.

———————————————————

Those, then, are the horizontal elements of our chart. Let's turn now to the vertical elements, beginning once again with the overall concept.

Microissues: the questions that matter most, both to the people living within a macroculture and to an external understanding of the people and their epoch. In all, we've identified seventeen microissues. They are:

- *Philosophy:* belief about the nature of man.
- *Mission:* the object of living.
- *Preoccupation:* what the mass of society is most concerned with and consumed by.
- *Work:* the activity that most results in economic survival.
- *Ritual:* the activity that most invokes the agency of God.
- *Travel:* the means to move.
- *Weapons:* the means for killing.
- *Status symbol:* the sign that most distinguishes the individual.
- *Defining activity:* that which the principal figures in society are distinguished by doing.
- *Recreation:* the activity most directly opposite to being at work.
- *Membership:* the defining group of the society.
- *Physical structure:* the defining building of the society.
- *Dominant resource:* the resource most directly correlated to dominance.
- *Dominant person:* the individual to whom the majority look for guidance, advice, and wisdom.
- *Learning:* the dominant method for processing stimuli and information and turning them into action and understanding.
- *Intelligence:* the quality of mind most celebrated by the society as a whole.

◆ *Visionary:* the person most celebrated for his or her ability to predict events to come.

Last, before we get to the chart explication, some instruction on how to use it. Earlier we referred to this chart as our tool. We meant that in both senses: It is first of all a tool that allowed us to unlearn our past approach and to create another way to organize our thoughts. And it is *our* tool, inevitably reflective of our experiences, our learning, our understandings, and our misunderstandings. Think of it as the weapon we have employed to commit serial future. Use the chart, as we have used it, to ask questions about the present, to review the past, and to project the past and present forward into the future. But don't let yourself be confined by our limitations or trapped in our reality. This chart is a complete guide to understanding the future if you happen to be us, but it's not a complete guide if you happen to be you.

The word "ethics," you'll note, does not appear among our microissues. Nor does "technology" or "structure," "war" or "politics." Other very important concepts—some that arguably have changed the history of man—have been omitted as well: food, for example. (Umberto Eco made the claim that the introduction of the bean in the diet of eleventh-century Europe produced the protein levels required for the population explosion that allowed for the Renaissance to occur three hundred years later.)

We discounted these and other concepts not because we fail to recognize their importance but because they fail to provide us with sufficient independent connection to the separate tracks industries and nations can take into the future. But because we avoid them does not mean you cannot embrace them or any others that allow you to sense the variables that operate to change your particular environment.

◆ Future Exercise

List the dozen microissues most critical to your life/your business/your industry.

The chart will help you, we think, to see the movement in your own life, and not just the movement itself but what's happening on the fringe of the movement, because that's finally where you have to look if you want to keep up with the future—just at the edge where it's about to spin off into something else. Once you understand that movement, though, once you find its fringe, you'll have to forecast your own vectors and follow them into your own future. As always, we provide Future Exercises at each step along the way to help you further refine your vision. As you'll see directly below, we also invite you at the front of each microissue to weigh our reality against your own.

Now, let's get to work.

PHILOSOPHY

HUNTER-GATHERER	AGRICULTURE	CONSUMER	KNOWLEDGE	UNCERTAINTY
Holism	Pantheism	Mechanical Causality	Complexity	?

Our reality: Paradox

Your reality: _____

Hunter-gatherers had no explanation for tree-ness or ground-ness, sun-ness or cloud-ness, birth-ness or death-ness or anything else that formed the core of their sensory and intellectual experience. Because they lacked an explanation for why anything existed, their principal philosophical issue was why everything existed, and out of that came a single explanation: a god-force. Why was stuff made? Why did things happen? Because a single god-force caused it to be made and caused it to happen, and all things that could be made or could happen were attributable to the same reason.

Agriculturalists had every bit as much need as the hunter-gatherers did for explanations of their universe, but as one epoch bled into the other, something complexly critical happened: Life became differentiated—we didn't understand lots more specific things—and language became differentiated and codified as well. People also came to have specific responsibilities at specific times of the year—to plant, to cultivate, to reap, to lay up for winter. Social experience became differentiated as well: Nomadic tribes were displaced by relatively stable societies. Land shared in common became land defined by feudal borders, which meant that land could be encroached on, which meant that wars for land and the people who came with the land had a reason to exist. Rituals developed, too, to mark the great turning points in life—birth, puberty, and so on. And with each of these differentiations, the single god of the hunter-gatherers became differentiated, too, into fertility gods and crop gods and war gods and house gods.

Thus, holism was layered over by pantheism. And then at the very tail end of the Agricultural Epoch, two new and radical things happened: The monotheistic God of the Judeo-Christian tradition began to dominate Western culture, as did the ten rules, or commandments, for living handed down by the tradition, and geometry was invented just in time for Archimedes to devise the first primitive concepts of cause and effect. From Archimedes' work would flow the mechanical theory of the universe that underlay the Industrial Revolution. Time ordering became transcendent. The physical world entailed such inevitable relationships that they could be captured in a series of laws and principles that themselves came to be the scientific analogs of the Ten Commandments, and mechanical science itself came to be seen as a philosophy and very nearly as a religion in its own right . . . except that as we came to know more and more about electronic relationships, mechanical theory was able to explain less and less about them.

The sinking of the *Titanic* in 1912 was the precursor of the collapse of mechanical causality—God had more than enough surprises left to combat the hubris of man—but its death knell was IBM's ENIAC computer, which increased calculating speed a thousandfold by substituting electronic impulses for mechanical switches. The Knowledge Era, it turned out, was going to run on electricity, and electricity simply wouldn't cooperate with the prevailing notions of cause and effect. As the world spun off into neutrinos, antimatter, mesons, scions, and quarks, mechanical relationships thought to be impossible were found to be, instead, commonplace. Find the right slot in the right curvature of space, and even Newton's famous rock would actually roll up the hill.

Out of a philosophy based on causality, then, emerged one based very nearly on its opposite—on the complexity that quantum physics and mechanics sought to drive to the heart of—and out of that is emerging a new philosophical construct based on the irresolvability of much of the complexity that had consumed the Epoch of Knowledge.

One quick example before we leave philosophy: The main issue affecting the speed of computers today is the side effects of the speed of light. The more you accelerate electrons toward the speed of light, the greater the speed of the computer, but the more you accelerate electrons, the more heat they give off. Removing that heat is perhaps the principal issue in chip design today, and yet there is a relatively easy solution close at hand: a fan. Put it in the computer and you can blow the heat away just fine. The only problem is that once you do that, you won't be able to sell the computer because people don't like the noise the fan makes. On the one hand you have a demand for the greatest possible speed; on the other, to achieve that speed you have to create an auditory phenomenon that would have annoyed the most primitive hunter-gatherer four million years ago. The critical battle in business life today isn't between the central tendencies; it's between the radical and conservative fringes of virtually every issue, every product, every consideration. And thus a philosophy built on the absorption of paradox because as with the speed of computers, so it is with just about everything today.

Calvin Klein, by the way, means for "absorption" to be taken literally. As we were writing, he introduced his newest fragrance: Contradiction, for Men.

◆ Future Exercise

On the left-hand side of the page, list five paradoxes of your personal or work life. (To express my love for my mother, I have had to place her in an assisted-care facility that she hates living in. To advance in my career, I have changed it. Etc.)

Next, create a middle column and, beside each paradox, note how you have attempted to resolve it:

♦ By being "reasonable"   _____
♦ By "living with it"   _____
♦ By resisting it   _____

In a right-hand column, note how you feel about your resolution of each paradox:

♦ Happy   _____
♦ Satisfied _____
♦ Miserable _____

Finally, read this over, and then go back to the schematic at the beginning of this section on "Philosophy" and fill in the blank beside "Your reality."

WEAPONS				
HUNTER-GATHERER	**AGRICULTURE**	**CONSUMER**	**KNOWLEDGE**	**UNCERTAINTY**
Personal Strength	Eye to Eye	Remote	Mass Destruction	?

Our reality: Surgical

Your reality: _____

Not surprisingly, the development of weapons tends to track the development of travel as both move through the history of humanity. Modern cartoon retellings of the myths of Xena, Hercules, and Conan clean up the action—there's no biting or fingers gouging eyes from their sockets—and they make it all look politically correct as well. But in broad stroke, they get the story right: The weapon of choice for hunter-gatherers was what it had to be: personal strength, the ability to wield a club or bring a bone or boulder crashing down on an enemy's skull.

Agricultural warriors could travel farther—by horse or boat— than hunter-gatherers, and they had finer weapons to fight with when they got there, most notably the sword and all its variants. But they still had to stand eye to eye to do combat. Gradually, archers, catapults, and early rifles would extend that space, but just as Aristotle and Thomas Jefferson occupied the same travel world, so the first Battle of Thermopylae in 480 B.C. and the Civil War Battle of Antietam were fought according to the same rough rules even though they were separated by almost 2,350 years: two armies occupying a single field of combat. Even with snipers, whether they used arrows or bullets, killing was still dependent on line of sight.

The growing remoteness of weapons during the two great world wars—mortars, navy guns, V-1 and V-2 missiles, aerial bombardment—yielded at the end of World War II to weapons of finality. As delivery systems moved into missile silos or planes traveling at fifty thousand feet above sea level or nuclear submarines traveling well beneath the surface of the ocean—and thus became ever more remote—the weapons themselves became both horribly impersonal (mass destruction kills everyone) and deeply personal (everyone includes me).

And then, just as rituals grew singular and unique in the Age of Uncertainty, so weapons grew singular and unique as well. The Gulf War of 1991 was to the new generation of surgical weapons what the Spanish Civil War had been to the German war machine: a tryout of sorts, and in both cases a spectacularly successful one. Not every Tomahawk missile went down a Baghdad smokestack exactly as U.S. military simulations said they should, but enough did to validate the concept, and enough have done so in forays against Iraq and Yugoslavia in the years since to validate the validation.

As we write, the Abilene Project connecting thirty-seven U.S. universities via Internet 2 is about to be launched with, among other events, a gall-bladder surgeon standing in Union Station in Washington, D.C., participating via media travel in a gall-bladder surgery in Columbus, Ohio. In essence, that is no different than a Tomahawk missile technician based on a battleship participating, via remote travel, in the destruction of a communications tower in Belgrade. Nor, really, is it any different in kind than a terrorist participating, via latent activation, in the release of biowarfare agents into the drinking water of New York City or Tokyo or Paris or Jerusalem. The more exact we get with our weapons, the more uncertain they tend to make us. Not everything surgical cures what ails you.

◆ Future Exercise

Our reality says that the Abilene Project we have described just above stands to be a seminal moment for surgical weapons because the remote gall-bladder surgery couples the tools of death with the tools of life. After you decide what weapons are becoming central to your reality, list the seminal moments that will allow you to know that the future you have envisioned has arrived.

MEMBERSHIP				
HUNTER-GATHERER	**AGRICULTURE**	**CONSUMER**	**KNOWLEDGE**	**UNCERTAINTY**
Tribe	Family	Hierarchy	Networks	?
Our reality: Neotribes				
Your reality: _____				

Just as most of human history has been a movement toward socializing and belonging, so the majority of human history has been a movement away from tribalism. The Agricultural Epoch replaced membership in the tribe with family membership, including the family of God. Associations never before codified—wife-husband, parent-child, aunt-nephew, grandparent-grandchild, cousins—came to define not just one's blood associations but who one was, where and how one fit into the group, and to whom one owed deference and respect.

The industrial era took the concept of family and extended it to the workplace and society generally. In America, there were no titled aristocrats, no lords and ladies, but there were the lower class and the lower middle class and all the other classes and subclasses straight up to "the Four Hundred," the crème de la crème of late-nineteenth-century New York society. (The number was determined by the number of the socially elite who could fit into Mrs. John Jacob Astor's Manhattan ballroom.) The Knowledge Epoch took those hierarchies, flattened them, and turned them into networks: women's networks, prayer breakfast and Bible study networks, young black professional networks, and finally—once the world was wired and everyone was logged on—cyber-networks. And as the focus of each network became more and more tightly defined and the view the network projected became more and more self-feeding and self-rewarding (survivalist magazines and talk-radio shows and cyberstores for the survivalist network, *Cigar* magazine and Cap Juluca for the young bond trader network), the networks began to evolve their own reality and the members formed themselves into . . . neotribes!

Just like the tribes of three million years ago, and the Stone Age tribes that survive today, neotribes distinguish themselves by their markings: outerwear logos, hip-hop pants, Turnbull & Asser shirts, nose rings and tongue studs for the Heavy Metal tribe, racist tattoos for the tribe of the White Aryan Nation. Tribes had to create their own reality because they lived for the most part in utter isolation. Neotribes impose their own reality by isolating themselves from competing claims and other versions of reality. In practical effect, the differences between tribes and neotribes are indistinguishable, but there is one large change: Then, you joined a tribe for life, and if you were driven from it, it was to an almost certain death. Now, the difficulty of leaving a tribe is determined by the depth of the commitment required to join it and by the severity of the crimes a tribe collectively commits: The neotribe of the Presbyterian Church is easy to join and just as easy to depart: Say "I believe" one Sunday and don't show up the next. The neotribe of the Ku Klux Klan or the Crips is another matter because of the secrets you inevitably carry away with you when you depart and because, in the Crips' case, you allegedly have to shoot someone to get in.

But leave we can, and leave we do, sometimes via the Federal Witness Protection Program but more often simply by chucking our logos and changing the nose rings for a Coco Chanel handbag. Even the tattoos can be removed by laser. Appropriately in an age that makes a fetish of singularity and uniqueness, we belong to our neotribes only as long as they reinforce what we have chosen to be, right here and right now, because, finally, neotribes are about *us*, not *them*. Once we change who we choose to be, we change neotribes as well and find a new support system (from personalized merchandise to single-interest chat rooms) to match the slice of omnireality that we have chosen for the moment to call our own. Diversity in the workplace isn't about race or ethnicity. It's about just this: neotribes and constantly shifting bandwidths of allegiance, which is why the workplace has no choice but to embrace omnireality, too.

◆ Future Exercise

List all the neotribes that can be found within the largest distinct group you work closely with: unit, division, regiment, board, whatever. Beside each neotribe place an arrow pointing up, down, or sideways to indicate whether the tribe is increasing, decreasing, or holding steady in terms of its relative importance within your workplace. Next, ask yourself what you and/or your company have done within the last month to bond each neotribe to your corporate values. Finally, write down the name of the neotribe you belong to.

TRAVEL

HUNTER-GATHERER	AGRICULTURE	CONSUMER	KNOWLEDGE	UNCERTAINTY
Foot	Natural Effects	Mechanical Propulsion	Jet Propulsion	?

Our reality: Media

Your reality: _____

Conan the Barbarian—the *first* Conan—could travel no farther in a day than his feet would take him. By Aristotle's time, mankind had learned to harness natural effects for transportation. Two millennia later, as the Agricultural Epoch was drawing to a close, not much had changed. Thomas Jefferson's life was fundamentally no different than Aristotle's: He could still go only as far in a day as the winds would blow him or the river would flow or a beast of burden would carry or pull him.

Trains and later autos and planes changed all that, and did so in a remarkably brief period of time. By 1879, when Thomas Edison was inventing the lightbulb that would lead a little more than a decade later to the founding of General Electric, a man could go as far in a day as a train would travel—New York to Chicago, say. Thirty-five years later, when Thomas Watson quit the National Cash Register company to rescue the Computing-Tabulating-Recording Company and eventually turn it into IBM, daily travel had been extended for the very daring to the range of an airplane. Soon, the mechanical propulsion of the Consumer Epoch would give way to jet propulsion, and as moving parts diminished, the length of travel available in a day became global. Rockets, with fewer moving parts still, took travel for a select few beyond the Earth and its atmosphere. For the first time, mankind could out-travel its ability to adapt. Jet lag became a problem, then an illness. Finally, for the flight-warrior businessmen of the age, jet lag became a clinical condition, and proof of their worth.

And today? Today with virtually no moving parts whatsoever you can travel as far as the wavelength of the Internet will take you, into outer space, and you can do so at the speed of light and without ever leaving home. Instead of jet lag from dragging our physical systems through myriad time zones, the travel-warriors of the Age of Uncertainty earn their purple hearts with carpal tunnel syndrome. The farther out we go, the broader the net we cast in our travels, the more we also climb inside ourselves and to very precise spots to lick our wounds.

◆ Future Exercise

Estimate all the miles you have traveled by foot (jogging counts) over the last ten years, all the miles you've traveled by automobile over the last year, all the miles you've traveled by airplane in the last month, and all the miles you've traveled by Internet in the last day. (Forget the satellite bounce. Point-to-point e-mail traffic alone should do it.)

Next, calculate the cost per mile (figure four pairs of shoes a year at $75 a pair) and the time per mile in hours (there are about 87,600 hours in ten years, 8,760 in a year, and 720 in a 30-day month).

Finally, figure the proportional waiting time for each means of travel over the relevant time frame (crossing lights, stoplights and traffic jams, flight delays and cancellations, log-on glitches, etc.). Who says the world isn't getting better?

PHYSICAL STRUCTURE				
HUNTER-GATHERER	**AGRICULTURE**	**CONSUMER**	**KNOWLEDGE**	**UNCERTAINTY**
Tent	Farm	Factory	Office	?

Our reality: Theme Park

Your reality: _____

Whether it was a tent, a farm, or a factory, the defining physical structure for untold centuries was married to the physical reality of the life people led. As work moved from production to the manipulation of knowledge, the defining physical structure moved from the factory to the office place, and structurally, the office was something different: part for work, part for politics; part a place to process paper and part a place to preen. Ultimately, every office building is less a collection of job-related spaces than it is an egoplex.

The Age of Uncertainty has separated physical structure from the physical life more thoroughly still. Today, the defining structure of a people whose defining activity is the dream is the theme park—dreams writ large and brought to life. Disney, of course, is the most obvious example: the storybooks and fairy tales turned into rides; EPCOT, where whole nations and cultures are reduced to pavilions with little rivers running through them and spotless restaurants where everyone can drink the water; even Celebration, the new Disney city outside Orlando where real people live in real houses in the apparent hope that their real children will never do real drugs or get real pregnant out of wedlock. But Disney is only the most obvious manifestation. There's also the restaurant as theme park (Hard Rock Café), the mall as theme park (Mall of America has virtually saved Northwest Airlines and made Minneapolis the shopping theme park of America), and as just suggested, the city as theme park, too.

We visit New York not because it's America's largest city and a surprisingly hospitable place but because it's the theme park of financial power, the nexus of all the money in all the world. Go to Detroit, and you're visiting the Theme Park of Bad Boys. You can even buy T-shirts that say, "I'm so bad I vacationed in Detroit." Both cities have a reality where real people work, eat, sleep, love, hate, and die. But it is their illusion we want, just as the fans of *The Truman Show* (the TV show that lay at the heart of the movie) wanted the illusion, not the reality, of Truman trapped in a life he seemingly couldn't escape. Only in the Age of Uncertainty could the defining physical structure be so clearly what it's not.

◆ Future Exercise

Beside each city below write what it is the theme park of (we'll give our own answers below):

◆ San Francisco
◆ Honolulu
◆ Amsterdam
◆ Frankfurt
◆ Singapore

Our answers:

◆ San Francisco (Disneyland for Adults)
◆ Honolulu (Polynesia Lite)
◆ Amsterdam (Sex and Drugs)
◆ Frankfurt (Just Sex)
◆ Singapore (Municipal Cleanliness at Any Cost)

Now, fill in the following three blanks:

◆ My office building is the theme park of _____.

◆ My office is the theme park of _____.

◆ My home is the theme park of _____.

PREOCCUPATION				
HUNTER-GATHERER	AGRICULTURE	CONSUMER	KNOWLEDGE	UNCERTAINTY
Survival	Reason for Being	Ascension	Quality	?

Our reality: Immortality

Your reality: _____

Just as microissues layer as they move horizontally through time, so they layer on themselves within any epoch. The preoccupation of a people whose mission is to survive is simply survival: life stripped to the basics. By the best estimates, even the oldest hunter-gatherers rarely lived past age thirty-five. No one could wait for the slowest member of the hunting party, nor could a mobile people tolerate the immobile sick or the marginally dying. The more complex society of the agriculturists created leisure time, which created leisure thought, which led to a preoccupation with the reason for being. Survival was still a struggle, but life was no longer constant movement. The Consumer Age both flooded the market with consumable goods and created power structures in the workplace, from foreman through vice presidents and CEOs, where such tiering never existed before. The goods provided a tangible measure by which people could gauge their relative position in the world of possessions. To help them along, General Motor's Alfred Sloan invented a hierarchy of needs that had you moving along from a Chevrolet to a Buick to a Cadillac as your capacity to possess increased. Meanwhile, the power structure gave them a title by which they could gauge their relative position in the world of work. Thus ascension became the preoccupation of consumerists.

The Knowledge Epoch dawned just as the preoccupation with ascension was playing itself out in novels like Sloan Wilson's *The Man in the Gray Flannel Suit* and plays like Budd Schulberg's *What Makes Sammy Run?* Suddenly, the rat race seemed more about the rat than the race. Instead of keeping up with the Joneses, people began to keep up with themselves. The quality, the specialness of their own experience became the new preoccupation, and it expressed itself in everything from a vast increase in the consumption of ever more sophisticated forms of plastic surgery, to the rise of (ironically) wholesale niche marketing to bring "specialness" to the masses, to the realization of Andy Warhol's ironic promise of fifteen minutes of fame for everyone.

Today, the question that really matters is: "How long am I going to last?" Why? Because the demographic push of baby boomers into late middle age has brought mortality, and hence immortality, to the fore of public consciousness with unpredictable and maybe unprecedented consequences for social, economic, and political life. And because people are living very whole lives in very high states of health such as history has never known before. And because, quite simply, the potential for immortality exists in a way—and in ways—it has never existed before.

The Soul Catcher project has shown that by attaching a silicon chip to the optic nerve you can take a moving picture of everything a person sees throughout his or her entire life. The same can be done with smell, taste, touch, and feel. In effect, total recall is now a total reality. Expand that a small step: Download that totally recalled conscience into a host human form. Are we now an alien memory occupying its body, or are we a continuation of ourselves in that new human form? If we are the latter and if we can repeat that downloading time and again through the centuries, layering conscience on conscience on conscience, haven't we escaped this mortal flesh and achieved immortality?

Better still, of course, what if we just have ourselves cloned and perpetuate memory, cells, DNA, and all? Impossible? Biologically, only if you happen to believe that the aging problem with cloned cells can't be gotten around or that humans represent a level of complexity infinitely far beyond that of mice or even sheep and cattle. (And it's worth noting here that a human being and a fern share about 97 percent of the same DNA.) Legally, though, cloning is another matter. Strictures within the mainstream scientific community actively discourage human cloning, and almost certainly laws will soon be on the books in the United States that do the same. But what could better testify to the preoccupation with immortality than the fact that we are on the edge of making it illegal?

As with mission, so with everything else: We live today in the tension between the present and future and in the tension between the extremes of our collective desires. One side tells us that we must outlaw immortality; the other says that we must pursue it full tilt. One side says that we can know an immortal afterlife only through an all-embracing spiritualism that escapes specific religious understandings of God; the other says that it is only through a rigidly defined religious sectarianism that we can come to our immortal home. Who's right? Who knows? The extremes drive the debate and shape the central tendencies for us all, and thus it is only by moving inside the debate and absorbing its contradiction that we can begin to see where we are going.

◆ Future Exercise

What are the half dozen most critical products and/or services your business offers? Assume for the moment that our reality is right and that immortality is emerging as the dominant preoccupation of the Age of Uncertainty: How does that change the positioning and/or market for each of your six critical products and/or services?

Now, fill in the section beside "your reality" at the start of this section, and if it's different from ours, do the same exercise with your preoccupation.

Last, do the same thing with the product of yourself: What are the six most critical qualities you bring to the marketplace? How does a preoccupation with immortality—or with whatever you choose—change the market for you?

DOMINANT PERSON

HUNTER-GATHERER	AGRICULTURE	CONSUMER	KNOWLEDGE	UNCERTAINTY
Chief	Head of Household	Owners	Celebrity	?

Our reality: Storyteller

Your reality: _____

Tribes pay homage to their chief because his rule is binding on the members and because it is with the chief and between chiefs that other tribes must negotiate. In the Agricultural Epoch, the head of household was the chief of the tribe known as family—again, whether it was a family defined by blood, a monarchy that embraced a royal family even unto the lowest serf, or the family of God at the head of which sat the Pope, appropriately from the Greek for "father."

With the rise of the Consumer Age, dominance passed to owners because it was the owners who sat at the top of the hierarchy that produced the possessions by which consumerists defined their status. Sometimes those owners were robber barons; sometimes they were land barons; sometimes they were studio heads. What was important—and the communists were right all along about this—was that dominance was established by owning the means of production, whether the object being produced was harmonicas, Stutz Bearcat coupes, corn, or Busby Berkeley musicals.

United Artists may have been the first clear precursor of the seismic shift that lay ahead for ownership and the entire macroculture of the consumer. Founded in 1919 by silent-film stars Charlie Chaplin, Mary Pickford, and Douglas Fairbanks Sr. and by director D. W. Griffith to wrest control of film production, distribution, and profits from the studio heads, UA began a transfer of power in Hollywood that has continued to this day and spread well beyond the movie industry. Stars of the so-called Golden Age of Hollywood were still owned mostly lock, stock, and barrel by the studios. By the mid-1980s, stars themselves were choosing their own projects, taking points in the gross, and demanding and getting artistic control over the product, and the people of a new macroculture that recreated by viewing and defined itself through creation were in complete accord.

In sports, too, it was the celebrity who dominated, not the owner. Michael Jordan had virtual control over the entire Chicago Bull franchise. It was Jordan who okayed the coach, Jordan who was consulted on trades, Jordan who brought the fans in and the television dollars in and the merchandise endorsement dollars, too—so much so that the Bulls franchise went into an almost total tailspin when Jordan finally retired, so much so indeed that there was serious question whether the National Basketball Association itself could survive his absence.

And adoration of celebrity wasn't limited to just the usual suspects. Peter Lynch and Warren Buffett brought the cult of celebrity to the financial world. Lee Iacocca and later Ross Perot and Steve Forbes became the celebrity businessmen-turned-presidential contenders, just as Colin Powell became the celebrity warrior and presidential mystery man.

Celebrity, though, doesn't exist in a vacuum. It sits at the top of stories that exalt its deeds, or it gains its fame or notoriety or singularness by the execution of a script that separates it (whether the "it" is inanimate or inanimate) from the common masses. Thus, as we enter the Age of Uncertainty, dominance is passing yet again, this time to the storyteller.

It's the storyteller who holds the intellectual property, the storyteller who shapes our dreams, the storyteller who creates the plots in which are embedded the promises that our brands reflect, the storyteller who expresses our belief systems for the world to see and hear. It's also the storyteller who can best pretend to rationalism in an irrational world. Not long ago, we asked one of America's leading venture capitalists what was the most important criterion in securing financial backing for a start-up. The ability to write a coherent business plan, he said, by which he explained he meant the ability to disguise the necessary fiction of a business plan as fact. More and more, it also will be the storyteller who gets the money.

The storyteller's job is to imagine a future in which neither the problems nor the solutions are known, and the better they are at it, the more they will destabilize what they cannot see, and thus the less likely it will be happen. And therein lies enough paradox for any one life: The greatest measure of dominance won't be the size of the tribe or family you command. It won't be the height of the ownership pyramid you sit atop of or the number of people who recognize your name or brand. True dominance will be measured by the capacity of your imagination to conceive a story that cannot come true.

◆ Future Exercise

Forget all past associations, all past history: the nuns and coaches and mentors to whom you looked for advice and guidance once upon a time. Beginning at this moment in time, who are the five dominant people in the society of your life? Write their names in the spaces below, but leave the parentheses blank.

_____ (   )
_____ (   )
_____ (   )
_____ (   )
_____ (   )

In the parentheses, write the description from the following choices that best characterizes each person: chief, head of household (broadly defined), owner, celebrity, storyteller.

MISSION				
HUNTER-GATHERER	AGRICULTURE	CONSUMER	KNOWLEDGE	UNCERTAINTY
Survival	Structure	Power	Well-being	?
Our reality: Omnireality				
Your reality: _____				

For hunter-gatherers the mission was both extraordinarily easy and extraordinarily hard: Their individual choices were made in accordance with the primitive need to survive—survive starvation, survive the elements, survive large animals and small ones, survive combat with other nomadic tribes over the same hunting grounds and killing fields.

Because they created the concept of society, agriculturists also created the concept of structure and made that their mission. From physical structures to house nonnomadic families and to protect crops from rodents and other forms of degradation, the mission expanded to include villages, towns, and eventually the structure of national governments.

Consumerists expanded the concept of structure in the Industrial Age to the structure of power, both the physical power to run factories and the political power that is the analog of physical power. Thus, the Consumer Epoch gave us not just steel and railroad barons but also Metternich and the stress on political "balances of power." The Knowledge Age didn't lose its interest in power, but under the influence of Sigmund Freud, Benjamin Spock, and many others, it came more and more to define power in physical and psychological terms. Its mission was to be healthy by avoiding sickness, and to that end, it consumed so much health care over the course of its scant half century that the management of health care costs came to dominate both the economic and political landscapes.

The omnireality of the Uncertainty Age takes that impulse both a step further and a step backward. Omnireality allows us to manage paradoxes that otherwise might well overwhelm us with their potential for sadness or despair; it allows us to be ourself and not ourself at one and the same time. For IBM, that means participating at the extremes of what is possible to be real in the world of computing while producing computers that represent technology that is already two generations old. Through omnireality, companies can explore their end points and live at their fringes while concentrating resources at the center. They also can plan strategically while knowing that every product they make will be either obsolete in ten years or made by someone else and while knowing, too, that they have to continue what they are doing if they hope to escape it.

To go back to the two-by-two matrix we introduced in Part I, omnireality allows companies to pay people to fill their Fool Box, knowing that if the people in the box are truly effective, they will end up plotting the destruction of the company as it is.

◆ Future Exercise

On the left-hand side of the page write down the same five paradoxes you listed for the exercise on page 188. Be sure to leave a space between them. Now, note the two realities you have to occupy to operate at the extreme edge of each paradox:

To place my mother in an assisted-care facility that she hates living in, I have had to be:

- ◆ A loving son or daughter
- ◆ A cold-blooded realist

Chances are, you'll find that omnireality has already become your mission.

WORK				
HUNTER-GATHERER	**AGRICULTURE**	**CONSUMER**	**KNOWLEDGE**	**UNCERTAINTY**
Group	Personal Labor	Service	Knowledge	?

Our reality: Spiritual

Your reality: _____

Hunter-gatherers labored in groups because they had to. Someone needed to find the animal. Someone else had to drive it toward the killers. Others had to dress the dead meat and salvage bones, skins, and the like. Still others gathered the nuts and berries that sustained the tribe between kills. A preoccupation with survival created a dependence on group. In the Agricultural Epoch, group labor remained a seasonal necessity, at planting and especially at harvest time and in times of war and conflict, but generally stable conditions and the necessarily isolated life of farming created the icon of the personal laborer that persists to this day, whether it's as the lone frontiersman blazing new trails for settlers to follow ("Elbow room," cried Daniel Boone) or as the ruggedly self-reliant farmer played by Jimmy Stewart in the Civil War epic *Shenandoah*.

It was the industrialists of the Consumer Age, not the information barons of the Knowledge Age, who created the concept of the service economy, at least from the worker's point of view. Work was service to a God who demanded evidence of industriousness as an admission ticket to His ultimate kingdom. It was service to factory owners and foremen, service to the clock that divided the day into the artificial shifts that best served production schedules, and service also to country in the form of military duty, taxpaying, voting, and the other duties of citizenship.

In the Knowledge Epoch, a worker's value came to be measured not by strength or endurance or team play or individual ruggedness but by the ability to assimilate and accumulate knowledge. The game of the Knowledge Epoch, appropriately enough, was *Jeopardy!* as hosted by Alex Trebek. As in the quiz show, a narrow slice of knowledge (" 'British prime ministers' for $500, Alex," or the capacity to write software codes) could be spectacularly rewarded. As in the quiz show, too, not knowing placed you in a jeopardy that was both immediate and painful: You couldn't come back next week or next job or for the next paycheck.

Appropriately enough, in an epoch that longs for immortality and makes choices based on a sense of omnireality, work has become spiritual for the people of the Age of Uncertainty. Every company today harbors people who view their jobs as their life's work—people for whom mind and body and spirit all come together at the moment they step into whatever function they fulfill in the corporate whole. You'll find them doing your Website or your most important law work. They're designing your molecules and analyzing your accounting systems. Undefined problems are for them the elixir of the workplace; unknown solutions occupy their waking and sleeping moments, whether they work on the assembly line or in logistics. If they knew the problem, they would stop being spiritual about it; if they knew the solution, the spirituality of work would disappear as well. Life, for them, is a journey through mystery, and the perpetual mystery is what gives life its meaning. The more they work, the deeper they delve into mystery, the more spiritual the work becomes. Such people are at the edge of what is really driving your business. They are your future. And yet as an executive, you have no way of evaluating their contribution. Thus, the most spiritual workers at the most vital edge of your business tend to make life spiritual for you, as well.

How do you tell the crackpots from the visionaries when there is sometimes not a dime's worth of difference between them? One way is to remember that the further out from the mean you get, the better and worse the ideas are going to be. Remember, George Lucas followed *Star Wars* with *Howard the Duck*. The first was the work of a visionary; the second the work of a crackpot; and both were the work of the same person. In the Age of Uncertainty, servicing the median isn't the point. The median is driven by the extremes. What creates value in the workplace is the capacity to function both at and between the extremes, and to be comfortable with both sides of the equation, with both ranges of possibility.

◆ Future Exercise

Write down the names of the three people in your department or company who are most valuable to short-term results. Do the same thing for the three people whom you consider most valuable to long-term results.

Next, score each person on the spiritual continuum, with one being the lowest score (least driven by spiritual needs in the workplace) and ten being the highest (most spiritual). Do the same thing on the crackpot continuum—with ten as the highest crackpot score.

Now, add up the spiritual score and the crackpot score for each group. Do the results tell you anything?

RITUAL				
HUNTER-GATHERER	**AGRICULTURE**	**CONSUMER**	**KNOWLEDGE**	**UNCERTAINTY**
Hunt	Seasons	Day	Access	?
Our reality: Singularity & Uniqueness				
Your reality: _____				

When a boy barely pubescent has his face painted with the blood of the first deer he has killed, he is taking part in a ritual of the hunt as old as the human experience. So is a gang member when he slices his finger and mixes his blood with that of his fellow gang members. Rituals connect us to what most matters in a society, and they permeate and change—but almost never die out—as societies change and one epoch yields to the next. The dance of the hunt becomes the dance of the seasons when crops matter more than slain mastodons. The stone cairn that might have marked a great killing field is replaced as a ritual site by a Stonehenge, which for all its eerie splendor is nothing more than a seasonal metric, a way of marking when to plant and harvest.

To meet the need of factories, the consumerists divided the day into parts and assigned to each part the functional roles of life— shaving in the morning, punching the clock when you entered and left the plant, eating when the time whistle said eat, going home when the time whistle said go home, recreating when the plant was closed on Sunday, vacationing when the factory shut down to clean the boilers—and thus the day itself became a ritual that celebrated the new mechanistic view of life.

As knowledge became ascendant, people began to use ritual not to celebrate the power of the gods but to celebrate instead their own access to the ritual sites and tokens of knowledge and quality. The "ta-da" of a computer was a tiny ritual of congratulations for gaining access to the World Wide Web. Celebrities celebrated their own ritual access by dancing and drugging the night away at clubs where bouncers held the hoi polloi at bay. The right college degree became treasured for its ability to open doors and launch graduates into the networks that would provide access to the jobs that could then be used to grant and deny access to others in an almost priestlike fashion.

And then suddenly knowledge was everywhere, access to it was universal, chains like Planet Hollywood promised to make every tourist Arnold Schwarzenegger's best friend, and everyone, it seemed, was connected to everyone else. As we became embraced in a culture of ubiquity, our rituals began to celebrate its opposite: singularity and uniqueness. The great moments of sports involved not teams but lone heroes beating seemingly unconquerable odds: Cal Ripken's 2,632 consecutive games played, Tiger Woods's winning the once lily-white Master's golf championship and doing so in his very first year as a pro. Popular nonfiction began to celebrate the lone adventurer doing battle against the elements: *The Perfect Storm, Into Thin Air*. Adventure travel—to the Galapagos

Islands, the rain forest, the Brooks mountain range of Alaska—extended the ritualism to our leisure life, and the rarer and the more difficult to get to and the more dangerous once you got there, the better. As Jon Krakauer shows so brilliantly in *Into Thin Air*, the upper reaches of Mount Everest, an area monstrously inhospitable to human life, became a virtual trash heap of used oxygen bottles and other abandoned survival gear.

Nothing perhaps better captures the spirit of ritual in an uncertain age than the personal Website. What else is it but a shrine to singularity? And nothing else also better illustrates the abiding paradox of this pursuit of the eternal unique because a Website has to be both eternally different every day in every way and eternally the same. Let it go stale, fail to renew your site on a continuous basis, and no one will come back, ever. Fail to keep it the same, and no one will know where they have come back to.

◆ Future Exercise

If you haven't yet done so, design your personal Website right now. What are you going to say about yourself? What elements, visual and text, can you include to make your site—and thus you—unique? What are you going to change about your Website on a continuing basis to refresh its uniqueness continuously, and what will stay the same about it, and thus about you as well?

STATUS SYMBOL				
HUNTER-GATHERER	AGRICULTURE	CONSUMER	KNOWLEDGE	UNCERTAINTY
Offspring	Land	Possessions	Awareness	?

Our reality: Events

Your reality: _____

Rarity always has status value, but rarity has the greatest status value when it is tied to the deepest aspirations and needs of a culture. Hunter-gatherers needed to build groups in order to survive; otherwise, they were at the mercy of animals far stronger than they and far better equipped individually for battle. Thus, the number of offspring—a measure of longevity and masculine vitality as well as the most practical and ready means of group building—conferred the greatest status. Agriculture changed that because agriculture required fertile, watered land first and foremost. Without land, even if you were strong as an ox and the sire of dozens, you were cut off from the means of sustenance. With land, you had status even if you were impotent and puny.

Consumerists converted status from the ownership of land to the ownership of the possessions that their factories began to turn out on a mass scale. "Whoever Has the Most Toys Wins," as the bumper sticker put it, but by the time the bumper stickers caught up with status, the cutting edge of the Knowledge Age had moved well beyond things and stuff. Everybody had things and stuff, and as Tom Wolfe's Sherman McCoy learned so painfully in *The Bonfire of the Vanities,* stuff and things were no protection. What conferred specialness in an age that worshipped knowledge was awareness, whether it was an awareness of the complexities of science, the manipulability of information, or the nooks and crannies and critical levers of cyberspace. But such status can last only as long as rarity underlies it, and when every third person is writing software codes or working in tech services, awareness is everywhere.

Instead, status has migrated yet again, this time to events, because special events and unique moments are where people who ritualize both specialness and uniqueness want to be. Tens of thousands of Americans saved the front page of their newspapers, or the whole sports section, on the morning after Mark McGwire hit his sixty-second home run even though they knew at any logical level that the very popularity of the moment diminished any future souvenir value their newspapers might harbor. People pack into Lollapalooza concerts, manufactured events in the realm of rock music, just as they packed into the Clintons' Renaissance weekends and their fourteen official inaugural balls in 1996—manufactured events in the realm of politics—even though they knew that any glance of the First Couple would be fleeting, if they appeared at all. Send the Rolling Stones out on tour these days, and you'll get an enthusiastic response from both the boomer and the retro crowd; send U2 out on tour and you might do marginally worse. But have the Stones appear with U2 at the base of the Great Pyramids on New Year's Eve as one millennium ticks into the next, and you've created an event attendance at which is instant proof of status at the highest level, even though the only true New Year's Eve celebration is the one held every year at Times Square in New York City and open to anyone who can crawl out of a bar and squeeze into the streets. A real event can't be manufactured out of whole cloth; it can only happen of its own critical mass. But only manufactured events can draw the media coverage necessary to make them defining events, and attendance at defining events is what confers the highest instant value. Thus, the absorption of paradox entails status, too.

◆ Future Exercise

Rank the following items one through seven (or one through whatever depending on how many "others" you add) based on their status value within your organization:

- ◆ Office space
- ◆ Office location
- ◆ Salary, wages, benefits, etc.
- ◆ Title
- ◆ Number of subordinates
- ◆ Attendance at the organization's defining events (board retreats, Future Council, etc.)
- ◆ Colleges and graduate schools attended
- ◆ Other: _____

_____

_____

Now do the same for your extended family. (For "Attendance at . . ." substitute "family." Examples would include funerals of patriarchs, weddings, reunions, etc.)

Adjust "your reality" accordingly.

DEFINING ACTIVITY

HUNTER-GATHERER	AGRICULTURE	CONSUMER	KNOWLEDGE	UNCERTAINTY
Hunting	Growing	Buying	Understanding	?

Our reality: Dreaming

Your reality: _____

Nothing defined life more readily for the first humans than hunting, whether it was for animals, wild fruits and vegetables, or the food of other humans. When your preoccupation is survival, you survive at any cost. Domesticated crops and animals slaked the hunger, and as they did, growing came to replace hunting and blood-letting. Animals were husbanded to produce the best genetic strains even though any specific knowledge of DNA was millions of years in the offing. In time, "husband" in the modern sense emerged as well. Monogamy was a social convenience, even a social necessity, among isolated people because in theory it bound them together for life, but monogamy also served human husbandry as well. You picked a mate for strength or beauty or durability or even spirituality, and you set about to produce a strain of like-qualitied humans who could help you work the farm or preach the gospel even as the union also carried your blood forward into the future.

Consumerists defined themselves by buying. Production created objects on a mass scale, and the ownership of objects became the measure of the person. A country's total production of objects (expressed either as gross national product or gross domestic product) became the measure of national worth, too. The Knowledge Epoch began the dematerialization of the consumer one. Things—*toys*—still mattered, but understanding mattered more. Intangibility came to outstrip tangibility in value; brain capital replaced physical capital as the ultimate measure of valuation. And then one day (if you can assign a defining event to a defining activity) Frank Gehry, the architect who designed the new Guggenheim museum in Bilbao, Spain, broke into tears as he explained that anything he could dream of, he could now build. And the truth is he was right, and dreaming itself had replaced understanding.

Being a slacker, it turned out, was okay, even cool. "Oh, he's just a dreamer, just pie in the sky" is no longer a put-down. Instead of sending dreamers to MBA programs to learn about ratiocination, the smartest companies have begun to put them on the Future Committee or in the Fool Box, with orders to dream the business's tomorrow because when you know neither the problem nor the solution, dreaming is not a bad place to begin. Advertising had been the defining business of the previous era; its job was to take the creative impulse and make it commercial, convert it to dollars and pounds sterling, marks and guilders. Dreamworks SKG has become the defining business of the Age of Uncertainty, and appropriately enough, since its capacity to produce a profit remains highly uncertain still. And dreaming has become the age's defining activity despite the fact that by all the normal measures dreaming is hardly an activity at all.

◆ Future Exercise

Put down this book, find a quiet place, close the door, and let yourself dream. What is the best thing you can imagine that could happen to your company? Your career? When you're through, open your eyes and write down the sequential steps that would be necessary for your dream to come true. Under what conditions might the first of those steps be achieved?

Then repeat the entire process for the worst possible scenario for your company and career. In the Age of Uncertainty, nightmares can come true as easily as dreams. Your job as a leader—of yourself or your company—is to be prepared for life at either extreme.

Our understanding of the importance of dreaming, by the way, leads us to believe that Steven Spielberg will be a totemic figure in the world that is emerging. Who will be the totemic figure created by your defining activity?

RECREATION				
HUNTER-GATHERER	**AGRICULTURE**	**CONSUMER**	**KNOWLEDGE**	**UNCERTAINTY**
Storytelling	Socializing	Belonging	Viewing	?

Our reality: Being

Your reality: _____

For 99.9 percent of human history, the evolution of recreation was defined by a steady coming together. Hunter-gatherers recreated—and still do in the primitive tribes of New Guinea and the Amazon rain forest—by storytelling, either by word or through petroglyphs. And, of course, we recreate still by the same means: The need to tell and hear stories is embedded in the human psyche. But as cultures complexified, recreation complexified with them. Agriculturists invented the concept of socializing as recreation: Barn dances, quilting bees, covered-dish suppers, even the more utilitarian barn raisings of the current-day Amish—all are a drawing together of people in a necessarily scattered community. As the industrial era pulled people into the cities, isolation was less a problem than the loneliness of the newly displaced. Trained to mechanistic solutions in their work lives, the consumerists created clubs and membership and initiation rites. Socializing wasn't enough. Belonging—to the Lions Club, the Elks, the Rotarians, the Klan, the YMCA and YWCA—became paramount. Along with "inventing" socialization, the agriculturists had invented play. The consumerists took play and wrapped it in rules—the Marquis of Queensberry rules for boxing, Abner Doubleday's rules for baseball, James Naismith's rules for basketball—and created recreation associations to enforce those rules.

Television, in a sense, changed that, but it wasn't just television. Passive viewing generally became the dominant form of recreation in the postwar years. Movie attendance continued to grow despite movies on TV; once VCRs were introduced, home viewing of movies soared, too. But nothing grew faster or established itself more firmly in the global pantheon of recreation than museum going: The Louvre, the Prado, the Metropolitan Museum of Art in New York had once been haunts of the effete or those on the Grand Tour; now they became totemic recreational moments. The House of Representatives during the 104th Congress made many mistakes under the leadership of Newt Gingrich, but none was greater than trying to close down government when crowds were clamoring to get into the Vermeer show at the National Gallery of Art. Recreation trumps politicization, and Dutch masters are mightier than the sword.

In the postindustrial, postinformation age, belonging and viewing have been replaced by being. The definition of who we are—European bicycle racer wannabe, NASCAR fan, cybersurfer, day trader, whatever fits our individual sense of reality—is the most important recreation we engage in. We can all discover the me we wish to be, we all can have our discovery reinforced by whatever media input we choose to expose ourselves to, and we can rediscover ourselves continuously, which is why the highest price tag in business soon will be the price tag of making "me" you—paying disparate people whose recreation is to occupy different realities to be in accord with the corporate whole. Stock options serve the purpose okay until the options are vested. Then, friend, what's the point?

◆ Future Exercise

On the left-hand side of your page, write down a product or service line that is critical to your business. On the right-hand side, list the five methods of recreation associated with each epoch, substituting your reality for ours where appropriate. Now, in the space between the two columns, jot down ways in which you might market your product or service line to each epoch.

When you're through, rate the methods 1 through 5 in terms of how close each comes to the way you are now marketing the product or service (even if it's only the product or service of yourself). Repeat this as often as you like for other products and services that are important to your business.

Finally, ask yourself if you are marketing the right product or service, and marketing it to the right epoch.

DOMINANT RESOURCE				
HUNTER-GATHERER	**AGRICULTURE**	**CONSUMER**	**KNOWLEDGE**	**UNCERTAINTY**
Territory	Fertilizer	Raw Material	Process	?

Our reality: Intellectual Property

Your reality: _____

Hunter-gatherers needed territory, and they needed animals and gatherable vegetative foodstuffs on those territories. Otherwise they starved, or moved on. Agriculturists needed fertilizer. With seed, they could plant a field and harvest for a season or two or even ten. But once the land played out, they starved also, or moved on. The Phoenicians may not have known hoot about crop rotation, but they knew where the guano was and how to get it to the farmers who knew about crop rotation, and thus Phoenicia, not the turn-of-history Farm Belt, was where economic power lay. Factories needed raw material; without it, they starved, too, and all the people in all the hierarchies that depended on the factory starved as well.

For the Knowledge Age, the dominant resource became process management. Industrialists knew how to make things, but they made them all in batches. The intellectualists streamlined that: Manufacturing created a product; the product was fed into a distribution channel; ancillary services—advertising, brand management, public relations, end-point sales—assured that the product controlled the market. The dominant resource wasn't the raw material that went into the product but the process that assured market domination.

Perhaps the ultimate expression of process management was the Vietnam War, a flawlessly conceived campaign that failed spectacularly. The U.S. military took the lessons of Vietnam to heart almost immediately. Two decades after the fall of Saigon, the rest of society seems to have caught on, too. Today, distribution channels have grown fuzzy; products are everywhere and everywhere duplicatable; the most successful companies seem to have dematerialized themselves the most; and the dominant resource is—sweet paradox—the intellectual property for which the Knowledge Epoch created such an appetite. Do you want to make computers or own the brains that make the computers run? Dell, for one, has voted for the latter, just as Ford is voting for owning the intellectual content of their cars, not manufacturing the mechanical brains or any other part.

The message hasn't been lost on divorce lawyers, either, or on their clients. When Wanda Clancy was going through an acrimonious divorce with her husband of twenty-eight years, novelist Tom Clancy, she didn't ask merely for an equal share of the family assets, even though those were substantial enough for Clancy to make a serious bid on the Minnesota Vikings football team. Ms. Clancy also demanded an equal share of the future income from her husband's intellectual property, most notably the one-time Naval Academy graduate and frequent world saver Jack Ryan. Given that Jack Ryan in print or cyberform or in the movie-person of actor Harrison Ford has a forecastable income of seven to eight figures annually for many years to come, Ms. Clancy made absolutely the right call, and she was in just the right position to make it. In an age devoted to dreams, theme parks, media, and the innate spirituality of things, the greatest value in intellectual property accrues not to the property with the most intellectual substance but to the property with the best story line, including the brand with the best story line, because brands finally are nothing but stories and the artifact of the promise contained within them.

◆ Future Exercise

Create three pie charts for your company across the page. (You can do the same thing for the company of yourself or for your family.) In all three pie charts, you are going to apportion the real value (not just the book value) of your enterprise among finished goods, intellectual property, process, raw materials, physical plant, and whatever else is appropriate to your reality, but each chart will represent a different time frame. In the left pie chart, do this as it would have appeared ten years ago. In the middle chart, do the same as it is today. In the chart on the right, project how this relative value might be apportioned ten years hence.

If intellectual property is not gaining an ever larger share of the pie as the charts progress, is our reality different from yours? Or is your enterprise living in a past epoch?

LEARNING				
HUNTER-GATHERER	AGRICULTURE	CONSUMER	KNOWLEDGE	UNCERTAINTY
Instincts	Cycles	Interactions	Scientific Method	?

Our reality: Probability

Your reality: _____

Hunter-gatherers survive on their instincts, and thus their biggest learning challenge is to hone those instincts and live by them. For farmers the difference between success and failure is learning the natural cycles: when to plant, when to reap, where and when to winter the cattle. In a mechanical world, success accrues to those who know how things work—the interactions between parts, the way one part meshes into another, the multiple system of causes and effects that results in a gasoline-powered engine running or a hydroelectric turbine spinning. Because scientific innovation relies on process, the Knowledge Epoch moved the scientific method to the center of the educational agenda. In the era of chaos what you need to learn is probability: how to evaluate the odds.

As much as it relies on trial and error, the scientific method also relies on absolutism: Change A on the x-axis has a 100 percent chance of producing Change B on the *y*-axis, or a 0 percent chance of producing Change C on the same axis. Chaos teaches differently. Instead of the certainty of cause and effect, you have the certainty of the failure of cause and effect. Why? Because embedded in any probability is the chance that the opposite is also true. Perhaps it's only a 10 percent chance; perhaps it's a 40 percent chance or a 70 percent chance. But the chance is there—nothing is certain but uncertainty—and unless you can evaluate that probability and absorb that paradox and do so immediately, you are no more ready to sit down at the business table than you are to take a chair at a Texas Hold 'Em table at Vegas. In both cases—poker deals and business deals—it's the risk of failure, not the certainty of outcome, that determines the potential for gain. If there were perfect certainty how every deal would come out, no one would have cause to sweat; but if no one had cause to sweat, guess what? No one would play. And so another paradox to ponder and try to fit into your own story line: In a chaos-driven world, it's only uncertainty that can produce the certainty of loss and gain.

◆ Future Exercise

Divide your paper into four columns, and number them 1 through 4, beginning at the left.

In column 1, take any deal you are now working on and list all the variables you can think of that might affect the outcome of that deal.

In column 2, write "100 percent" at the top of the page, and "0 percent" at the bottom. Then take all the variables you have listed on the left-hand side and arrange them in order of the probability that they will occur.

In column 3, take the variable you have decided is most likely to occur, and put it at the absolute top of the column, in the 100 percent slot. Now rearrange the probability of all the other variables to reflect the absolute certainty of this variable's coming true.

In column 4, take the variable you had judged least likely to occur in column 2 and make it your 100 percent factor. Again, rearrange all other variables accordingly.

Repeat this exercise with every variable you have listed in column 1, and you will be prepared to take control of your future, instead of your future taking control of you.

VISIONARY				
HUNTER-GATHERER	**AGRICULTURE**	**CONSUMER**	**KNOWLEDGE**	**UNCERTAINTY**
Shaman	Priest	Ideologue	Economist	?

Our reality: Futurist

Your reality: _____

The visionary who defines a macroculture has traveled the path from the shaman who read the bones to the priest who read the Bible to the ideologue who read the doctrine to the economist who read the numbers to the futurist who has to do all those things and do them over and over and over again because, unlike the shaman or the priest or the ideologue or the economist, the futurist can never allow him- or herself to think that he or she has got the story right.

One more thought on the matrix we have just parsed: The whole history of humankind has been a layering on of experience in the search for better ways to accomplish always changing ends, a piling up of information in the service of decisions about always shifting problems, and a constant and relentless learning process that always culminates in the extinction of the macroculture that has done the learning.

Hunter-gatherers made themselves extinct by learning to plant seed and domesticate animals. Hello, farmers. Good-bye, club-wielders. Agriculturists became so adept at making tools that they were able to create the factories that would satisfy the consumerists' demand for the ownership of things. Consumerists gave us mechanical causality, which laid the foundation for the scientific method, whose faith in absolute principles helped us discover the fundamental instability of the universe and introduced us to uncertainty and the chaos that underlies it. Nothing today works the way it should: not career, not space, not time, not procreation, not anything. Everything contains its opposite potential.

Just as earlier macrocultures learned to stalk and kill and plant, so we are having to learn today to manage the paradox of our personal and professional lives, and just as those who learned to stalk and kill best and plant in the most fertile soil prospered the most, so those—the individual "those" and the corporate "those"—who are learning to manage paradox the best are beginning to prosper best in our own time. And just as all those macrocultures learned their way out of existence, so ours will, too, just at the point when we have finally reformed the social, political, religious, relational, economic, and structural elements of our culture to deal in perfect harmony with the uncertainty that surrounds us. That's paradox, but that's life, too.

INTELLIGENCE				
HUNTER-GATHERER	AGRICULTURE	CONSUMER	KNOWLEDGE	UNCERTAINTY
Language	Literacy	Education	Creativity	?

Our reality: Intuition

Your reality: _____

Hunter-gatherers invented the concept of tool; they had the first primitive understandings of family and shelter. But for them, language was the great intellectual accomplishment—they began talking, and no one has stopped since. In the Agricultural Epoch, language gained abstract representation in the form of symbols that eventually became codified as letters and numbers. Now language wasn't enough. To succeed, you had to be literate. You had to know the code so you could count and name things. The Consumer Epoch added education to literacy. To participate in the consumer society, you had to be educated to the concept of value-relative work and to the concept of moral choice. As education became democratized, a new concept rose up: Einsteins, it turned out, were randomly distributed, not systematically created by an aristocratic genetic transfer. Individuals had self-worth because everybody in society had the potential ability to invent something worth knowing by somebody else. Thus, creativity came to supplant mere education as the highest expression of intelligence: It wasn't just the number and quality of degrees you held; it was the suppleness with which you played with what you had learned.

Today, creativity still counts, in critical ways more than ever. Unless we want to live by and in someone else's story, we all must become the authors of our own individual futures. To write that story, we need to gather our own trends, identify where we want to go, establish the path we are on, and figure out what course corrections are required and what it will mean if we arrive at the destination we've set out for. What is that but the work of a novelist or a scriptwriter? But here's the difference: We need to do all the work we've just cited constantly and on the fly. Rather than plotting our way, we need to trust our capacity to intuitively resolve the contradictions among a large number of forces and trends and variables, all of which affect the vector along which we are journeying through our years. And thus it is not just creativity but the intuitive capacity to integrate that spells the real difference between each of us and anybody else.

As your own visionary, you will soon learn that this intuitive approach to understanding does not always win friends. Intuition is largely nonliterate. It resists telling and it resists reason, and because it resists both, futurists often have difficulty defending their rationale. So intuitive have some people become that the left side of their brain can tell a joke that the right side has never heard. Oddballs and crackpots proliferate along the margins of the intuitive mind.

Your comfort will be that you are in good company. George Orwell's *1984*, Anthony Burgess's *A Clockwork Orange*, and George Lucas's *Star Wars* movies were not just works of creative genius; they were also intuitive guesses about what the future would become. Each looked at the trend lines of his time. Each accepted the inevitability of being human, integrated his experience, and made a subjective forecast that could never be validated until it was too late to know.

One more comfort, too: While intuition has grown as the means by which decision models are silently resolved, the sciences themselves have become equally obscure and unexplainable: the physics of subquarkian particles, the cosmology of the big bang, and theoretical mathematics that require no reference to objective reality have proliferated. We would argue that this decoupling of human intelligence from the quantifiable rigors of reason has liberated science to go where no mind has ever gone before.

The more we know, the less we rely on empirical knowledge.

◆ Future Exercise

Imagine yourself as a driver approaching a traffic circle at twenty-five miles an hour. To your left another car is about to enter the same intersection at the same speed. Your best estimate is that you are both twenty yards from the traffic circle and will be arriving at your respective entrances to the circle at exactly the same moment. And both you and the other driver know that for most people in most of the world, the phrase "right of way" really means "right to dominate."

List below all the intuitive judgments you and the other driver will be required to make in the next few seconds. (And while you're doing that, marvel that 99.9999-plus percent of the time all those intuitive judgments are correct ones.)

Now take any recent hour from your office calendar, and list all the intuitive judgments you were required to make within that time frame.

◆ Third-Term Exam

In this exam, you'll be creating a chart like the large one we've explicated in this section, but you are to ignore our microissues and macrocultures. The left-hand margin of your chart should consist of the independent variables that cause the greatest change in your world. The right-hand variables are the things being changed whether the change is desirable or not. Call the left-hand variables "indicators" and the right-hand variables "consequences." You'll probably want to turn your pad sideways because you will need plenty of space between the two columns.

Go ahead and fill in the left-hand margin now. For example, if you are a steel distributor, we would guess that the independent variables causing change in your world would have to include transformations in the weight-to-size ratio of nearly everything, the distances over which finished goods travel and the supply-chain economics in between, the difficulty of finding enthusiastic staff, and probably tremendous changes in the nature of metallurgy itself—changes that have introduced the concept of obsolescence into something that was once poured to last forever.

Once you've got your indicators listed, go to the top of the chart and arbitrarily break your industry or company—or life if you want to make this chart even more personal—into four epochs that will divide the space between "Indicators" and "Consequences." (You might want to use the four epochs and dozen microissues you had jotted down early in this section, if they still seem valid.)

Next, determine the total time span covered by these four epochs and write that at the very top of the chart. (Our advice is to make the time span as long as the history of your industry, or company, or life.) Note that the consequences you'll be dealing with in the right-hand margin should project as far forward as your industry/company/life projects backwards. Your job as leader is not just to execute the tasks of today but to predict the tasks that will matter in the near term and long term, but if you are in an industry that began only relatively speaking yesterday (e-commerce, for example), you'll be able to predict consequences only through, relatively speaking, tomorrow.

By now, you should have a chart that looks more or less like this:

[time span = x years]   [time span = x years]
          Epoch 1   Epoch 2   Epoch 3   Epoch 4

Indicators   Consequences
    A.   A.
    B.   B.
    C.   C.
    etc.   etc.

Fill in the chart, showing how each independent variable, or indicator, has morphed over whatever time horizon you have chosen. To return to steel for our example (and with no real knowledge of the subject), let's say that when it comes to processing, you have the epoch of the ceramic oven, the Bessemer oven, the conglomerated factory, and the micro-steel processing plant.

Now, go to consequences and ask yourself one simple question for each microissue: What next? Once you've done that for each microissue, you'll have maybe a dozen trend lines all pointing into the future. Your job now is to intuit their convergence. Study their overlaps. Look at the speed and magnitude. And then go ahead and make a single bold guess about the future.

To go back to steel one last time as an example, we can see now how the absorption of a giant, complex technology led to the offshoring of production in the 1960s. We've pored over the capital value of the industry in the 1970s and followed the technological road map that led to the tremendous growth in the 1980s, which became stalled by the diffused availability of that technology in the 1990s, coupled with the globalization of distribution. Would we build a steel mill next week? No. Would we build a Website that gathered surplus metal from throughout the four corners of the world and emphasized transportation? Probably, yes. But that's steel, and that's our reality interpreting steel's reality. Your reality might arrive at a single bold guess that's entirely different.

This is a thought process, in short. If you are prepared to think hard, you can do this. And having done it once, you'll need to come back and do it again every six, eight, or ten months, or whenever the rhythms in your industry or company or life change. Your conclusion won't have changed because you have changed: You're the constant. The conclusion will have changed because what you are looking at has changed. In that regard, serial futuring is just like watching a child grow up.

Last of all, name your right-hand column: the Age of _____.

IV

THE PARADOX OF REALITY

Your reality is ours alone.

If you are sitting on a commuter flight reading this book, or reading it in the evening propped up on your bed, or in a lounge chair on a deck overlooking the ocean, take heart. Three billion people in the world today—half of all living humans—aspire to your momentary reality, to the lifestyle you are leading at this very second in time. But each of those three billion people interpret your reality differently, by the lights of their own separate experience. And therein lies the paradox of reality: There is none, at least collectively. Every person on the planet Earth today has the potential to be connected to every other person, and every single one of us inhabits a world of our own and is a marketing segment of absolutely one.

We've talked throughout this book about what that means in terms of your life, of your own reality: the need to tap into the global metaphors to which all those separate worlds respond in like kind, the need to atomize your organization so that it reflects in its bones the atomized world you must operate in, the need to go to where those separate worlds are instead of expecting them to come en masse to you, the need to be constant in the things that matter and inconstant in the things that don't. You can't change a product from market to market. Do that and you'll be selling nothing but a blur. Instead, you have to keep your product the same in every market and let it constantly redefine its meaning so that it becomes a different product in different markets while always being one product in all of them.

A Zip Drive allows multimedia people to store multimedia images and reproduce them quickly. That is its meaning in that market, for that person. For a mom it's something else again entirely: A Zip Drive is a way to keep games stored for—and sometimes from—the kids. For a photographer, it's yet another product: a safe for protecting a library of photos. Mention "Zip Drive" to any of those three people, and they'll know exactly what you mean. They should even be able to provide a reasonably accurate drawing of the product, and the drawings should look more or less the same. But the product they have described will be a separate and distinct item to each of them.

That's part of doing business in an irrational world. Another part is that you have to be prepared to accept that your deepest and most closely held conviction—even the one we just cited—will turn out to be wrong in the end, or at least no more right than its opposite. The reality of a reality-less world is that two precisely incompatible outcomes can and do exist simultaneously, and that each is true and each is false in equal measure. One of the things that means is that the more dearly you value something because it has never proved untrue in life, the more you are setting yourself up to discover that its opposite is also true and possible.

The world of reason that we lived in not long ago liked to talk about polls and standardized tests as having a "margin of error" of plus or minus X percent, as if there were one right answer and anything that didn't conform to that linear line of truth was wrong. Today, in order to survive and thrive in our business, professional, and personal lives, we have to live at precisely the opposite point: We have to make both edges of those "margins of error" our drivers because only by becoming both can we move inside them and absorb the fundamental paradox this irrational world presents us with.

* * *

To achieve a satisfactory future today we also have to be able to imagine it. That's why we contend that the dominant person of our society is becoming the storyteller. It's our reality, after all, and our own individual future that we're talking about, not anyone else's. And once we do imagine that future, once we declare a major in our ambition, we have to be prepared to so comport and alter our own reality that it comes into alignment with the future reality we have chosen for our self.

What does that mean? Let's say your ambition today is to become a CEO in five years. What will you need? Well, general management experience, certainly. If that is not yet part of your reality, you will have to make it so, and in short order. You cannot be ignorant of general accounting principles, either, and you'll have to make your media universe synchronous with your future. You may love *People* magazine, but once you've declared yourself as a CEO major, *People* is part of the wrong reality. Put it down. Pick up *Business Week.* That's the reality you need to embrace. You've got to begin now to walk the walk and talk the talk.

You'll also need to eliminate those things not involved with your ambition. You want to be a CEO before the decade is out? Fine. But realize that you've eliminated the possibility of being a minister or of making husbandhood or father- or motherhood your number one ambition. Yes, you can still be good at parenting or good at spousing, but you can't be great, and if you are not yet married, it is your utter obligation to tell the person with whom you fall in love that he or she will always be number two in your life. And you'll need to learn to live simultaneously in two worlds.

Many years ago, we saw an experimental movie built around the French adage that, in order to change, a thing must both be itself and not itself at once. To illustrate this phenomenon, the director showed the evolution of Spencer Tracy's face as seen in mirrors in film after film over many years' duration. (Tracy's reflected image, it turned out, was a staple of his career.) What you saw on-screen was the face growing older, but what you knew was that Tracy himself couldn't see this.

So it is with all of us. The continuous nature of daily existence blinds us to the small changes that are guiding us, yet it's the accumulation of those small changes that causes the big changes that mark our years, aging among them. Only when you freeze frames and look hard at yourself can you decide which things you must learn in order to thrive, which you must forsake in order to feel good, and which you must control in order to accommodate disaster. Yet to do so opens you to the mental anguish that inevitably arises from the inherent contradiction of being something and liking it even as you are becoming something else with no promise of advantage.

To achieve a satisfactory future, you also need to decide what you believe, on the big questions as well as the small ones. Do you believe in God or don't you? Do you believe in democracy? Do you believe in the inevitable triumph of the human will? Do you believe in the ultimate victory of good over evil? The answers you arrive at are less important than that you stop dithering around with the questions, because for corporations to succeed in a world of splintered and infinite realities, they must have a shared belief system, and that shared belief must begin at the top. That's you—or at least it's the you that you want to be.

There's a second reason to decide what you believe in, a more personal one: The only way to really succeed in life, whatever ambition you set for yourself, is to have other people around you who are interested in your success, and the people who are most interested in your success are always those who share the same beliefs you do. With kids, the connection is easy to see. To a high degree, they turn out to be as adults what their parents, close relations, siblings, and friends had advocated for them in their youth. But as with kids, so with all of us. Surround yourself with people who do not believe that you can become what you wish to become, and it's highly unlikely that you will get there.

You'll have to deal with the small questions, too. Do you believe in teamwork? Or are you uncomfortable working with others? If your present reality is that you work best as a lone wolf, you'll have to change that if you hope to be a CEO, or you'll have to change your ambition. The choice is up to you, but you can't be both.

Two other things you have to do to bring your reality into synchronicity with your ambition: You have to tell yourself the story of what you are going to be and retell it again and again until you believe it absolutely and until there's not a thread of inauthenticity left in what you aspire to. Only by doing so can you blend the future and present tenses together and make yourself live in the pressure tense and be completely comfortable with living there. And you can't be afraid to fail along the way.

Bill Clinton knew he was going to be President of the United States long before the rest of us did, because even when he was growing up in Nowhere, Arkansas, with an alcoholic mother, he was able to imagine himself as captain of the Free World. Steven Spielberg could have been many things, but he knew he was going to be a great moviemaker almost before he knew anything else about himself, and he told himself that story time and again, very silently, just as great stories about the future should be told. Madonna imagined herself as a famous femme fatale, and by doing so, and doing so consistently over many years, she made herself come true, just as Richard Holbrooke imagined himself as a diplomat and John Elway saw himself from grade school forward as a great quarterback and Jasper Johns was a great painter—*never* a starving artist—from the moment he picked up a brush. And because they all knew what they wanted to be, because they could imagine themselves so clearly in the future and thus make their futures live in their present, they all also rearranged their realities to fit where they wanted to go. Failure was never failure for them; it was just another step on the road to success.

Ron Howard has no business being successful today. Howard was a phenomenal hit as a child star—Opie, on the old *Andy Griffith Show*—and almost by definition phenomenally successful child stars fail on the larger stage of life. Why, then, is Ronnie Howard so highly regarded today? Because he wanted to make great pictures from the time he first started acting in great television shows and because he consciously created a reality that served that end: by being a nice guy, by avoiding the pitfalls of early fame, by getting close to people who could help him, and by doing everything he could to master what he knew he would become. Macaulay Culkin spent his adolescent years arguing with his parents and becoming a caricature of the aging child star; Howard spent his adolescence learning how to write a script and manipulate lights. Both have created their own reality, but only one of them, we would bet, wants the reality he has.

And a final thing: Be patient, for fame and for fortune. Accept the paradox of recognition: that you're less likely to get recognized for what you do deserve than for what you don't. And trust to the gods for ultimate right. The world today is so heavily mediated that if you are good—*really* good—at what you do, you *will* become famous for it. And if you become famous for it, you're likely to become rich as well. But to pursue the fame and fortune first is inauthentic by its very nature.

What else can you do to prosper today? At the very start of this book, we mentioned four rules. In closing, let us pose them as questions and accompany each question with a last future exercise to send you on your way. As always, we encourage you to answer each of our questions and perform each of our exercises as truthfully as you can and in as much detail as you feel necessary. When we do this exercise with companies, we find that on average it takes about two years to work through all the layers of misunderstandings and deception that any organization indulges in when it faces the future. We also find that when companies do this work well, they end up with a five-hundred-year plan for their own futures. Here's to a great five hundred years for you as well.

♦ *Do you know who you are?* The first oracle of Delphi is the same as the first rule in Sun-tzu's *Art of War:* Know thyself. What are the absolutely unchangeable issues of you that will always be sacrosanct and never discussed as negotiable? Identifying them can be truly hard work, but they are your bedrock and your anchor, and the more you know about them, the more you know yourself. Charles Lindbergh didn't make it across the Atlantic because it sounded like a neat thing to do. He did it because he knew who he was. Because he knew who he was, he knew what he could do. And because he knew who he was and what he could do, he wrote his own myth and defined himself for the future of aviation. Think back to that early exercise you did, way back in Part I (page 12), where we asked you to calculate your own mythic truths. This is what it was about: knowing yourself, not just the factual truths but the truths born of your belief system—ground zero of your character.

An aside: When we did CEO polling for PBS's *Nightly Business Report*, we found that when times get tough, top executives instinctively spend their time and energy in the discipline from which they came. They go back, in short, to who they are, and so do we all when we want to move ahead.

◆ Future Exercise

Think of your life at this moment in time as a job. Moreover, think of it as a job you want, and think of yourself as a candidate for that job. Now, write a résumé that would justify hiring you to do it. Don't leave anything out: race, nationality, sex, place of birth, education—every single item that makes you the ideal candidate to assume the job of your life right now, including what you believe in, what the people you associate with believe in, and what constitutes the media universe in which you live.

◆ *Do you know where you want to go?* This is the strategic planning question—the tipping point between present and future. Great companies and great executives honor their past and always know who they are at their heart's core: Coke has never forgotten that it started by selling patent medicine; the Marriotts have never forgotten that three generations back they were running a root-beer stand in downtown Washington, D.C. But great companies and great executives also know where they want to go next, and they take their people with them. Ninety-nine out of a hundred times, employees in such companies make the right decisions because they know the direction those decisions need to take them in. That leaves senior management free to become the promise police.

Great companies and great executives know that the only way to get from here to there, from the present to the future, is to be true to the values that have sustained them in the past. Beliefs are the eye of the hurricane, in our corporate life as in our personal ones. Everything else will and must change: Marriott is not only out of the root-beer stand business; it's not in the same business it was in less than two decades ago. But it's the same company nonetheless because it still pays homage to the same values. Thus it is with your own business or career. If either is to survive the torrents of change, your core belief system has to remain the same.

◆ Future Exercise

Write the résumé of the person you want to be in X number of years, and be sure to make X an exact number. (You might want to borrow one of the answers you gave for the second "Future Exercise" in Part II, chapter 5, "The Paradox of Action," but only if your future is still the same as it was back then.) Again, be exact and exhaustive. Race, nationality, and place of birth you can do nothing about, and sex isn't so easy either, but don't stop there. What talents large and small should you include on the résumé? What new beliefs would it be prudent to hold? What new ones will it be essential to embrace? And are they compatible with the core beliefs that must sustain you? How about media? What should you be reading? And what about associates? What should they be believing, and what do they need to believe about you?

Once you've characterized the you that you wish to be demographically and spiritually, by education, by associations, and by the media that you will need to attend to, pick up this résumé and compare it item for item with the one you wrote just a few pages back. In the space between the two lies the path to the invention of your future self.

And once you've done that, take a different-colored pen or a Hi-Liter and mark all the similarities between the person who applied for the job of your life as it is today and the one who is applying for the job of your life as it will be X number of years from now. These should reflect your core beliefs. If they don't, start over again.

◆ *Do you recognize your seminal moments?* And do you look beyond your own discipline to find them? First, an example of an institution that missed its seminal moment: When Elton John played his tribute to Princess Di at her funeral in Westminster Abbey, it was both the first time that an openly gay man performed rock 'n' roll at a royal English funeral and a watershed moment in the demythologizing of the monarchy itself. Hey, they're just like us! At that moment, the British crown had the chance to begin writing the story of its own future. Instead, Queen Elizabeth asked that the doors of the Abbey be closed, and thus she assured that her future and that of her bloodline would be written by others. Seminal moments can't be shut out, even by royalty.

A second example, this time of a seminal moment that was caught and used: When the Boeing 777 became the first modern aircraft built without a prototype, it was a seminal moment not just for the aircraft industry but for architecture and design generally. Frank Gehry, the architect of the new Guggenheim Museum in Bilbao, Spain, recognized the Boeing moment for precisely that. Like the new Boeing jet, his museum design was based on a scale model that was scanned into a computer. The computer itself did the final drawings, and the design has made Gehry famous.

There are seminal moments, in short, that can be plotted— ones that are deeply personal to individual ambition and ones that have to happen for you or your business to get where it wants to go. For an actress such a moment might be her first part; for a business it might be the first $-illion year. (Million, billion—the number matters less than the moment.) There are also seminal moments that will simply catch you by surprise; genius is knowing when they have. And there are seminal moments in history when everything gets turned upside down. Copernicus's discovery of the basic motion of the universe, the invention of the United States Constitution, the delivery of the Ten Commandments, the splitting of the atom, the creation of the Internet—every one of them gave mankind a choice: to go on with life the way it was or to find a new way of living in the world, and how each person chose has made all the difference. Make your own list of the seminal moments of history (it's a great parlor game), but remember that genius doesn't lie in being able to parse history for its turning points. True genius lies in recognizing your own seminal moments, the ones that bring good as well as the ones that bode ill.

One other caution: Just as we advised you earlier to be patient with fame and fortune, so we advise you here to be patient with the moments you think you can plot. If you don't make first vice president or first violin on Day X in Year Y, it doesn't mean you won't get there. Give it another two years. The future has a lousy sense of time.

◆ Future Exercise

List the seven seminal moments that have gotten you where you are. Now study the résumé you wrote for your future in the last exercise, and list the seven seminal moments that need to happen for your future to come true. Next, create a time line between now and whatever date you have set for your future ambition, and place each of the seven seminal moments on the continuum between Point A and Point B. Finally, write three notes in the margin: "All dates plus or minus two years." "What unexpected moments have occurred since I last consulted this time line that are sufficiently impor- tant to change the trajectory of where I want to go?" And "Has anything of such historical significance happened since I last consulted this time line that the future that was my ambition is no longer viable?" Now your future has a Day Planner.

◆ *Do you have the attitude of an insurgent?* You need to con- stantly rail against the established order of how you do the things you do. Fail to see yourself as a radical in whatever domain you aspire to, and you'll be just another player, which is fine if that is what your ambition for the future happens to be. If it's not, if you want to aim high, you have to aim high all the time. You have to be big or go home, and you have to defend your interests and defend them anew every time they change (and they will, they will). Allow others to set your agenda, and they'll set your future as well, and make you a bit player in it.

An attitude of insurgency means that you invent new doctrines, you coin new tactics. Differences make life interesting, not similarities. Differences create unique personalities that crawl out from the pack. But being different also means that you have to be willing to fail, willing to be an outcast, willing to put an idea in front of the world that the world won't buy and being all right with that because you know in your heart that the idea is honest to your own reality through and through. That, too, is part of the authenticity we've been talking about. The world wants you to live in the present, not the future. If you want to be well loved, you will let it do just that to you. If that isn't enough for you, though, read *The Loneliness of the Long Distance Runner*.

"There are always two parties," Ralph Waldo Emerson wrote, "the party of the Past and the party of the Future, the Establishment and the Movement." The choice is yours: past or future, the establishment or the movement. But if it's movement you want, if it's the future you want to live and thrive in, you'll need an insurgent's attitude to get there.

◆ Future Exercise

Brand the self you wish to be, or the company you wish to become. If you've stayed with us thus far, you've decided what you are. You've decided where you want to go. You've plotted the moments that will get you there. In the Future Exercise at the end of Part II, chapter 1, "The Paradox of Value," you even spot-priced yourself. (You might turn back and look at that exercise before you go on.) Now we're asking you to decide what you have to be that's different and unique—not so different and unique that you will simply be a freak, but so different and unique that you may stand a chance of having the world beat a path to your door.

◆ My business is _____.

◆ My meaningfulness is _____.

◆ My brand is _____.

Last, and very important, answer the following: In order to bring my business, my meaningfulness, and my brand into alignment and invest each with value, I will need to seize the following initiative(s):

_____

_____

_____

Good intentions are noble, but good actions are what count in the end.

===

Let us leave you now with a last exercise to perform. If you think you've done well to this point, feel free to skip it. No one's watching; no one's grading; and even if someone was, you're the sole custodian of this permanent record.

As for ourselves, it's time for us to heed our own advice. We've consulted our Future Committee, we've sat in the Fool Box, and truth told, we think we have the future just about right, which means that it's time for us to tear our assumptions apart and start all over again. We've loved writing this book. It represents everything we've learned to date from our collective half century in business. And we hope that when the dust settles, we'll be right once more. For now, thanks for coming along. We'll see you in our next book. And good luck.

◆ Final Exam

Ungraded, untimed, and if you do it right, seriously hard

Your final exam is to write yourself a letter telling yourself who you are and what you are becoming. You can do this as a literary exercise if you want to do, but you can also do it as a list. To take the latter approach, divide your paper in two, and create four categories for the left-hand column: _I am a_ . . . ; _I am going to_ . . . ; _My seminal moments are_ . . . ; and _I have an attitude of_. . . . At the beginning Part I, we asked you to answer these same questions in no more than sixty seconds each. You can take out those sheets now and have a look. But the clock's off: Use all the time you need.

To get you started on this deeper search into the reality of your future, we're going to give you a model below, an amalgam of our own realities.

By now, you know not to get trapped in us. Use this simply to jar your own thinking.

I am a:

◆ father
◆ husband
◆ senior executive
◆ casually religious person
◆ happy guy
◆ modestly wealthy person
◆ interesting person
◆ writer

I am going to:

◆ retire soon to Santa Fe
◆ consult
◆ write a column
◆ teach
◆ collaborate
◆ consult
◆ be a grandfather
◆ wear no suits forever

My seminal moments are:

◆ a great ad campaign
◆ a great quarter
◆ a win on the stock market
◆ my anniversary
◆ my daughter's wedding
◆ acceptance of this book

I have an attitude of:

◆ an aggressor
◆ a trainer
◆ a drover
◆ a time Nazi
◆ a reactionary

When you're through, go to the upper right-hand column and write: *I will be*. Again, we'll fill out the column, at least partially, from our collective reality.

I will be:

♦ without colleagues
♦ happy
♦ cultured
♦ religious
♦ healthy within my capacity to control it

That's our reality. Now find a relaxing spot, take a deep breath, and create your own. Note also that we've introduced two new sections in the right-hand column that only you can begin to answer: "My internal conflicts are" and "I will need to do."

In the first, you'll have to resolve the inconsistencies in all the items you have included to date. If you have said that you are going to "win an Academy Award" and later have written that you have an attitude of "self-reliance," you have a conflict that needs dealing with. To win an Oscar, you must kowtow to the motion picture industry, and such is the level of obeisance required that you no longer can call yourself self-reliant. Similarly, as we've pointed out before, you cannot be both a primary care giver to your family and CEO of your company. The two simply don't compute, and life is choice.

In the second section, "I will need to," ask yourself and answer these questions: Which of the items under "I will be" do you know how to do? Which can you now do? Which do you need help in learning or implementing? Which require someone else? Does that someone else exist? What initiatives will you need to take? Do you have the strength for this? The desire? The burn in the gut?

Okay? Here's the template again:

I am a: _____   I will be: _____

_____   _____

_____   _____

_____   _____

_____   _____

I am going to: _____   My internal conflicts are: _____
_____   _____
_____   _____
_____   _____
_____   _____

My seminal moments are: _____   I will need to: _____
_____   _____
_____   _____
_____   _____
_____   _____

I have an attitude of: _____
_____
_____
_____
_____

Finally, a question in the pressure tense—the future expressed in the present time. You get no more than three words to answer.

I am a:

Remember: The more prepared you are not to get there, the more likely the success of your journey will be. That, too, is paradox.

Index

ABC, 45
Abilene Project, 190–91
Access, 208
Accidental value, 69
Accounting profession, 106–107
Action, paradox of, 115–33
    academia and, 130
    activity traps and, 127–28
    colliding opposites and, 118
    comfort zones and, 128–29
    compartmentalizing and, 129
    farthest horizon and, 125–27
    Fool Box and, 129–31
    future exercises and, 132–33
    goals and, 116–17
    golf analogy, 115–16
    mistakes and, 126–27
    outsourcing and, 129–30
    Scenario Plan game and, 118–25
Activity traps, 127–28
Adaptation, 69
Advanced Research Projects Agency,
    11
Advertising, 213
Age of Possibility, 3–4
Age of uncertainty, 182–83
    microissues and, see Microissues
Agriculture epoch, 182
    microissues and, see Microissues
AirTran, 52–53, 76–77
Alcoholics Anonymous, 117
Ali, Muhammad, 61–62, 64
Allocation of resources, 30
Altering the future, 15–17
Amazon.com, 52, 67–68
Ambition, 231, 232–33
American Airlines, 160
Anecdotes, 147
Animal Planet Channel, 102

Anticipatory feedback, 85
AOL, 117
Apple computer, 86
Arafat, Yasser, 20
Archimedes, 187
Arizona Diamondbacks, 141
Arms race, 105
Arnaz, Desi, 45–46
Arthur Andersen & Company, 81,
    130
Ascension, 198
Atlanta Braves, 140
Atlanta Falcons, 106
AT&T, 20, 93, 117
Attention bandwidth exercise, 24
Automatic teller machines (ATMs),
    12
Avis, 161
Axioms, 34–35

Ball, Lucille, 46
BankAmerica, 99
Bank of Credit and Commerce
    International (BCCI), 74
Barnard, Chester, 32–33
Barnes & Noble, 52, 67–68, 168
Baseball, 117, 141, 143–44
Being, 215
Belief system, 30, 232
Beloit College, 20–21
Belonging, 214
Berkshire Hathaway, 147
Big companies, 64–70
Bin Laden, Osama, 140
Blair, Tony, 135, 137
Boeing, 11, 237
Book clubs, 168–69
Borden, 83
Borders, 168

"Brand equity," 101
Brand promise, 57–59, 111–12
Bristol-Meyers Squibb, 150
British Airways, 113, 129
British Petroleum (BP), 82–83
Brown, John, 82–83
Brown, Tina, 138
Brown Brothers Harriman & Co., 163–65
Bryant, Kobe, 170
Buffet, Jimmy, 14
Buffett, Warren, 138, 147, 201
Burgess, Anthony, 222–23
Burke, James E., 71
Business Week, 148
Buying, 212

Cable TV, 77–78, 102–104
Cadillac, 86
Campbell, William, 149
Capital markets, 64–65
  competition and, 99
Captain Morgan's Rum, 55
Carlucci, Frank, 143
Carroll, Lewis, vii
CBS, 45–46
Celebration, Florida, 196
Celebrity, 201–202
Change, 175–76
Channel competition, 99–100
Chaos, 218–19
  collisions with, 7–9
  denial of, 10
Chevron, 161
Chicago Bulls, 201
Chicken McNugget organizational model, 65–66
Chief executive officers (CEOs), 82, 235
  living inside the story, 146
Chiefs, 200
Children and leisure, 169–71
China, 27
Chopra, Deepak, 25
CIA, 130
Cisco Systems, 20
Citibank, 28
Clancy, Tom, 217
Clancy, Wanda, 217
Clepsydra, 90
Clinton, Bill, 74, 84, 135, 137, 138, 233
Clinton, Hillary Rodham, 137

Cloning, 199
Coca-Cola, 18, 54, 57, 113, 114, 146, 235
  insurgency and, 69–70
  spot pricing of, 42–44
Cold war, 105
Collision of opposites, 61–64, 118
Collisions with chaos, 7–9
Comfort zones, 128–29
Common cost tax basis, 129–30
Compartmentalization, 129
Competition, paradox of, 97–114
  cable TV example, 102–104
  capital and, 99
  channel competition, 99–100
  consciousness share and, 100–101
  definition of competition, 101
  employees and, 101
  excess choice and, 111–12
  external, lateral model and, 105–108
  future exercise, 112
  global metaphors and global brands, 113–14
  internal, vertical model and, 105–107
  lateral competition, 98
  market attention and, 99
  measuring yourself and, 105–106
  past, present, and future and, 97–99
  performance category and, 99
  symbiotic relationships and, 109–12
Complex emergencies, 64, 73–76
Complexity, 187–88
Computer hard-drive exercise, 21–22
Computer speed, 187, 188
Connectivity, 18, 62, 92, 107
Consciousness share, 100–101
Consumer Age, 182
  microissues and, *see* Microissues
Consumer Reports, 49, 50
Contextual Price Discrepancy Threshold, 44
Contradiction, 17–18, 135–38
Corning, 83–84
Corporate campuses, 130
Corporate culture and leisure, 157–67
Corporate injustice, 62–63
Corporate mission:
  leisure and, 163–67
  statement of, 79–80

"Correctness," 141
Coulter, Dave, 98–99
Crackpot dreams, 125–26, 206–207
Creativity, 222
Crips, 193
Cronkite, Walter, 102
Culkin, Macaulay, 233–34
Custer, General George Armstrong, 73
Customer involvement, 51–52
Cyber-piracy, 14
Cyber-publishing, 13–14
Czech Republic, 7

Daiwa Securities, 76
Day rituals, 208
De Beers, 78
Decentralization, 63
Deep ties, 83
Defining activity microissue, 184, 212–14
Dell computers, 51, 217
Delta Airlines, 129
Democrats, 105–106
Denial of reality, 23–26
Denver Broncos, 106
Desilu, 46
Destabilizing the present, 13
Detectives, 178
Detroit, Michigan, 196
Diamond cartel, 78
Diana, Princess, 237
Diebold, John, 12
Differences, 239
Direct TV, 78
Discovery Channel, 102–104
Discovery Communcations, 102–103, 104
Disney, 57, 88–89, 146–47, 148, 196
Divorce plan, 124
Dominant person microissue, 184, 200–203
Dominant resources microissue, 184, 216–18
Double-click technology, 107–108
Dow Corning, 84
Dow Jones Industrial Average, 180
Dreaming, 213–14
Dreams, 12
  crackpot, 125–26
Dreamworks SKG, 213
Dunlap, "Chainsaw" Al, 145

"Early adopters," 142
eBay, 139
Eco, Umberto, 185
Economic diplomacy, 30
Economist, 220
Ecosystem economics, 109–12
Edison, Thomas, 132, 194
Education, 221–22
Eisner, Michael, 148
Eliot, Charles W., 23
Elizabeth, Queen, 237
Emergencies, 64, 73–76
Emerson, Ralph Waldo, vii, 239
Encyclopedia Britannica, 23
Entertainment industry, 109–10
Entertainment Weekly, 84
Events, 210–11
  response to, 6–7
Exams:
  final, 240–43
  first-term, 35
  pretest, 4–5
  second-term, 171–72
  third-term, 223–25
Extremes, migrating to the, 19–21
Eye-to-eye combat, 190

Factories, 195–96
Failure in the future, 108
Faith, 120
Families, 191–92, 200–201
Farms, 195–96
Faulkner, William, 98
Federal government, 165–66
FedEx, 51
Feiler, Bruce, 84–85
Fermi Labs, 86
Fertilizer, 216
Fiber-optic cable, 83–84
First-quarter exam, 35
500-Year Delta, The (Wacker, Taylor, and Means), 175–76, 178
Fonda, "Hanoi Jane," 140
Fool Box, 33–35, 55, 120, 129–31, 204, 213
Foot, transportation by, 194, 195
Forbes, Steve, 201
Ford, 113, 152, 217
Fox Network, 45
Frontier Airlines, 160
Fuji, 126
Fundamental questions about yourself, 27–31

Future Box, 129, 131
Future Council, 28, 30, 31–32, 213
Future exercises:
   action, 132–33
   attention bandwidth, 24
   big and small organizations, 70
   calculating your own myth, 12–13
   competition, 112
   generational-technological
     bandwidth, 21–22
   insurgent attitude, 239–40
   knowing thyself, 234–35
   learning bandwidth, 24
   leisure, 171
   macrocultures, 183–84
   for microissues, *see* Microissues
   pressure tense, 95–96
   professional bandwidth, 18–19
   seminal moments, 238
   spot price, 56–57
   strategic planning, 236
Futurist, 220–21

Gaming industry, 131–32
Gates, Bill, 135, 136, 138, 145–46
Gateway, 86
Gehrig, Lou, 144
Gehry, Frank, 213, 237
General Electric, 78, 100, 111,
   131–32, 160, 194
General Motors, 20
   planned obsolescence and, 85–86
   tension between present and
     future in, 80–81
Generational-technological
   bandwidth exercise, 21–22
Genetic information, 53–54, 126, 199
Gerstner, Lou, 161–63
Gingrich, Newt, 215
Global brands, 113–14
Global ideas, 19–20
Globalism, 29–30, 113
   governance and, 151–53
   paradox of size and, 62–63
Global metaphors, 113–14
Goals and action, 116–17
   Scenario Plan game and, 118–25
God-force, 186–87
Golf, 158–59
Governance, 151–53
Green Bay Packers, 106
Greenpeace, 82–83
Grosvenor, Gilbert, 104

Groundhog Day, 85
Groups, 205
Growing, 212
Gulf War, 143, 190

Hallmark, 10
Hard Rock Café, 196
Hart, Gary, 105
Harvard Classics, 23
Harvard University, 46–48
Head of household, 200–201
Health care, 204
Hendricks, John, 102–103, 104
Heroism, 143–44
Hershey, Milton, 146
Hierarchies, 192
High technology, 86
Hingis, Martina, 170
Holism, 186–87
Homer, 145
Honda, 82
Honeywell, 111
Hot dogs, 39–42, 52–53
Houston Astros, 141
Howard, Ron, 233–34
Humility, 143–44
Hunsicker, Gerry, 141
Hunter-gatherer epoch, 180, 182
   microissues and, *see* Microissues
Hunting, 212
Hunting ritual, 207–208
Hussein, Saddam, 110–11

Iacocca, Lee, 201
IBM, 11–12, 152, 182, 187, 194, 204
   corporate culture at, 161–63
Iceland, 69
Ideals, leadership and, 138–40
Ideologue, 220
I Love Lucy, 45–46
Imagination, 231–34
Imitation, 104, 107
Immortality, 198–200
Immunization fallacy, 24–26
Imus, Don, 53
Inconsistencies, personal, 17–18,
   135–38
Information, 82
   acceleration and massification of,
     17–18
   attention to, 100
   global dispersion of, 19–20
   making a gift of your, 106–108

synchronously available, 92
value and, 49–55
Inherent obsolescence, 86
In-N-Out Burger, 112
Instincts, 218
Insurgency attitude of, 29, 81, 131, 238–40
seed bed of, 65–70
Intel, 88
Intellectual property, 109, 130, 217
Intelligence microissue, 184, 221–23
Interactions, 218
Intermediaries, 14–15, 53
Internet, 9, 11, 52, 53, 67–68, 91, 92, 176, 194
as the exoskeleton, 109
leisure and, 159–60, 161, 168
Into Thin Air (Krakauer), 208, 209
Intrinsic value, 39–40, 41
managing, 51–54
Intuition, 117, 222–23
Investing, 126, 127, 147
Investment clubs, 168–69
Iron Curtain countries, former, 7
Israel, 27

Japan, 176–77
Jefferson, Thomas, 18, 130
Jeopardy!, 206
Jet engines, 111
Jet propulsion, 194
Jiang Zemin, 135, 136–37
John, Elton, 237
Johnson, Randy, 141
Johnson & Johnson, 54, 71–72
Jordan, Michael, 201
Justice Department, 26

Kelley, Steve, 135
Kelly, Tim, 103–104
Kelly, Walt, 98
Kennedy, John F., 137
Killian, Linda, 104
Klein, Calvin, 188
Knowing thyself, 234–35
Knowledge, 206
Knowledge epoch, 182
microissues and, *see* Microissues
Knowledge extreme, 20–21
Kodak, 13
mission of, 79–80, 165
Krakauer, Jon, 209

Krzyzewski, Mike, 138
Ku Klux Klan, 193

Land, 210
Language, 221
L.A. traffic jams, 88–89
Leadership, paradox of, 135–53
continuum of leadership and, 142–43
examples of, 135–38
future exercise, 150–51
governance, patriotism, and loyalty, 151–53
heroism and humility, 143–44
living inside the story, 144–50
managing based on fact while leading based on an ideal, 138–40
personal contradictions and, 135–38
recognizing and separating short- and long-term value, 140–42
reputation and, 144
Leadership Moment, The (Useem), 149
Leaf, Ryan, 143
Learning bandwidth exercise, 24
Learning Channel, 102
Learning microissue, 184, 218–20
Leisure, paradox of, 155–72
children and, 169–71
convergence of work and play, 155–57
corporate rewards and, 166–67
everyday life and, 167–69
at the federal government, 165–66
future exercise, 171
at IBM, 161–63
identification and communication, 169
indivisibility of work and play, 157–59, 167–69
at Kodak, 165
play at work, 158–61
validity of corporate value system and, 163–65
Lewinsky, Monica, 74, 84
Library of Alexandria, 18
Library of Congress, 18
Lindbergh, Charles, 234
Liquidation value, 39, 147
Literacy, 221

Living inside the story, 144–50
  ambition and, 232–33
  anecdotes and, 147
  examples of, 148–50
  future tense and, 145
  heroes and villains and, 147–48
  meaningfulness and, 146–47
  mythic figures and, 145–46
  ring of truth and, 148
  rules for, 145
Living with the opposition, 26–27
Loyalty, 151–53
Lucas, George, 207, 222–23
Lucent Technology, 20
Lynch, Peter, 201

McDonald's, 18, 111–12, 113
  sense of play at, 163–65
McDonnell Douglas, 166–67
McGovern, George, 105
McGwire, Mark, 143–44, 210
Macrocultures, 180–225
  age of uncertainty, 182–83
  agricultural epoch, 182
  chart of, 181
  consumer age, 182
  future exercise, 183–84
  hunter-gatherer epoch, 180, 182
  knowledge epoch, 182
  microissues and, *see* Microissues
Madonna, 233
Mall of America, 196
Management:
  of emergencies, 64, 73–76
  facts, ideals and, 138–40
  of paradox, 22–24
  of relations, 29–30
  of single-incident disasters, 71–73
  of value, 51–54
Mandela, Nelson, 137
Manning, Peyton, 143
Manufactured events, 210–11
Maoist cells, 65–66
Market attention, 99
Market capitalization, 126, 127
Marketing window, 41
Market research, 58
Marriott family, 235, 236
Mass destruction, 190
Matrices, 183
Mattel Toys, 108, 160
Maximum concentration, unit of, 88
Meaningfulness, 72, 75–76

living inside the story and, 146–47
Measuring yourself, 105–106
Mechanical causality, 187–88
Mechanical propulsion, 194
Mectizan, 149–50
Medline, 50
Membership microissue, 184,
    191–93
Memories, 43, 54
Mercedes, 113
Merck & Company, 149–50
Metadata, 53
MetLife, 125
Michelin tires, 45
Microissues, 184–225
  chart of, 181
  defining activity, 184, 212–14
  dominant person, 184, 200–203
  dominant resources, 184, 216–18
  future exercise, 185
  intelligence, 184, 221–23
  learning, 184, 218–20
  membership, 184, 191–93
  mission, 184, 203–205
  philosophy, 184, 186–89
  physical structure, 184, 195–97
  preoccupation, 184, 197–200
  recreation, 184, 214–16
  ritual, 184, 207–209
  status symbol, 184, 209–12
  travel, 184, 195–95
  visionary, 185, 220–21
  weapons, 184, 189–91
  work, 184, 205–207
Micromanagement, 80
Microsoft, 8, 99, 126
Middle East, 27
Middlemen, 14–15
Migrating to the extremes, 19–21
Military weapons, 126
Mission microissue, 184, 203–205
Moceanu, Dominique, 170
Monogamy, 212
Motorola, 10, 28, 86
Moynihan, Daniel Patrick, 143
Murdoch, Rupert, 135, 136
Murray, Bill, 85
Museum going, 215
Mythic figures, 145–46
Mythology exercise, 12–13

National Football League, 45, 143,
    169

National Gallery of Art, 215
National genome, 69
National Geographic Ventures, 104
National Institutes of Health, 50
Natural cycles, 218
Natural effects for transportation, 194
Natural resources, 131
NEC, 93
Need and value, 45–46
"Negative capability," 147–48
Negative mass, 68
Neotribalism, 62, 63, 169, 192–93
Networks, 192
New Age religion, 25
New grammar, 5–7, 9
Newmont Mining, 129
News, 151
Newspaper articles, 84–85
New York City, 196, 211
New York Times, 84
Nike, 100–101
1984 (Orwell), 16
Nixon, Richard, 137–38, 153
Northwest Airlines, 196

Offerings, 44–45
Offices, 196
Offspring, 210
Oil industry, 82–83
Oldsmobile, 85–86
Omidyar, Pierre, 139
Omnirealty, 204
One-hundredth birthday plan, 120–25
On-line trading, 126
Opposiiton Box, 33
Optimists, 6
Organic, 9
Organizational models, 66–67
Orwell, George, 16, 80, 222–23
Oscar Meyer hot dogs, 39–42, 52–53
Outsourcing, 129–30
Owens-Corning, 10
Owners, 201
Oxford English Dictionary, 23

Pantheism, 187
Paper checks, 12
Paperless office, 11–12
Paradox:
    absorption of, 188
    denial of, 24–26

everyday, *see* Action, paradox of;
    Competition, paradox of;
    Leadership, paradox of; Leisure,
    paradox of; Size, paradox of;
    Time, paradox of; Value,
    paradox of
managing, 22–24
permanent, 17–18
of reality, *see* Reality, paradox of
triumph of, 27–31
of the visionary, *see* Visionary,
    paradox of the
Patriotism, 151–53
Pepsi-Cola, 43
Performance, 141–42
Performance category, 99
Perot, Ross, 201
Personal labor, 205
Personal strength, 189–90
Pessimists, 6, 28
Pharmaceutical companies, 53–54
Philip Morris, 45–46
Philosophy microissue, 184, 186–88
Photography, 13
Physical structure microissue, 184, 195–97
Picard, Dennis, 110
Planet Hollywood, 208
Planned obsolescence, 85–86
Possessions, 210
Possibility, Age of, 3–4
Powell, Colin, 143, 202
Power, 204
Predictions, 176–77
    for the U.S. in the year 2000, 15–16, 125–27
Preoccupation microissue, 184, 197–200
Pressure tense, 83–96
    consumers and, 86–87
    future exercise, 95–96
    industry and, 85
    newspapers and, 84–85
    products and, 85–86
    stocks and, 85
    time and, *see* Time
Price changes, 40–45
Price Discrepancy Threshhold, 44
Price-earnings (P/E) ratio, 127
Price points, 58–59
PriceWaterhouse, 106–107
Priest, 220
Principles for visionaries, 5, 234–40

Probability, 218–20
Problems and solutions, 31–34
Processing simultaneously input, 157
Process management, 216–17
Procter & Gamble, 54, 111
  globalism and, 62–63
Professional bandwidth exercise, 18–19
Prostate cancer, 50–51
Prostitution, 43–44
Publicity, 55
Publishing industry, 13–15

Quality of one's own experience, 198

Randomness, 23–24
Rarity, 210
Raw materials, 216
Raytheon, 110–11
Reading-material exercise, 18–19
Reality, 17
  denial of, 23–26
  dimming, 139
  multiple, 23
  shared, 23
  single sense of, 23
Reality, paradox of, 227–43
  ambition and, 231, 232–33
  belief system and, 232
  final exam, 240–43
  imagination and, 231–34
  insurgent attitude, 238–40
  knowing who you are, 234–35
  living inside the story, 232–33
  margins of error, 230
  patience and, 234
  products that are the same, yet
    separate and distinct, 229–30
  seminal moments, 236–38
  small changes and, 231–32
  storytellers and, 231
  strategic planning, 235–36
Real-time standards, 87–88
Reason for being, 198
Recreation microissue, 184, 214–16
Relations, managing, 29–30
Relative value, 40
Remoteness of weapons, 190
Repetitive actions, 127–28
Republicans, 105–106
Reputation, 144
Residual brand value, 44

Respect and disrespect, 88–89, 92
Response to events, 6–7
Ripkin, Cal, 144, 208
Ritual microissue, 184, 207–209
"Road rage," 87
Roast Chicken organizational model, 66–67
Robinson, Eugene, 20
Rockwell, 111
Rolls-Royce, 111
Ross, Chuck, 104
Royal Dutch Petroleum, 63–64, 152
Russia, 7, 26–27
Ruth, Babe, 144
Rwanda, 73

San Diego Union-Tribune, 135
Sarno, Vincenzo, 170
Saturn, 57, 128–29, 146
Scenario Plan game, 118–25
Schulberg, Budd, 198
Schwartzkopf, Norman, 143
Scientific method, 218
Seasons, 208
Seinfeld, 136
Self-contradiction, 17–18, 135–38
Self-determination, 19–20
Seminal moments, 8, 29, 171–72, 191, 236–38
Serial future, 173–225
  see also Macrocultures;
    Microissues
Service economy, 205–206
Shaman, 220
Shelley, Percy Bysshe, 33
Shell Oil, 63–64
Shopping malls, 167–68
Shultz, George, 143
Side businesses, 10
Silicon Valley, 151–52, 158
Single-incident disasters, 71–73
Singularity, 208–209, 210
Size, paradox of, 61–76
  accidental value and, 69
  big and small companies and, 64–70
  collision of opposites and, 61–64
  complex emergencies and, 64, 73–76
  future exercise, 70
  global opinion and, 62–63
  insurgency and, 65–70

single-incident disasters and, 71–73
Sloan, Alfred, 198
Small changes, 231–32
Small companies, 64–70
Socializing, 214
"Socratic gadflies," 30
Somalia, 73
"Some assembly required," 43
Sony, 113, 114
Sosa, Sammy, 144
Soul Catcher project, 199
Southwest Airlines, 160
Soviet Union, 105
Specialization, 25–26
Spielberg, Steven, 214, 233
Spiritual workers, 206–207
Spock, Benjamin, 204
Spot pricing, 40–43, 47–49
  exercise, 56–57
Star Wars, 113, 207, 222–23
Status symbol microissue, 184, 209–12
Steel industry, 110
Steinbrenner, George, 135, 136
Stocks, 85, 92
Story, the, see Living inside the story
Storytellers, 202, 231
Storytelling, 214
Strategic planning, 235–36
Structure, 203–204
Success, paradox of, 101
Super Bowl XXXII, 106
Surgical weapons, 190–91
Survival, 198, 203, 212
Swissair, 72
Swiss banking, 74–75
Symbiotic relationships, 109–12

Teachers, 125–26
Television networks, 77–78
Ten Commandments, 187
Tents, 195–96
Territory, 216
Texas Instruments, 161
Theme parks, 196, 197
Tier pricing, 46–48
Time:
  abuse of, 88, 89
  business's sense of, 93–95
  calibration of, 89–90
  clocks, 90
  discontinuities in, 94–95

fantasy, 87–88
fungibility of, 91–93
hyperbolic discounting of, 90–91
latent, 93
as money, 88
order cycle and, 94–95
relationships and, 90
repacking your concept of, 28–29
respect and disrespect, 88–89, 92
situational changes in, 91–95
at the speed of light, 92
"time rage," 87
Time, paradox of, 77–96
  corporate mission and, 78–79
  duality between present and future, 77–83
  future exercise, 95–96
  pressure tense, see Pressure tense
  reporting on the future, 84–85
Titanic, 22–23
Travel microissue, 184, 194–95
Trebek, Alex, 206
Tribalism, 191–93, 200
Triumph of paradox, 27–31
Truman Show, The, 196
Turino soccer club, 170
Turner, Ted, 139–40
Tylenol, 71–72

UMB Financial, 160–61
Uncertainty, age of, 182–83
  microissues and, see Microissues
Understanding, 213
Uniqueness, 208–209, 210
United Artists, 201
U.S. Air Force, 81
University of Virginia, 130
Useem, Michael, 149

Vagelos, Roy, 149–50
Value, paradox of, 39–59
  brand promise, 57–59
  Contextual Price Discrepancy Threshold and, 44
  future exercise, 56–57
  information and, 49–55
  intrinsic value, 39–40, 41, 51–54
  managing value, 51–54
  marketing window and, 41
  need and, 45–46
  offerings and, 44–45
  price changes and, 40–45

Value, paradox of *(cont.)*
  Price Discrepancy Threshold and,
    44
  relative value, 40
  spot pricing and, 40–43, 47–49
  tier pricing and, 46–48
Values, 28
  leisure paradox and, 163–65
  short- and long-term, 140–42
ValuJet, 53, 75–76
Vending machines, 42–43
Vietnam War, 216–17
Viewing, 214–15
Visionary, paradox of the, 1–35
  Age of Possibility, 3–4
  altering the future, 15–17
  collisions with chaos, 7–9
  critical issues in becoming your
    own futurist, 5
  destabilizing the present, 13–15
  first, 11
  first quarter exam, 35
  Fool Box, 33–35
  future exercises, *see* Future
    exercises
  immunization fallacy, 24–26
  living with the opposition, 26–27
  managing paradox, 22–24
  migrating to the extremes, 19
  new grammar, 5–7
  pretest, 4–5
  problems and solutions, 31–34
  second, 13–15
  self-contradiction, 17–18
  third, fourth, and fifth, 16

  triumph of paradox, 27–31
  visions false and true, 9–12
Visionary, role of, 177–80
  see also Macrocultures;
    Microissues
Visionary microissue, 185, 220–21
Visions, 9–12, 138–40
Vision statements, 9–10, 11
Volvo, 57

Warhol, Andy, 198
Warren Court, 16
Washingtonian, 104
Watson, Thomas, 194
Weapons microissue, 184, 189–91
Weinberger, Caspar, 143
Well-being, 204
Welsh, Jack, 138
Westinghouse, 10
What am I?/what will I be?, 27–31
Wilson, Sloan, 198
Wolfe, Tom, 210
Workaholics, 156
Work and play, *see* Leisure, paradox
  of
Work microissue, 184, 205–207
World Jewish Congress, 75
www.persiankitty.com, 53

Xerox, 107–108, 130

Yahoo!, 116
Yale University, 175–76
Yankelovich Partners, 6
"Your:)Ware," 86

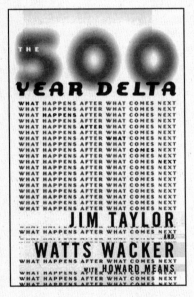